THIRD WAVE CAPITALISM

THIRD WAVE CAPITALISM

How Money, Power, and the Pursuit of Self-Interest Have Imperiled the American Dream

JOHN EHRENREICH

ILR PRESS

AN IMPRINT OF

CORNELL UNIVERSITY PRESS

ITHACA AND LONDON

First published 2016 by Cornell University Press
Printed in the United States of America

Library of Congress Cataloging-in-Publication Data

Names: Ehrenreich, John, 1943– author.
Title: Third wave capitalism : how money, power, and the pursuit of self-interest have imperiled the American dream / John Ehrenreich.
Description: Ithaca ; London : ILR Press, an imprint of Cornell University Press, 2016. | Includes bibliographical references and index.
Identifiers: LCCN 2015038554 | ISBN 9781501702310 (cloth : alk. paper)
Subjects: LCSH: Capitalism—United States—History—20th century. | Capitalism—United States—History—21st century. | United States—Social conditions—20th century. | United States—Social conditions—21st century.
Classification: LCC HC103 .E373 2016 | DDC 330.973—dc23
LC record available at http://lccn.loc.gov/2015038554

Cornell University Press strives to use environmentally responsible suppliers and materials to the fullest extent possible in the publishing of its books. Such materials include vegetable-based, low-VOC inks and acid-free papers that are recycled, totally chlorine-free, or partly composed of nonwood fibers. For further information, visit our website at www.cornellpress.cornell.edu.

Cloth printing   10 9 8 7 6 5 4 3 2 1

For Sharon
and
for Rosa, Ben, Alex, Anna, and Clara

CONTENTS

ACKNOWLEDGMENTS

It takes a village to write a book.

First there are the "ancestors." The intellectual influences on this book are too numerous to mention, but several individuals whose personal influence on me was great deserve mention. The late Leo Huberman at *Monthly Review Press* encouraged me to write, taught me a great deal about U.S. social history, and advised me that the way to write a book is "one chapter at a time." The late Harry Becker profoundly influenced my understanding of the American health system. My ideas about health care, U.S. social structure, and ideology have been shaped by years of discussion and collaboration with my former wife and present good friend Barbara Ehrenreich. For chapter 5, Barbara also graciously agreed to permit me to draw heavily on an article we coauthored.

Then there are the "tradespeople, craftspeople, and professionals." Fran Benson, editorial director of ILR Press (an imprint of Cornell University Press) was a constant source of support, providing repeated and valuable insights on the content and organization of this book. My copy editor,

Chris Dodge, and Cornell University Press staff, including Susan Barnett, Jonathan Hall, Mahinder Kingra, Karen Laun, and Emily Powers, shepherded me through the process of publication with kindness and competence. I also owe a debt of gratitude to the many other staff members at Cornell—from administrators and designers to clerical workers and custodial workers—who make a book possible. Sara Bershtel provided enormously helpful practical advice on publishing. Courtney Schuster capably helped prepare the references. Justin Hargett provided able publicist services. Millie Loeb, Florrie French, and Karen Borneman at the Sherman, Connecticut, public library cheerfully put up with my endless demands for interlibrary loans.

Of "friends and neighbors" I have many to thank. Alfred Guzzetti, Frank Hoeber, Bob Lobis, Wayne Saslow, Lincoln Taiz, and Edmond Weiss helped me think about the title. In the course of researching the book, I had extensive conversations with numerous people, many of whom also read and commented on drafts of chapters. Henry Abraham, Laura Anker, Stanley Aronowitz, Minna Barrett, Ros Baxandall, Bill Berg, Howard Berliner, Robb Burlage, Michael Clark, Ofelia Cuevas, E. J. Dionne, Peter Edelman, Oli Fein, Duncan Foley, Julie Fraad, Nick Freudenberg, Norman Fruchter, Todd Gitlin, David Kotelchuck, Ronda Kotelchuck, Eileen Landy, Hedva Lewittes, Steve London, Jeff Madrick, Tim Noah, Fran Piven, Ken Porter, Len Rodberg, Richard Rothstein, Alix Shulman, Joel Spring, David Sprintzen, Ida Susser, Jon Weiner, and Lisa Whitten all generously offered their time and wisdom, and I am grateful.

Finally, there is "family." My children, Rosa Brooks, Ben Ehrenreich, and Alex Ehrenreich, encouraged me to write this book, commented on drafts of proposals and early versions of chapters, discussed the substantive issues, advised on the process of getting published, and provided constant love and support. My wife and fellow traveler through time and the universe, Sharon McQuaide, read and reread drafts, talked about ideas and arguments, edited, reined me in when I let my passions overwhelm my reason, and encouraged me when my energy or confidence flagged. Her suggestions and criticisms immeasurably strengthened the book. More importantly, her love, energy, and generosity sustained me and made my year of writing joyful.

THIRD WAVE CAPITALISM

INTRODUCTION

I remember myself as a child growing up in the fifties, thinking, "How lucky I am to be an American." How sad it would be to come from somewhere else, I thought, to be French or Italian, perhaps. Wouldn't everyone, if they could, choose to be American? By the late eighties, three decades later, David Remnick, then a writer for the *Washington Post*, complained that the United States had become "second-rate in business, culture, even sports," and today this lament is echoed from left to right. America is "in warp speed decline," writes C. J. Werleman for the liberal activist news service Alternet. "America is in trouble," writes centrist *New York Times* columnist Thomas Freidman. "America is disintegrating," writes conservative political commentator and former presidential hopeful Pat Buchanan. Hector Barreto, former chief of the U.S. Small Business Administration and chair of the Latino Coalition, asks, "Are we the land of the American Dream, or the American Decline?"[1]

The repeated concern that the United States is in decline is odd. In many ways the America of today is a far, far better country than that of the fifties and sixties, a period frequently idealized as the high-water mark of U.S. prosperity and power. Living standards have risen. Life expectancy is up, and infant mortality are rates down. The air and water are cleaner. Crime rates are down. High school has become universal, and college is more accessible. Expression of sexuality is freer. Transportation is cheaper, safer, easier, and more efficient. Information is more available. Health care is more effective and finally—maybe—about to become more universally available. The danger of the United States engaging in nuclear war (at least all-out nuclear war between states) is lower. For huge groups of once marginalized people—women, African Americans, Latinos, other people of color, gay and bisexual men and women, transsexuals—the United States provides far greater freedom, far more opportunity, and far greater safety than it did a generation or two ago.

Given the gains in American society, the pervasive belief in decline and the pessimism infecting both pundits and the wider public calls out for explanation. Dating back a quarter of a century or more, it can't be dismissed as nothing more than the result of the sluggish recovery from the Great Recession of 2008, the political gridlock of the Obama years, and the anxieties bred by the threats of terrorism, Ebola, and climate change. The national malaise reflects longer-term discontents and perhaps a distant, often-distorted memory of post–World War II America and a dim sense of the paths not taken. Though "decline" may be the wrong word, *something* has changed in the United States, and that something has produced a sense of looming crisis.

James Truslow Adams, who coined the phrase "the American Dream" in his 1931 book *The Epic of America*, defined it as "not a dream of motor cars and high wages merely, but a dream of social order in which each man and each woman shall be able to attain to the fullest stature of which they are innately capable, and be recognized by others for what they are, regardless of the fortuitous circumstances of birth or position."[2] The American Dream was to live in a country characterized by freedom, based on the proposition that "all men are created equal," a country ruled by "government of the people, by the people, and for the people."

In the years after World War II, the American Dream seemed alive and thriving. Free at last from the Great Depression, Americans looked forward to steadily rising incomes and upward mobility. Advances in medicine, communications (television), transportation (jet planes), and energy ("the promise of the peaceful atom") promised ever-improving health and well-being. The United States had become the world center of both high culture (art, dance, music, literature) and mass culture (Hollywood movies, comic books, rock 'n' roll, and television). The country was certainly too large to be a community, but in cities and in small towns, despite ethnic, racial, and religious friction and hostility, a sense of community, shared values and purposes, and collectivity survived. In the wake of the New Deal, the belief that government could and should intervene to guarantee the common welfare was generally accepted.

In retrospect, it is easy to see the illusions and fantasies that underlay the American Dream. In the South, Jim Crow still ruled, and lynching was far from a thing of the past. In the North, rigid housing segregation, job discrimination, and hostility of whites towards blacks were the rule, not the exception. Throughout the land, a third of Americans lived in poverty. The "red scare" made neighbor suspicious of neighbor and suppressed dissent, and the threat of nuclear annihilation hung over all. A cult of conformity masked deep divisions in society. Still, imperfect though things might be, there was a widespread belief that the country's story was one of progress and the gradual expansion of democracy. The progressive social gains of the New Deal were a beginning, not an end. "Our marching song will come again," proclaimed leftist Earl Robinson's "Ballad for Americans," sung at the 1940 Republican National Convention, at the 1940 Communist Party National Convention, and by two hundred African American soldiers at a wartime concert in London. The song was recorded by both Paul Robeson and Bing Crosby. And the faith seemed justified. Only a few years later, the civil rights movement, the black liberation and community control movements, the Great Society and the War on Poverty, the New Left and the sixties counterculture, and the modern feminist, gay rights, and environmental movements transformed the country and its people.

Now, however, half a century later, despite easily documented gains in wealth and well-being, that world of faith in the American Dream seems long gone. Politics are gridlocked and impotent in the face of a faltering economy, climate change, and a dozen other problems. We have lurched, apparently rudderless, from the dot.com boom of the late nineties to the financial crisis of 2008 and the following recession, from the triumphal end of the Cold War to a disastrous preemptive war in Iraq and an apparently endless "war against terror." The country's public schools, once the wonder of the world, seem to lag behind those of a dozen other, poorer countries. The American health-care system is the most expensive, least accessible, and one of the least effective in the industrialized world.

In 2015, the economy of the richest country in the history of the world seems to be unraveling. Long before the Great Recession, we were losing competitiveness to the Chinese and others, and today, years after the financial crisis, we are still unable to climb out of the financial pit dug for us by the banks. For decades, wages have stagnated, income and wealth inequality has grown, the poverty rate has remained stuck at mid-1970s levels, and the social safety net has deteriorated. Families have only been able to maintain their standard of living by working more (the dual-income family is now the norm) and by borrowing to stretch their income. The price, not surprisingly, has been increased pressure on individuals and on the family as a unit, with concomitant political tension.

While racial attitudes of whites may have softened, racial inequities persist at an institutional level, and individual racism and bigotry is still widespread. Poverty in America remains concentrated among people of color. The rate of incarceration of black men (mainly for nonviolent drug offenses) is five times that for white men, and, sixty years after *Brown vs. Board of Education*, well over a third of black students nationwide (and almost two-thirds of black students in New York and Illinois) attend a school with fewer than 10 percent white students.[3] Hundreds of thousands of "illegal immigrants," most of them people of color and many raised in the United States since childhood, are unceremoniously deported each year. Other issues, such as abortion, gay and transgender rights, and gun control, provoke bitter division along the familiar Red State and Blue State lines.

As for the government's role in providing for the common welfare, it has lost out to free market ideology and a belief in unbridled individualism. In the United States these days, freedom seems to be less about the absence of constraint than about freedom from obligations to one another. Social critics have documented a decades-long decline in the sense of community and decried the rampant greed, litigiousness, consumerism, and belligerent egoism of today. The very idea of the common well-being has all but disappeared from political discourse. U.S. citizens, even before 2008, seemed to be experiencing a loss of optimism with respect to the future and with respect to the country's collective ability to solve pressing problems.

So what happened? How did we go from "how lucky I am to be an American" to "the American Dream is in trouble"? What complex shifts in American society have led to the perception of irreversible decline despite the real gains for so many? What do they mean for families and personal lives, for the way we educate children, for the way we deal with sickness and health, for our chances of personal happiness? Is it possible for us to recapture that sense of community and hope that once bound us together? Or are political polarization and paralysis, growing inequality, ongoing racial disparities, popular alienation from government, virulent individualism, concern about what our schools are teaching, and inability to confront challenges such as climate change and globalization here to stay.

Some of the fears of decline may be transient, rooted in the depth and intransigence of the post-2008 recession, and some of the claims that the sky is falling may be motivated chiefly by ideological agendas. Yet to describe what has happened in recent decades as nothing more than "the inevitability of change" is insufficient. There is a *coherence* to the changes, distinguishing the United States of recent decades from that of my childhood. Beginning in the early 1970s, the American political economy underwent a major transformation. Just as the Industrial Capitalism of the nineteenth century gave way to the Corporate Capitalism of the first two-thirds of the twentieth century, in recent decades the latter has given way to a new phase—the era of "Third Wave Capitalism."

Conceptualizing the last five decades as the onset of a new phase in the history of American capitalism helps resolve and explain the apparent contradictions of recent history—the growth of poverty amid growing wealth, the apotheosis of individual freedom and the paralysis of democracy, the election of a black president and the incarceration of a million black men, the increase in educational attainment and the growing mismatch between student skills and the needs of the job market, and the increasingly sophisticated medical technology and the decline in health indicators compared to other affluent countries.[4]

Chapter 1 provides a deeper, more systematic look at the sources and essential characteristics of Third Wave Capitalism. Like Industrial Capitalism and Corporate Capitalism before it, Third Wave Capitalism is marked by distinctive forms of economic enterprise, new technologies, a dramatic expansion of markets, new modes for the accumulation of wealth, a changed relationship between the public and private sectors, new patterns of social conflict, and shifts in ideology.

Subsequent chapters provide examples that flesh out these somewhat abstract conceptualizations. Chapters 2 and 3 look at the U.S. health-care system and educational system, respectively. The health-care system, which evolved into its current form over the years after World War II and especially since the 1960s, is a "mature" Third Wave system, fully revealing the characteristic features of Third Wave Capitalism. By contrast, the school system was forged during the eras of Industrial and Corporate Capitalism. The drive to reform it, based on the claim that our schools are failing, is a concerted effort to transform American schools into a Third Wave system that can generate profits for the private sector as efficiently as the health-care system does.

Chapters 3 and 4 turn to the impact of Third Wave Capitalism on various groups of U.S. citizens. Chapter 4 focuses on the collapse of sixties' efforts to "eliminate the paradox of poverty in the midst of plenty" and "close the springs of racial poison" (to use President Lyndon Johnson's phrases) and examines the persistence of poverty and racial disparities. The abandonment of the poor, the retreat from commitments to end racial discrimination and racial disparities, and the turn to the criminal justice system to exert social control reflect the most extreme version of Third Wave Capitalism's more general retreat from collective solutions to societal ills.

Chapter 5 looks at the fate of the privileged upper end of the American middle class. The liberal and creative professions (e.g., lawyers, teachers, writers) were once able to maintain a position of relative autonomy, largely outside the corporate framework. From their privileged positions, professionals could dream of a society ruled by reason. But in recent years, cuts in public spending and the rise in new technologies, offshoring, and direct ideological attack have undermined their position, and along with it, their dreams for America.

Chapter 6 explores the cultural and psychological impact of Third Wave Capitalism. It examines the rise in individual distress in recent years, expressed sometimes as depression, anxiety, and loneliness, sometimes as political rage. These join economic inequality and political gridlock as central components of our national malaise. The distress is rooted in changes in typical personality patterns, a response to the demands that Third Wave

Capitalism places on its citizens, and in the decline in social integration and economic and cultural stresses that Third Wave Capitalism has created.

The epilogue that follows is less a conclusion or set of proposals or plan for political action than exploration of the potential for progressive change—and of obstacles to it.

A few caveats: I have made no effort to make Third Wave Capitalism encyclopedic. Many important aspects of the American experience of recent decades will appear only incidentally. These include the changing status of women, the situation of economically disadvantaged ethnic groups such as Latinos, the national debates about reproductive rights and gay marriage and gender identity, the impact of massive immigration (documented and undocumented), and the threat of global warming.

I also focus on what has happened within the United States and do not address the country's decline in power relative to the rest of the world. I have treated world events such as the Vietnam War and the "war on terror" as external, making no effort to explore the reciprocal interaction between what happens here and what happens elsewhere. The two are not independent, of course. The decline of U.S. power on a world scale, the confusion of purpose, the lack of moral compass leading to our war of aggression in Iraq and to waterboarding and "external rendition" certainly contribute to the national malaise.

I also do not examine the development of capitalism in other countries. Many of the changes in the United States in recent decades can be seen in other "advanced" democracies as well, but I have not attempted to address the similarities and differences between what has happened here and elsewhere. While history may be shaped by grand forces, its working out is full of particularities and the influences of very specific and local histories.

Others have analyzed many of the specific issues addressed in this book, of course, and I have relied judiciously on these secondary sources. My hope is that putting these analyses together in a new way will be illuminating.

Finally, the passage of time creates an inherent problem with any book about current affairs. Events inevitably outrun the production cycle of a book. Congress or the Supreme Court may yet cripple the Affordable Care Act. The Common Core Curriculum (or at least the testing regime associated with it) may implode under the pressure of the "opt out" movement.

The minimum wage may be increased. Revulsion at police killings of un-armed black people may lead to reform of policing tactics. But none of these developments would invalidate the insights into the dynamics of the health-care system, the politics of the school reform movement, or the state of the black community provided by my analysis of the dynamics of Third Wave Capitalism.

1

Third Wave Capitalism

Looking back on the decades since World War II from the vantage point of 2015, the gods would seem to have looked with favor upon America. Our economy has boomed. New technologies have transformed our lives. Our standard of living is much, much higher than it was. Americans are healthier and better educated than ever before. While inequalities and bigotry certainly remain, people of color, women, and gays and lesbians now know far greater freedom, opportunity, and security than in the years immediately following the war.

But if we look back more carefully, the view gets more complicated. From the end of World War II until the 1970s, despite turmoil and ups and downs, evidence of progress in the United States is clear. But somewhere in the 1970s or early 1980s the road turned sharply. In some areas, progress came to a dead halt. In other areas, we, the American people, took what now seems to be a wrong road. In a few areas, progress was even reversed.

Consider a few examples (all of which I will return to later, in more detail):

- From World War II until the early 1970s, Americans from all socio-economic strata benefited from economic growth. But beginning in the seventies, productivity and incomes became uncoupled, and inequality grew. In the late 1970s, the richest .01 percent of Americans owned 7 percent of our aggregate wealth, a 30 percent *lower* proportion than thirty years earlier. Today they own 22 percent. In the late 1970s, the richest 1 percent took home 10 percent of aggregate wages; today they take home over 20 percent. Though productivity has increased by 120 percent since 1979, inflation-adjusted average hourly earnings for production and nonsupervisory workers (everyone but higher paid managers and supervisors) went up only 0.1 percent per year between 1979 and 2014.[1]
- By virtually any measure of health status, Americans are far healthier today than they were decades ago. Life expectancy is up, mortality rates are down, and effective treatments for many diseases, nonexistent fifty or sixty years ago, have become routine. But the price has been high. Health-care spending as a percent of GDP has risen 250 percent since 1970. Inability to pay medical bills accounts for more than half of all family bankruptcies. And by international standards, at least, what we get for the $2.9 trillion we pay each year for health care isn't very good. Americans experience more illnesses and have shorter lives than people in other high-income countries. In 1960, the country's infant mortality rate ranked twelfth among the thirty-four countries in the Organization for Economic Cooperation and Development (OECD), ahead of Japan, Canada, Germany, and France. Today the United States has fallen to thirtieth in infant mortality, behind Greece, Poland, and Slovakia. Most of the relative decline has occurred since 1980. Within the United States, huge disparities remain. A male black infant born today can expect to live four years less than his white counterpart, and for poor people with less than a high school education, mortality rates are actually rising.[2]
- Americans today are far better educated than years ago. The average number of years spent in school, the percentage of Americans of all social classes who are high school graduates, the percentage who are college graduates, and (despite what you may have heard) students' test scores are all up dramatically. Students from all over the world come to attend U.S. colleges and universities and even high schools. But most

of the reduction in the gaps in academic achievement between white and black and between white and Latino students occurred during the 1970s. The gap barely changed in the two decades following and has narrowed only slightly over the last fifteen years. The difference between the proportion of children of poor people and the proportion of children of rich people attending or completing college has doubled since the 1970s. And at least since "A Nation at Risk," the 1983 report of the Reagan administration's National Commission on Excellence in Education, we have been inundated with claims that our schools are failing, that students' skills are falling behind the rest of the world, and that U.S. students are not being prepared for the job market.[3]

- Jim Crow is no more, and the income, health, and educational statuses of African Americans today are dramatically better than in the 1950s. For most white Americans, open expressions of racism have become unacceptable. A large black middle class has emerged, and we have a black president and countless elected black officials at lower levels. But the gaps between black and white in schooling, unemployment rates, and income have barely narrowed since the mid-1970s. Since the 1980s, school segregation has been rising again, in both the North and the South. Today one quarter of all of black children in New Jersey attend super-segregated schools, with fewer than 1 percent nonblack children. A growing proportion of blacks live in predominately poor neighborhoods. And, beginning in 1980, the rate of incarceration of black men has risen dramatically. Today, the *New York Times* headlines, some 1.5 million black men are "missing" from their communities, either languishing in prison or prematurely dead.[4]

- Between 1960 and 1975, the proportion of Americans living in poverty dropped by more than half. By 1973, the poverty rate was down to 11 percent. But it then rose a bit, and it has never again reached its 1973 low point. Meanwhile, the proportion of the poor who are in "deep poverty"—who have incomes less than half the official poverty level—has steadily risen, from 30 percent in 1975 to 44 percent today.[5]

- Despite rising wealth, personal misery and a sense of personal isolation have increased. Rates of depression are up and levels of self-reported anxiety among young people have doubled since 1980. Meanwhile, sources of social support have declined. The number of Americans who say that they have no "confidant" rose two-and-one-half-fold between 1985 and 2004. Sociologists have documented a decline in social trust in recent decades, especially among the less educated. Despite increasingly shrill proclamations of religiosity, church attendance, once a source of solace for many, has dropped precipitously since the mid-1970s.[6]

- The first two-thirds of the twentieth century brought wave after wave of progressive reform—the Progressive Era of Teddy Roosevelt and Woodrow Wilson, FDR's New Deal, Truman's Fair Deal, and Johnson's Great Society. Regulation of banks and of the transportation, food, drug, and other industries, the development of the "social safety net," governmental guarantees of minimum wages and maximum hours and the right to unionize, unemployment compensation, workplace safety rules, anti-discrimination laws, and controls over air and water pollution made Americans safer, less exploited as workers and consumers, and more secure in the face of the vagaries of employment and the inevitability of old age. There were periods of backsliding, of course, but rarely for long. Looked at from a distance, progress was steady. But in the early 1970s, the reforms came to an abrupt halt and militant conservatism became increasingly triumphant. There was Republican Nixon's "southern strategy" with its withdrawal from aggressive enforcement of civil rights, Democrat Jimmy Carter's onslaught against transportation industry regulation, Republican Ronald Reagan's proclamation that "government is not the solution, government is the problem," Republican George H. W. Bush's deregulation of the energy industry, and Democrat Bill Clinton's embrace of deep cuts in welfare, bank deregulation, and harsh prison sentences for minor offenses. After Republican George W. Bush's effort to cut taxes for the rich, and in the face of ever-more-entrenched and ever-more-powerful conservative opposition, Barack Obama's claim of "yes we can" seems ever more hollow.

Many other examples could be given. In sphere after sphere of American life, the seventies and early eighties are an inflection point. Before, there was progressive change. After, there was not.

There are what seem to be exceptions, of course, most notably in the gains in the status of women. But looked at more closely, the course of modern feminism shows a similar pattern, peaking in the early 1970s, then falling back. State ratification of the 1972 Equal Rights Amendment had stalled out by 1977. The 1973 *Roe v. Wade* decision (disallowing most state and federal restrictions on abortion) was followed by a wave of increasingly successful efforts to chip away at women's reproductive rights. By the 1980s, the feminist movement had become increasingly fragmented, fraught with dissension, and imperiled by backlash. Even the gains in women's employment and income may have reflected the growing need for families to have two wage earners, if they were to maintain their living standard in the face of stagnant wages, as much as support for women's rights.

So what's going on here? Let's step back for a moment. The change of course that is evident in U.S. history since the 1970s is not merely a superficial, retrospective grouping together of unrelated events. Inequality, political paralysis and the conservative onslaught, the crises in the American health care system and in American education, the collapse of efforts to end poverty and racial disparities, the rise in personal misery and political rage, all traceable to the 1970s and early 1980s, are not just a random collection of isolated problems. They represent the emergence of a new stage in the history of American capitalism.

Historians often divide American social, political, and economic history since the early nineteenth century into two phases, the age of Industrial Capitalism and the age of Corporate Capitalism. Each of these phases was characterized by the emergence of distinctive forms of economic enterprise, by novel technologies and radically new modes of transportation and communication, by expansion in the extent of the market, by changes in the modes through which wealth was accumulated, by shifts in the relationship between public and private sectors, by evolution of the typical forms of social conflict, and by distinctive ideologies. Since the 1970s, we have entered a third phase, the phase I call "Third Wave Capitalism." (For discussion of this terminology, see below).

The First Two Waves: Industrial Capitalism and Corporate Capitalism

The age of Industrial Capitalism—the era of the Erie Canal and the transcontinental railroad, of Morse's telegraph and McCormick's reaper and Edison's electric light bulb, of small entrepreneurs but also of hyper-rich "robber barons" such as Andrew Carnegie and John D. Rockefeller—extended through most of the nineteenth century. The steam engine and the factory system revolutionized production. Railroads, steamboats, and the telegraph and telephone revolutionized transportation and communications, widening markets. Great fortunes were made in railroads, mining, and basic industry. Though its role was minimal by later standards, the federal government subsidized the railroads, indirectly subsidized manufacturing through the tariff system, and promoted the settlement of the West. Local and state governments helped maintain order, which included helping to break strikes and repress the recently freed black population in the post-Reconstruction South. This was a turbulent period in the United States, with social and economic conflict manifest in the Civil War, pitting region against region and manufacturers against plantation owners, in widespread strikes, pitting workers against their employers, and in regional political battles such as the Populist struggles, pitting southern and Plains State farmers against banks and railroads and their allies.

Then, around the end of the nineteenth century, Corporate Capitalism began to emerge. Giant joint stock companies and giant banks increasingly dominated the American economy. Technological advances in chemistry and electricity, the rise of the petroleum industry, and the development of the internal combustion engine—what some called "the second industrial revolution"—led to the emergence of the automobile industry, electrical utilities, and broadcasting. Soon the automobile and the truck and the radio permitted the development of a truly national marketplace. Rapid urbanization, wave upon wave of immigration from eastern and southern Europe, and the great northward migration of blacks from the rural South transformed the American workforce and the American landscape. "Scientific management" reorganized work processes, turning individual workers into little more than appendages of the machines they operated. In response to financial crises, labor unrest, and middle-class outrage over excesses of industrial capital such as those described in Upton Sinclair's *The Jungle*, both government and corporations were forced to accommodate to some degree to the needs of workers, farmers, and consumers. At the same time, corporate leaders began to see the state as a mechanism that could directly serve their needs. Progressive Era reforms such as railroad rate regulation, the Pure Food and Drug Act, and the Federal Reserve Act not only protected consumers and small businesses but also helped rationalize industries, stabilize the economy, and protect corporations against more radical demands from workers and farmers.[7]

The increasing scale of enterprises and the rise of a national market created the possibility of raising wages to permit higher consumption. In 1914, Henry Ford increased the wages he paid his workers to five dollars a day, doubling their previous rate. In legend, at least, Ford realized that paying higher wages to his workers would make it possible for them to buy his products. It was actually probably more an effort to reduce worker turnover in his plants and was accompanied by vastly increased scrutiny of the workers' lives. But regardless of Ford's own intentions, the understanding that higher wages would, in the end, help corporations make profits, triumphed. Of course, the argument that higher wages lead to higher consumption really only works at the level of society as a whole, not at the level of a single company. No matter what Boeing pays its workers, they won't be able to themselves afford a 747. But if everyone pays their workers more, capitalists can benefit from higher sales. The Boeing workers may be able to afford to buy tickets from American Airlines to fly on a 747 and a Samsonite suitcase to carry their belongings from one city to another.[8]

Struggles between workers and owners persisted at the level of individual corporations, of course (as the great 1941 strike against Ford itself, among other labor battles, showed), but something new had been added. Now what happened to workers at a specific company was often inseparable from what happened to workers in general. Struggles for economic justice took on an intercompany or even national form. In earlier times, most strikes had been local, pitting workers against the owners of an individual company. The new model was reflected in the emergence of industry-wide strikes, such as the steel strike of 1919, the textile workers' strike of 1934, and the coal miners' strike of 1946, and even citywide strikes such as the San Francisco general strike of 1934. It can also be seen in the development of explicit or implicit industry-wide collective bargaining, as in the auto industry's adoption of "pattern" settlements after World War II: Once the union reached a contract with one of the Big Three auto companies, the other companies copied it.

Sometimes big strikes took on an anticapitalist, "class struggle" tone, but in the wake of the 1946 strike wave, a general social compact emerged. Unions would accept the underlying class relationships of society, agree to long-term contracts that protected employers from the threat of frequent strikes, and give up the right to bargain over some issues, in exchange for employment stability, a steady increase in real wages, and extensive health and pension benefits and vacation time (all underwritten, of course, by increases in productivity and monopoly control over pricing).

Unions, an insurgent force in earlier days, became a powerful institutional force throughout the United States, backed by federal laws protecting workers' right to organize and bargain collectively. By 1954, more than one in three wage and salary workers in the United States (and more than half of all manufacturing workers) belonged to a union. Unions provided the organizational underpinning for the post-FDR Democratic Party's electoral machine and served as what John Kenneth Galbraith, in his 1952 book *American Capitalism*, termed a "countervailing" force, capable of partially offsetting the enormous power of the giant corporation.[9]

Reflecting the newfound power of unions and the national integration of the economy, wages and working conditions became not just a matter of negotiation between an individual company and its workers but a matter for governmental action as well. Labor conditions were regulated by the New Deal's minimum wage and maximum hours laws, the workman's compensation system, and, later, by workplace health and safety laws. Progressive taxes (on corporations and on all citizens, including bankers, landlords, and factory owners) were paid out as a "social wage" to workers of all sorts, in the form of benefits such as unemployment compensation, Social Security, subsidized mortgages, and later Medicare, Medicaid, food stamps, and the Earned Income Tax Credit. The modern welfare state had emerged. In addition to providing greatly increased security for most Americans, these developments led to a dramatic redistribution of income. The share in national income of the top 1 percent fell from almost 24 percent in 1928 to less than 10 percent by 1970.[10]

At the same time, in the wake of the Great Depression, the federal government took on responsibility to manage the well-being of the country's economy as a whole. This responsibility became official U.S. policy with the passage of the Employment Act of 1946, which gave the federal government responsibility for maintaining full employment at fair rates of pay and low inflation. (The act did not prescribe specific policies.)[11]

The "national-ization" of the economy, corresponding to the development of a national market, became increasingly evident in other ways. FDR's National Industrial Recovery Act, intended to regulate wages, production, and prices, was declared unconstitutional by the Supreme Court, but similar, if smaller, efforts to provide a nationally uniform system appeared in oil production, coal mining, agriculture, trucking, and shipping. Under government sponsorship, the nation's uniform electrical grid was completed, telephone service was made available even in rural areas, federal control over the airwaves was completed, and the interstate highway system was developed.

The Rise of Third Wave Capitalism

Since the 1970s, American capitalism has evolved into a distinctive third phase, Third Wave Capitalism. This third phase of American capitalism is marked off from the preceding Corporate Capitalist period by the dramatic growth of globalization. Capital markets were internationalized. Foreign trade and investment grew dramatically, and the new multinational corporations created globally integrated supply chains, uniting under the control of a single enterprise the extraction of raw materials, production of parts, assembly of final products, and sales, with each process occurring in a different geographic location. At home, U.S. manufacturing declined, its once proud place in the national economy taken over by service industries and the financial sector. Meanwhile giant nonprofit enterprises arose, coming to account for more than 10 percent of U.S. employment by the end of the twentieth century. Another wave of technological innovation, this time in electronics and materials, fueled another historic shift in production, communications, and transportation. Free market, highly individualistic ideologies flourished, promoted by a well-financed and self-conscious propaganda barrage from conservative business leaders and media. The relationship between government and business became ever more intimate, and, correspondingly, the protections that the federal, state, and local governments offered the poor and the middle class began to fray (see table 1).

A word about my use of the term "Third Wave Capitalism" to describe this phase in American history. Many others have explored changes in the United States over recent decades (though not always focusing on the same changes or on precisely the same time frame) and have sought a way to name them. Each of the other leading candidates is deeply problematic, however. "Global capitalism" implies that the economic world is far more integrated than the real world actually is and falsely suggests that developments in the United States are closely mirrored in other capitalist countries, including not only the countries of Western Europe but

TABLE 1. The phases of American capitalism

	Pre-Industrial	Industrial	Corporate	Third Wave
Dominant economic sectors	Agriculture	Manufacturing	Manufacturing; finance	Services (often organized as nonprofit); finance
Scope of market and production	Very Local	Local	National	International
Form of dominant economic enterprise	Family farm; artisanal workshop	Privately owned company	Joint-stock corporation	Multinational corporation; nonprofit organization
Technological frontier		Steam power; mechanization of manufacturing; steel	Electricity; electronic devices; chemicals; petrochemicals; motor vehicles and airplanes	Computers and information technology; biotechnology; ceramics and composites
Modal forms of communication	Newspaper	Newspaper, telegraph	Newspaper, telephone, radio and later, television	Television, Internet
Modal forms of transportation	Horse	Train, steamboat	Automobile, truck	Automobile, truck, airplane
Relationship of government and private sector	Mercantilism; colonial economy (pre-1776)	Direct and indirect subsidies (e.g., railroads, tariffs); maintenance of order	Regulation; provision of social wage and social safety net; macroeconomic intervention	Deregulation; welfare state as source of profits; blurred boundaries between government and private sector; outsourcing and privatization; macroeconomic intervention
Modal domestic social conflict	Anticolonial movement, slave resistance	Local strikes, Civil War, regional politics (e.g., Populism)	Industry-wide strikes; national politics	National politics; rent-seeking
Modal personality pattern		Inner-directed (internal goals)	Other-directed (interpersonal goals: getting along)	"Me-directed," narcissistic, anxious (external goals: money, status)

countries such as China, Russia, and Brazil.[12] "Finance capitalism" focuses on a very important shift in our economy, but financialization alone has little power to explain the many changes in U.S. politics, economics, and culture.[13] "Late capitalism," espoused by many in the humanities, is vague and leaves us with the problem of what we will call the inevitable next phase of capitalism ("later capitalism"?).[14] "Neoliberal capitalism," a favorite among many Left scholars to refer to the renewed popularity of laissez faire economic ideas, uses the word "liberal" in a sense completely opposite to historic American usage.[15] In Europe, "liberalism" implies small government and laissez faire economics, but in the United States the word is virtually synonymous with strong government and support for the welfare state. None of these terms will do. "Third Wave Capitalism" simply sets off the current phase of American capitalism from the two earlier phases, with no obvious downside.

In a deeper sense, the difficulty in coming up with a more precisely descriptive label is itself telling. The Industrial Revolution was the overwhelmingly dominant force in shaping the era of Industrial Capitalism, and the rise of the giant corporation was equally central to the era of Corporate Capitalism. But no one institution or process dominates the changes in of recent decades. If anything, in Third Wave Capitalism the boundaries between institutions and between processes—between business and government, money and politics, profit and nonprofit, race and class, war and peace, police and military, private and public, cultural practice and commodification, male and female—are increasingly blurry. The very vagueness of "Third Wave" turns out to be descriptive.

The Corporate Imperative

Where did the Third Wave come from? The most basic engine driving the transition to the new stage of American capitalism was the relentless search for corporate profits, at home and abroad. U.S. corporations have long sought foreign markets and invested in sources of raw materials. Foreign investment and international trade grew gradually until the 1990s, then explosively penetrated into the most remote corners of the world. Today, at the top of the heap, some sixty giant international corporations, including companies such as General Electric, Exxon, AT&T, Walmart, and Pfizer, account for $30 trillion in annual revenues and $119 trillion in assets, and they employ seventy-two million people worldwide.[16]

In their relentless search for profits, corporations moved into areas previously left to families or to the nonprofit sector. The most human of relationships, such as educating children and caring for the sick and the aged, were turned into commodities, whose availability and quality are subject to the vagaries of the market and the imperatives of profits. The interests of the market trumped all others. Young children were targeted by toy and breakfast food advertisements, pharmaceuticals were marketed to television viewers (even though their sale is controlled by physicians and pharmacies), and powerful corporate interests prevented or distorted reform in areas central to social well-being.

Within the corporation, restructuring of corporate reimbursement policies so that top management compensation became linked to the company's stock price resulted in the triumph of a short-term perspective: short-term profits (and as a result, higher stock prices) were generated, even at the expense of long-term planning and growth. Corporations became increasingly unwilling to make long-term investments in activities that did not guarantee rapid and large-scale payoffs, unless they were accompanied by massive government subsidies or guarantees (for example, guarantees for drug companies developing vaccines).

Corporate greed, of course, is nothing new, but well into the sixties, recalls *Washington Post* business columnist Steve Pearlstein, "Corporations were broadly viewed as owing something in return to the community that provided them with special legal protections and the economic ecosystem in which they could grow and thrive." The law does not actually require corporations to be run to maximize profits or share prices, points out Pearlstein, nor do the executives and directors have a special fiduciary duty to the shareholders (as opposed to the corporation itself). All the corporation contractually owes its shareholders is "a claim to the 'residual value' of the corporation, once all of its other obligations have been satisfied."[17]

In the past, CEOs did consider the needs of a variety of stakeholders, at least rhetorically. "The job of management," said Frank Abrams, chairman of Standard Oil of New Jersey, in 1951, "is to maintain an equitable and working balance among the claims of the various directly interested groups . . . stockholders, employees, customers, and the public at large." As late as 1981, the Business Roundtable, an organization of the CEOs of the country's biggest firms, proclaimed: "Corporations have a responsibility, first of all to make available to the public quality goods and services at fair prices, thereby earning a profit that attracts investment to continue and enhance the enterprise, provide jobs, and build the economy. . . . The long-term viability of the corporation depends upon its responsibility to the society of which it is a part."[18]

Beginning in the 1970s, however, American businesses shifted from this "stakeholder model" to a "shareholder model," in which the immediate interests of shareholders were practically all that mattered. By the late 1990s, the Business Roundtable had changed its tune. The principle objective of a business enterprise, it now said, "Is to generate economic returns to its owners . . . [If] the CEO and the directors are not focused on shareholder value, it may be less likely the corporation will realize that value." The shareholders had won. Or, as Gordon Gecko said in the movie *Wall Street*, "Greed is good."[19]

The long-term struggle between individual large corporations and their workers, clients, and smaller-scale competitors escalated, with the large corporations going on the offensive. In the face of a wave of labor unrest in the 1970s and growing competition from abroad, employers placed renewed emphasis on labor flexibility and on control over their workers. At home they shifted from long-term commitments to their employees to the use of temporary and part-time employees, freelancers, and other workers deemed "outside contractors." Ever larger parts of both production and administration were outsourced to other domestic or foreign companies. Advances in automation technology increasingly permitted replacement of potentially obstreperous workers with lower-cost, more docile machines. Companies also showed a growing resistance to the pay and benefit demands of unions, and a greater willingness to vigorously fight union organizing campaigns and strikes. In the marketplace, Walmart, Home Depot, and other huge national retail chains used the savings from their enormous scale of operations, along with aggressive use of loss leaders, to drive millions of small retailers out of business. Small mom-and-pop retail establishments providing day-to-day commodities such as food, clothing, hardware, and books were driven out. This, in turn, contributed to the collapse of smaller scale, "people-friendly" neighborhoods.[20]

The aggressiveness of large corporations was especially evident in banking and other financial institutions. Before the 1960s, banks were staid, heavily regulated institutions, investing mainly in government bills and bonds and short-term loans. Most corporate investment came from funds generated internally by the corporations themselves. But then, with Citibank's CEO Walter Wriston leading the way, banks surged into retail banking and credit cards and into investing in equities and derivatives. As federal regulations were loosened, both consumer banks and investment firms began to invest heavily, often recklessly. The line between what in retrospect get called "reckless" sub-prime loans and "predatory" loans became harder and harder to see, and the banks' products—"derivatives" and other complex financial instruments—became less and less easy to understand. Today, four banking groups (JP Morgan Chase, Citigroup, Bank of America, and Wells Fargo) have assembled assets equal to 43 percent of the Gross Domestic Product of the United States, four times the relative amount they controlled twenty-five years ago.[21]

The Rise of Nonprofits

A second change in the organization of private enterprise, easily overlooked amid the rapid growth of multinational corporations, was the emergence of the giant nonprofit organization. There is nothing new about nonprofits, of course. What is new is their dramatic growth in numbers and in size. Today elementary and secondary schools, universities, hospitals, think tanks, social welfare organizations, charities, unions, trade associations, social clubs, fraternal societies, churches, foundations, and other types of organization categorized by the Internal Revenue Service as "not for profit" enterprises account for about 10 percent of U.S. employment, up tenfold since the early twentieth century and threefold or fourfold since 1960. By official estimates, nonprofit enterprises are responsible for 5.4 percent of the GDP, but this figure may significantly underestimate their impact, due to the way the statistics are gathered. Their annual revenues, $2.16 trillion in 2012, are the equivalent of more than 13 percent of the GDP.[22]

What defines an enterprise as being "nonprofit" is not the absence of profits in the usual sense of the word (that is, revenues in excess of expenses). A more accurate name would be "non-taxpaying organization." A nonprofit is defined by the U.S. tax code as an organization ostensibly organized for purposes other than making a profit and that has no shareholders to distribute profits to. In return for presumably serving some socially beneficial purpose or providing charity or other forms of community service, the organization is exempted from most income, property, and sales taxes.

Despite their benign name and aura of doing good, nonprofits are simply a variant form of business enterprise, and they are thoroughly integrated into the for-profit business system. Some provide essential services to for-profit businesses. For example, the National Football League (NFL), the trade association for the $9-billion-a-year professional football business, was a nonprofit until it voluntarily relinquished its tax-exempt status under heavy political pressure in 2015. The NFL (as opposed to its individual franchises, which have never been nonprofit) had revenues of over $300 million in 2012. The U.S. Chamber of Commerce, another nonprofit, spent over $1 billion between 2004 and 2014 lobbying for business interests.[23] Other nonprofits serve as conduits for other companies to make profits. Nonprofit hospitals, for instance, provide an enormous market for the products of the pharmaceutical industry, and nonprofit charter schools provide a market for the products of testing companies such as Pearson. (I'll have more to say about this in chapters 2 and 3.)

Nonprofits are also central to the research endeavors of for-profit enterprises. The 1980 Bayh-Dole Act (the Patent and Trademark Act) permitted universities and hospitals to patent products or processes discovered by their researchers using federal tax dollars and license them to for-profit companies. For example, the anticancer drug Taxol was developed by Florida State University (FSU) scientists with almost half a billion dollars in federal grants. FSU licensed it to drug maker Bristol Myers Squibb, which, after more research and testing, marketed it, accounting for almost $10 billion in wholesale revenue for the company. Other highly profitable drugs, including the anti-HIV drug Truvada (developed at Tufts and marketed by Gilead), the anti-allergy drug Allegra (developed at Georgetown and marketed at Sanofi), and the anti-wrinkle drug Renova (developed at the University of Pennsylvania and marketed by Johnson and Johnson), have similar histories. A former president of the technology-heavy NASDAQ Stock Exchange estimated that no less than 30 percent of its value stems from university-based, federally funded research results, commercialized due to the Bayh-Dole Act.[24]

In all of these cases, nonprofits serve a legitimate role (though whether one deserving of tax exemption is debatable), but other nonprofit activities are less defensible. For example, a nonprofit may make purchases from companies linked to their board members. One 2007 study found that administrators and directors were involved in insider arrangements at nearly half of large nonprofit organizations, including universities. Fraud and embezzlement associated with nonprofits is also common, totaling more than $40 billion a year from charities alone.[25]

Though they may not pay profits to shareholders, nonprofits may legally use their income to pay their executives very well. In 2012, Cleveland Clinic paid its CEO, Delos Cosgrove, $3.17 million; Goodwill Industries paid CEO John L. Miller $3.21 million a year, Northeastern University paid its president Joseph Aoun $3.12 million; and the National Football League (while it was still claiming its tax-exempt status) paid its commissioner Roger Goodell no less than $44 million. The pay of nonprofit CEOs, including bonuses, like that of their counterparts in for-profit companies, may be linked to their institution's financial performance, with higher pay contingent upon the organization's financial success.[26]

As if to emphasize the lack of any large difference between nonprofits and profit-making enterprises, nonprofits sometimes even decide that the business benefits of not having to pay taxes are not great enough to forego openly making profits for shareholders, and they seamlessly shift to become for-profit endeavors. In the 1990s, for example, the nonprofit Blue Cross and Blue Shield insurance plans were transformed into very profitable for-profit companies, shedding their former obligations to the community (which had included providing insurance coverage regardless of a customer's health status and charging the same premiums to all consumers). Anthem, the second-largest health insurer in the United States and the thirty-eight largest company altogether, with 2013 revenues of $71 billion and profits of $2.5 billion, is the most prominent member of this group.[27]

The Role of Technology

The shift to Third Wave Capitalism was also driven by the emergence of new technologies. Often these were the result of federal government investment, later adopted by and benefiting the private sector. Computers, originally developed in the 1940s as part of the war effort, were first adopted by big companies in the 1960s to control automated industrial processes and to maintain business records, and they have since become ubiquitous. Container ships revolutionized the movement of goods. Cheap air transport (also the product of military development) moved passengers and goods rapidly. Communications satellites and the Internet (both developed by the federal government) made rapid long-distance communication cheap and reliable.

New technology transformed the way U.S. companies operated. Many routine jobs were eliminated, taken over by machines, and many new kinds of relatively skilled jobs were created. The transportation revolution made globally integrated production systems, export of production jobs abroad, and expansion of world trade possible and profitable.[28] The communications revolution permitted outsourcing of many backroom operations—from routine clerical tasks to accounting, design, and legal services—and enabled coordination of increasingly global enterprises. By century's end, home computers and the Internet, and then laptops, smart phones, and tablets, profoundly influenced popular culture as well as business practices, undermining traditional senses of privacy and altering patterns of interpersonal interaction.

Some have argued that technological advances themselves have driven economic growth in recent years and that recent technological change has transformed society in an unprecedented way. Some perspective is in order, however. Though recent technological developments have certainly had major economic, social, and cultural impacts, their uniqueness can be easily overestimated. With the possible exception of the computer, most technological changes of the last half-century had counterparts in earlier phases of capitalism. Ever since the beginnings of the Industrial Revolution in the first half of the nineteenth century, transportation and communication have become ever more efficient, ever faster, and ever cheaper. In comparison to what went before, industrial capitalism's railroads, steamships, and telegraph brought different parts of the world into contact with one another even more dramatically than has the Internet. Corporate capitalism's tractors, insecticides, and fertilizers revolutionized agriculture around the world, leading to massive immigration, rural depopulation in the United States, and the continued rise of the country's great cities. The medical advances of corporate capitalism saved children from infectious diseases and prolonged life, forever changing our perceptions of childhood, adolescence, and aging. The computers of Third Wave Capitalism may have dramatically reduced the need for certain types of labor and increased the need for other types, but so did the steam engine and the reorganization of production into factories in the era of industrial capitalism. And despite the claims to the contrary of those star-struck by the cyber age, the jury is still out as to whether the rise of digital technology, mobile computing, and the Internet and their competition with the printed word and the physical phonograph record will turn out to be comparable in their social and cultural implications to the invention of moveable type.

Seeing technology as the major driver of economic and social change, blaming it for the ills of contemporary society or, conversely, looking to technology for solutions to our contemporary woes, can divert attention from underlying economic and political explanations. Yes, the improvements in communications and transportation of recent decades certainly facilitated globalization, but, as nineteenth-century British imperialists could testify, globalization could proceed quite well with ships and handwritten manifests. High-tech created vast fortunes (e.g., Microsoft, Google, Intel, and Facebook), but so did coal, oil, and railroads, and so did radio, television, and airlines. Sophisticated medical equipment has transformed health care, but the rise of the health insurance industry in the 1950s and the consolidation of hospital systems that began in the 1960s predated it.

New technologies may create a demand for new products or undercut old business models or enable new behaviors, but nothing automatically links invention to demand. It is not the impersonal progress of technology and its inevitable impact on society that explain history, but human actions. As C. S. Lewis wrote, "What we call Man's power over Nature turns out to be a power exercised by some men over other men with Nature as its instrument."[29] Take the 1960 introduction of the birth control pill, which helped foster the sexual revolution and the new feminist movement of the late 1960s on. The origins of the pill lay in a Mexican pharmaceutical company's commercially motivated synthesis of progestin analogs, intended as the basis for a fertility drug. But the road to the pill coming into use as a contraceptive and having a massive cultural impact led through a series of deliberate human actions: private funding by women's suffrage activist (and International Harvester heiress) Katharine McCormick; a 1965 Supreme Court ruling (Griswold v. Connecticut) establishing the constitutional right to use contraceptives; the liberalization of Catholicism by

Vatican II; and disingenuous advertising by pharmaceutical giant G. D. Searle (who initially marketed the pill as a treatment for menstrual disorders).[30] In short, the introduction and impact of the pill were not the inevitable consequence of new technology. They were the product of political demands and social change and corporate profit-seeking as much as their cause.

To take another example, the current crisis in the publishing industry is often ascribed to technology. To be sure, millions of people have switched from a daily paper to the 24/7 news sites on the Internet, ads on Craigslist and eBay have eaten into newspaper want ad revenues, the ebook has undercut publishing companies' traditional pricing, and Internet journals such as *Slate* have become an alternative to printed magazines for readers and for writers. But the publishing crisis long predates the World Wide Web and the ebook. Leveraged corporate takeovers in the publishing industry in the 1980s and 1990s resulted in the new owners demanding profit margins that their market could never sustain (see chapter 5). The poster child for failure due to leveraged over-expansion was the Chicago-based Tribune Company, which by 2008 owned twelve newspapers, twenty-three television stations, a national cable channel, and assorted other media holdings, but which also was $13 billion in debt. Faced with declining circulation and ad revenues, it was unable to pay its debts and in 2008 it declared bankruptcy.[31]

The result of the financial pressures on publishing has been a substantial narrowing in what kind of book can get published and a decline in the willingness of newspapers to meet the demands of any but the largest mass audience. At the next remove, we see a narrowing of readers' expectations and of taste, a narrowing of the formal possibilities that most writers are able to imagine, and a narrowing of the imagination for all. But although new technology may have delivered the deathblow, it was not the source of the underlying disease.

Assessing the interactions between technology and other social processes is crucial. If advances in technology are independent of social forces and if technology per se is responsible for economic and social change, then negative changes in people's experience are no one's fault, and change—at least social and political change—is both irrelevant and impossible. Only technological fixes are possible.

The Nature of Third Wave Capitalism

Whatever its sources, Third Wave Capitalism is characterized by a distinctive ideology, a distinctive relationship between business and government, and a distinctive way of getting rich.

The Triumph of Ideology

The emergence of Third Wave Capitalism was accompanied by the triumph of ideologies that centered on the belief in market-based solutions to all social problems and the exaltation of the rights of the individual over the needs of the community. The so-called free market was equated with freedom itself. Businesses demanded direct and indirect government aid while insisting that the right to remain free of government supervision was the essence of the American Dream. Corporations are persons, declared the Supreme Court, and free spending is free speech.

This conservative ideology didn't just develop on its own. It was developed systematically and self-consciously at the initiative of conservatives in the religious, business, and political communities. It was elaborated by academics, promoted by wealthy individuals and corporate executives, assertively promulgated through local and national political campaigns, and spread by conservative talk radio, Fox News, and thousands of local and national groups, ranging from the organizations of the religious right to the Tea Party (see chapter 6 for more on this).

Along with conservative ideology came an attack on liberalism, including an effort to demonize the very word. Liberalism, Bill Moyers once said, consists of "public action for the public good."[32] Proponents of such liberalism have been on the defensive in the United States since the early or mid-seventies. By the standards of 2015, at least, the last "liberal" president was the not-very-liberal Republican Richard Nixon, who expanded the Food Stamp program, applied cost-of-living adjustments to Social Security, expanded the role of affirmative action, proposed what became the Earned Income Tax Credit, and signed the Clean Air Act of 1970.[33] But the Vietnam War and the decade of stagflation that followed combined with the rise of free market ideology to undermine popular trust in government. From the cautious centrism of Presidents Carter and Clinton, through the outright assault on the liberal tradition by Reagan and both

Bushes, to the political stalemate of the Obama years, little of liberalism has survived. In its absence, all that is left is an exalted belief in the rights of the individual, unfettered by any moral requirement to consider the well-being of others.

In the booming nineties, it sometimes seemed as if free market capitalism might be able to provide some of the social benefits that liberals in earlier years had assumed could only come from the public sector. During the Clinton years, there was, in fact, some decrease in overall inequality. In some measure this resulted from relatively rapid economic growth and the lack of serious recessions, but it was not entirely the free market at work. It was also the result of government action, including an increase in the top income tax rates, an increase in the Earned Income Tax Credit, and increased government spending for both K–12 schools and higher education. Even so, the top 1 percent widened their advantage over everyone else.[34]

It took the 2008 financial crisis to finally reveal the hollowness of the free market solution. At the level of the individual, the free market had brought rising incomes only for the upper levels of U.S. society. For the rest it meant stagnating wages, intransigent unemployment and sub-employment, and the unraveling of the social safety net. Far from being convinced that the automatic functioning of the market was in any way dysfunctional, however, conservatives doubled down. The failures of the last decades, brought on by the failure of government to act and the overreliance on the free market to solve all problems, led to an even more concerted right-wing attack on the idea that government can (or should) help. To conservatives, Adam Smith's "invisible hand" rules, and even the possibility of public action for the public good grovels before it. It is the pursuit of self-interest alone that leads to the good of all.

The now four-decades-long retreat from public efforts to systematically address social problems is a correlate of the rise in free market ideologies and of the collapse of organized countervailing forces such as unions (see below and chapter 4). At a societal level, efforts to reduce poverty and eliminate racial and ethnic inequities faltered, and wages for working families stagnated. The conservative response was to blame poor people for their own misfortune and to shift attention to street crime, the federal deficit, and the rights of gun owners.

The New Private-Public Intimacy

The rise of multinational corporations and of giant nonprofits, the new technologies, the spread of free market ideologies glorifying the individual, and the collapse of liberalism interacted with one another to produce a second major defining characteristic of Third Wave Capitalism: a vastly increased intimacy between the private sector and the state. The state had always served the needs of business, of course, but in Third Wave Capitalism the economic and political distinctions between the state, private enterprise, and the nonprofit sectors have become increasingly blurred. Whether in health care, military equipment, education, technology, or finance, it's very hard to make money any more without major government involvement.

Recall what came before. Until the 1960s or 1970s, the federal government and many state and local governments, with prodding from unions, civil rights organizations, a wide range of advocacy groups, and other components of civil society, served as a partial counterbalance to the power of the private sector. The basic operations of the capitalist economy were never challenged (howls of protest from the right notwithstanding), but federal and state regulatory systems did counter many of the worst excesses of private enterprise. At the federal level, at least, a moderately progressive system of taxation prevailed, and compared to pre-Depression days the distribution of wealth and income became less unfair. Federal fiscal and monetary policy moderated recessions. Americans' economic security were underpinned by governmental programs such as Social Security and Medicare, minimum wage and maximum hour laws, unemployment compensation, mortgage and housing subsidies, and Food Stamps. Quality of life was sustained by environmental and occupational health and safety regulation. The government protected the position of labor unions and, from the sixties on, the rights of racial and ethnic minorities and women. These government roles helped maintain an implicit social contract: working-class and middle-class Americans would accept the economic and political structure of society in exchange for a steady increase in their standard of living, quality of life, and political and social rights.[35]

Then, beginning in the late 1970s, everything changed. Against a background of the largest strike wave since the post–World War II shutdowns of 1945–46 (with many of the strikes initiated by rank-and-file workers without the approval of the union bureaucracy), business went on an anti-union crusade, aided by its allies in government.[36] Manufacturing employment, the most important source of union membership, began a steady decline, the victim of automation, outsourcing, and foreign competition. The federal government became increasingly hostile to unions. National Labor Relations Board (NLRB) decisions impeded union organizing. The Internal Revenue Service allowed corporations to redefine an increasingly large part of their staffs as independent contractors, supervisors, part-time workers, or interns, exempting them from the protection of the NLRB. And in 1981, the Reagan administration decided to break the air traffic controllers' strike. Individual companies stepped up their war on unions, or picked up shop and moved production to non-unionized facilities in the American South or in low-income countries. Not surprisingly, union membership and union power plummeted. Union membership, expressed as a percent of employed workers, dropped by two-thirds from its 1954 peak.

At the same time, the civil rights movement, the militant black and Latino community movements, the New Left, and the feminist movement of the late sixties and early seventies also declined or were defeated. The FBI's COINTELPRO (an acronym for COunterINTELligence PROgram, a series of covert and often illegal efforts to infiltrate, discredit, and disrupt "radical" social movements), played a major role in their decline. The collapse of these movements combined with the decline in the union movement dramatically reduced the pressure on government to sustain the social gains and worker and consumer protections of earlier years.[37]

The decline in countervailing forces, the rise of conservative free market ideology, and the pressures of globalization together provide the context in which government and the private sector cozied up. Government became ever more closely allied with business interests, and deregulation of business became a permanent project of both Republicans and Democrats. In the late 1970s, Democrat Jimmy Carter led the way, deregulating airlines and trucking. Republican Ronald Reagan followed, loosening regulation of savings and loans, oil and natural gas production, interstate bus service, and ocean shipping, and weakening the vigor with which remaining regulations were enforced. Under Republican George H. W. Bush, some environmental regulations were strengthened but regulation of the electric power industry was loosened. Democrat Bill Clinton continued the tide of deregulation, repealing the 1930s Glass-Steagall Act, which had separated commercial and investment banking, and deregulating the financial products known as derivatives. In the wake of the financial crisis of 2008, some re-regulation of financial institutions became inevitable, but in the years since the passage of the Dodd-Frank Act, efforts to roll back the new regulations have reappeared, with support from Republicans and some Democrats.[38]

Under Democrats and Republicans alike, programs that had historically been governmental were spun off to semi-autonomous "authorities" such as the Long Island Power Authority (electricity) and the Massachusetts Water Resources Authority (water and sewer services). Other programs were simply given to the private sector: Federal government-sponsored private enterprises such as Sallie Mae originated, serviced, and collected private education loans and Freddie Mac guaranteed home mortgages. The operation of these programs became less accountable and less transparent, and the private agencies running them took a cut of the taxpayer-provided funds as profits and as high executive salaries.

The U.S. government bailout of banks and auto companies in the wake of the 2008 crash is well known, but long before that it had bailed out, among others, Lockheed in 1971, Chrysler in 1980, savings and loans in 1989, and the airline industry in 2001. Governments also directly contracted with private, for-profit firms to carry out what had long been government functions. Such contracting now adds up to more than $500 billion a year at the federal level, more than one-third of all federal government discretionary spending. State and local governments outsource billions more. Private firms were hired to carry out military functions (Blackwater, for example), intelligence functions (e.g., Booz, Allen, Hamilton), and information technology and communications functions (EDS). They were hired to operate prisons and Immigration and Naturalization Service detention centers (e.g., Corrections Corporation of America), to operate public transport systems (e.g., Accenture), to run schools (e.g., KIPP, Gulen, Success Academy), to develop and maintain roads (e.g., Infrastructure Corporation of America, Plenary Roads Denver, VMS Inc.), and to administer Medicare and Medicaid (e.g., United Health Care, Humana). At the same time, wealthy people, working through nonprofit foundations and think tanks, undertook previously governmental tasks, such as developing, promoting, and financing education "reform," with little or no input from the public (see chapter 3).[39]

Sometimes the outsourcing was not deliberate but was the result of the private sector's ability to compete effectively with the public and nonprofit sector (often by cherry picking the most profitable lines of business). Thus chains of proprietary general and psychiatric hospitals such as Hospital Corporation of America and Psychiatric Solutions have taken over an ever-growing part of health care, and Fed Ex and UPS have taken over an ever-increasing portion of mail delivery. There is little evidence that out-sourced or privatized services are more efficient than government-run services. To take one example, FedEx and UPS use the U.S. mail to ship the more than one-third of their ground deliveries that are not cost-efficient for them to do themselves. That is, they shift their high-cost deliveries to the government.[40]

Generally the last decades have seen the emergence of what have been called "complexes" of intimately interacting businesses, nonprofit, and governmental enterprises. First came the "military-industrial complex," against which President Eisenhower warned in his 1961 farewell address. By 1970, the lineaments of a medical-industrial complex had begun to emerge (see chapter 2). Today, an educational-industrial complex (chapter 3), a prison-industrial complex (chapter 4), and, for all intents and purposes, a banking-industrial complex have joined the others.

Elections themselves have come increasingly under the sway of private enterprise. With the Supreme Court's 2010 *Citizen United* and 2014 *Mc-Cutcheon* decisions, what few barriers remained between money and political power disappeared. Reflecting the decline of organized labor, the rise of new technologies such as social media, and the massive flows of corporate and individual money into politics, the basis of American politics shifted from a "community organizing" model, driven by grassroots activism and by unions, to a "mass communications" model, based on television, robocalls, social media, and other technology-driven approaches.

Increasingly the state, influenced by corporations, took on a direct role in shifting resources from poor to rich. Lobbyists (often circulating back and forth between government positions and the private sector), regulators (in cahoots with the regulated and often going from working for the regulatory agencies to working for the companies they had regulated), legislators (increasingly dependent on the corporate rich for campaign financing), mogul-controlled media, and other elite-controlled cultural institutions systematically sought to shift wealth toward the owning classes.

In many cases, industry lobbyists actually wrote tax regulations, to the benefit of the well-to-do. The maximum individual marginal tax rate, 70 percent in the seventies, was dropped to 50 percent, then to 28 percent under President Reagan. It was raised to 39.6 percent under Bill Clinton, cut to 35 percent by George W. Bush, and returned to the Clinton level under Barack Obama. It still remains far below the 1945–86 levels, however, and Obama era cutbacks in federal spending shifted a greater part of the overall tax burden to the states and cities, where the tax rates are much more regressive. At the same time, under the influence of free market ideology proclaiming that "big government" and deficits were at the root of all economic difficulties before and since the financial crisis of 2008, tax cuts and government subsidies amounting to an estimated $100–200 billion a year were provided to corporations.[41]

Other public policy changes directly undercut the economic position of working people. The federally mandated minimum wage, which underlies the entire wage structure, was allowed to decline simply by not raising it. The minimum wage peaked in purchasing power in 1968. If the 1968 minimum wage had merely kept up with inflation, the minimum hourly wage today would be $10.79, almost 50 percent above its current level. If it had increased proportionate to the gains in worker productivity, it would be nearly $18.50 an hour (and well above the $15 an hour which today is often denounced as a radical demand that would destabilize the labor market). As for the long-term unemployed, cash benefits under the federal welfare program, Aid for Families with Dependent Children, declined 47 percent, adjusted for inflation, even before the 1998 Clinton welfare reforms. Since then they have declined another 20 percent and are available to far fewer people in need. Failure to adjust the salary threshold entitling salaried employees to overtime pay and tax law changes encouraging the move from defined benefit pension plans to defined contribution plans (which shift the risk to the employee) further reduced worker security.

Ironically, the social safety net, which was developed in the era of corporate capitalism to enable workers to withstand temporary adversities, in the era of Third Wave Capitalism has been turned into a subsidy to enable employers to pay lower wages. One recent study found that nearly three-quarters of the people helped by programs geared to the poor are members of a family headed by a worker. Their employers are able to pay them low wages only because the workers can fall back on the more than

$150 billion a year that state and federal governments spend on four key programs used by low-income working families: Medicaid, Temporary Assistance for Needy Families, food stamps, and the Earned Income Tax Credit. Housing and child-care subsidies provide additional aid.[42]

Rent-Seeking and the Accumulation of Wealth

The third major defining characteristic of Third Wave Capitalism is the tendency for rewards to go not to those who create wealth but to those who succeed in using their power over government and private institutions to grab a greater share of the wealth that would have been produced in any circumstances.

Economists call this "rent-seeking." As Nobel Prize–winning economist Joseph Stiglitz and Harvard public policy professor Linda Bilmes explain,

> The word 'rent' was originally used, and still is, to describe what someone received for the use of a piece of his land—it's the return obtained by virtue of ownership, and not because of anything one actually does or produces. This stands in contrast to 'wages,' for example, which connotes compensation for the labor that workers provide. The term 'rent' was eventually extended to include monopoly profits [and] other kinds of ownership claims.[43]

Thus, the profits gained when the government grants a company the right to import a certain good, such as sugar, at a favored tariff rate, or grants the right to mine or drill on public land, or grants preferential tax treatment for particular industries, all constitute rents.

Every functional society since caveman days has produced more goods and services than are needed for bare survival, and in every society there has been an ongoing battle over how to divide up this "social surplus." Slave masters struggled with slaves over how much food the slaves would get, and feudal lords struggled with serfs over how many days of labor a year would belong to the lord. In more recent times, landlords battled renters, bankers battled borrowers, manufacturers battled workers, and merchants battled customers.

Historically there have been many tools and weapons used by those with power to seize a disproportionate share of the social surplus. Legal codifications of status underlay the slave-owners' ability to seize the surplus produced by their slaves. Tradition helped determine the share that feudal lords extracted from their serfs. Ownership of land or of the machinery of production gives landlords and manufacturers the upper hand over renters and workers. Reputation and status enable a few pop stars to earn far more than many equally talented singers. Intellectual and social capital, including access to government and corporate officials at home and abroad, enable Bill Clinton and Henry Kissinger to make fortunes offering up their opinions (labeled "consulting and speaking"), even though they are no longer in office.

In Third Wave Capitalism, the above mechanisms still apply, but increasingly it is *power* that determines the distribution of earnings and wealth. That is, rent-seeking is the route to wealth. Government determines what the tax rates are, what is fair competition, what business activities are legal, what portion of the social costs of air and water pollution corporations have to pay, what kinds of debts can be discharged through bankruptcy laws, what kind of personal assets can be protected when one is eligible for Medicaid, and what inequalities in access to financial information are permissible. With the increasingly tight ties between government and the private sector and the increasing centrality of federal, state, and local government policies to business operations, the road to riches lies in gaining control over those policies. It means working hand-in-hand with elected officials to limit regulation of business, to gain access to direct and indirect governmental subsidies, and to encourage the shift of potentially profitable activities from government to private enterprise (whether for-profit or nonprofit).

The rent-seeking sector par excellence is the financial industry. As Stiglitz and Bilmes write,

> [The financial industry] now largely functions as a market in speculation rather than a tool for promoting true economic productivity. . . . Rent seeking goes beyond speculation. The financial sector also gets rents out of its domination of the means of payment—the exorbitant credit- and debit-card fees and also the less well-known fees charged to merchants and passed on, eventually, to consumers. The money it siphons from poor and middle-class Americans through predatory lending practices can be thought of as rents. In recent years, the financial sector has accounted for some 40 percent of all corporate profits.[44]

Rent-seeking, put in blunt terms, is nothing more than the naked redistribution of wealth from those with less power to those with more. In the era of rent-seeking, social conflict increasingly focuses on laws and regulations, social benefits, private subsidies, and other governmental and corporate policies and programs that affect market share, credit, wages, and profits.

Even in the private sector, wealth more and more comes not from producing something or performing some service of value, but from power within the corporation. CEOs generally heavily influence the appointment of the members of their corporate boards, which in turn determine the CEOs' pay. In recent years, they have used that power to their own benefit. In 1973, the typical CEO at a top U.S. firm earned annually about twenty-two times what a full-time, nonsupervisory worker in their company earned. By 2000, the ratio had reached 383 to 1. Since CEO pay is usually tied to the value of the firm's stock, the CEO-to-worker pay ratio fell during the 2001 and 2008 recessions, when stock prices fell, but it recovered along with the economic recovery. Since 2009, while worker compensation has remained flat, CEO compensation has grown by more than 33 percent. Other top managers have shared in the gains. A significant part of the dramatic increase in income inequality in the U.S. over the last few decades stems from this factor alone.[45]

Another potent source of wealth is a different type of power—monopolistic power over markets. To take one example, drug companies' ability to obtain favorable patent laws, together with their ability to get Congress to pass a law barring the government from negotiating the drug prices paid by Medicare, enable them to charge whatever they will for their drugs. And where does the Bill Gates fortune come from? It is not a reward for his being a better computer programmer than anyone else, or even for his creating Microsoft Windows thirty years ago. Microsoft extracted an average of $180 (shall we call it the Gates tax?) from every man, woman, and child in the United States who bought a computer, through Microsoft's power to force computer manufacturers to make Windows their operating system and to bundle Internet Explorer and other software with Windows.[46]

Why Does It Matter to Call It Third Wave Capitalism?

I began this chapter with a question: how did America go off the track in the four decades following the mid-1970s? Since then we have seen rising inequality, stagnating wages, and a poverty rate that just won't go down, even in prosperous times. Health-care costs rise with no apparent limit, despite the failure of our health-care system to match those of other affluent countries. A chorus of demands to reform our "failing" schools continues, although those schools seem to be giving more Americans more and better education than ever before. Racial disparities in income, housing, schooling, health care, and criminal justice have not improved. Personal misery and rage are rife; and liberalism apparently has been defeated.

Viewed from the perspective of the transition to Third Wave Capitalism, these developments seem less puzzling. They are all the direct consequences of the workings of Third Wave Capitalism, with its blurring of the distinction between business and government, its absence of countervailing forces, its pervasive rent-seeking, and its individualistic, free market ideology. In the decades since the mid-seventies, conservatives and the wealthy have been able to roll back many of the earlier, hard-won economic and social gains of the poor and of the working and middle classes. As Warren Buffet famously said, "There's class war, all right, but it's my class, the rich class, that's making war and winning."[47]

In Third Wave Capitalism, great wealth is generated by the dynamic and relentless corporate search for profits. New technologies, developed through implicit or explicit government partnerships with for-profit and nonprofit corporations, are rapidly integrated into production, distribution, and other business operations. Government underwrites the vast and very profitable expansion of our health-care system, military industries, and financial sector. New opportunities for profit-making are seized from what used to be public systems, such as schools and prisons.

At the same time, the power of those who might have other agendas is destroyed. Governmental regulation of business is gutted. The very notion that people, acting collectively and deliberately through government, can address our common problems is ridiculed, and the capacity for government to do so (which may require raising taxes) is weakened. It often seems that the only legitimate roles left for government are to enable the already powerful to seize an ever-larger part of the wealth that is produced—and to control those who are left behind.

2

THE HEALTH OF NATIONS

Health care provides an example of a quintessentially Third Wave system. Today's health-care system has come a long way from the old family doctor, neighborhood drugstore, and community hospital. Although its major components date back to the era of Corporate Capitalism and even before, it developed into its current form only in the years after Medicare and Medicaid went into effect in the late 1960s, at the dawn of the Third Wave era.

Today health care in America is dominated by the medical-industrial complex, a characteristically Third Wave mix of intimately interacting for-profit businesses, nonprofit enterprises, and government agencies. Though generating enormous profits for the private sector, every part of it is completely dependent on government spending and completely integrated with public-sector institutions and programs. Huge non-profit enterprises play a central role not just in the actual administration of health services but also in the generation of profits for the for-profit sector. The well-known high costs of health care reflect the

control that drug and medical supply companies, insurance companies, and hospitals have over the health-care enterprise and over government health policy, rather than accurately reflecting the value of the
goods and services it provides. That is, much of the wealth generated
by the health-care system constitutes rent-seeking. And the American
health-care system is both built on and reinforces an individualistic,
free market ideology that simultaneously embraces government subsidization and scorns government intervention.

When I was very young, my father contracted tuberculosis, a disease then
treated by sending the patient to a sanitarium in the countryside. My father's sanitarium stay lasted over a year and a half. Tuberculosis in those
days was still the seventh-leading cause of death in the United States, and,
had my father become ill only a year or two earlier, he probably would
have died. But the year before he became ill, a clinical trial had shown that
the then-new antibiotic, streptomycin, could be used to treat the disease
successfully. My father was enrolled in an experimental treatment program (featuring fourteen intramuscular shots a day of the antibiotic) and
recovered, enabling him to live to age ninety-four. I was left with an almost
magical belief in the efficacy of modern medicine. After all, it had saved
my father's life.

Years later, as a graduate student in biology at Rockefeller University,
one of the temples of biomedical science, one of my mentors was Rene
Dubos. Dubos had played a key role in the development of antibiotics, in
1939 discovering gramicidin, the first commercially produced, clinically
useful antibiotic. He also had written a book, *The White Plague*, in which
he showed that even before the introduction of streptomycin, the death
rate from tuberculosis in the United States had dropped to less than a quarter of the turn-of-the-century rate. Modern medicine may have saved my
father, but what saved millions of other Americans from TB was not antibiotics but better hygiene and other public health measures.[1]

The goal of health care is, of course, better health—reduced sickness,
disability, and suffering, and longer, more productive lives. We do not desire to get injections, undergo surgery, take medication, or spend time in
a doctor's waiting room. We seek out health care because it is a route to
health. Any discussion of the problems in the American health-care system
will get us nowhere unless we recognize that that "medical care," is not a

synonym for "health care" that health care is not the only route to better health, and that reducing sickness and disability and suffering is not the only goal pursued by the health care system.

The Price of Health

Let us start with the conventional narrative, in which we equate improving health with improving health care and conflate "health care" with "medical care." From this perspective, the Affordable Care Act, President Obama's signature effort to improve the U.S. health-care system, will probably be the most important lasting achievement of his presidency. It has certainly been the most divisive political issue in the United States over the last few years. President Obama declared that passage of the Affordable Care Act "answers the prayers of every American who has hoped for something to be done about a health care system that works for insurance companies, but not for ordinary people. . . . It's a victory for the American people." Supporters such as former U.S. Senate Majority Leader Tom Daschle proclaimed that "every American's quality of life will improve as a result of its passage." Then-Senate Minority Leader Mitch McConnell retorted that the act was unnecessary, saying the United States already had "the finest health care system in the world." Neurosurgeon, conservative pundit and 2016 presidential hopeful Ben Carson upped the ante, calling Obamacare "the worst thing that has happened in this nation since slavery."[2]

The driving force behind the Affordable Care Act was costs. The American health-care system is the most expensive in the world. In 2013, Americans spent more than $2.9 trillion on health care. That represents more than 17 percent of the Gross Domestic Product, the equivalent of $9,255 for every person in the country. We spend 50 percent more per capita on health than Norway, the second-biggest spender, and more than twice as much per capita as Sweden, Germany, France, and Japan, all countries that provide health care whose quality matches or surpasses our own.[3]

Health-care spending consumes an ever-larger part of family budgets. Per capita spending on health care has grown more than 300 percent since 1990, four times faster than spending in other sectors of the economy. The rate of inflation has slowed somewhat since 2008, largely due to the lingering effects of the recession and slow recovery. But even by the most optimistic estimates, although some provisions of the Affordable Care Act may help moderate inflation in the health-care sector, they will not fundamentally change the disproportionate amount of resources going into health care.[4]

One might ask, "So what? What better thing is there to spend our money on than our health, on relieving pain and suffering and disability and extending our lifespans?" But the more we spend on health care, the less we have available to spend on other desired goals. For those with poor health insurance or none at all, the cost of medical care is borne directly. For those who do have good health insurance, it is reflected in higher premiums. For employers who pay all or a portion of their workers' insurance, the rising burden of health insurance premiums cuts into their profits. For state and local governments faced with rising costs for Medicaid (the governmental insurance program that pays the medical costs of poor people), the rising cost of care seems to leave little alternative but to cut back on schools and other needed programs. And the widely held fears that the federal budget is intractably in deficit, which has driven so much of our recent political gridlock, largely rests on the belief that costs for Medicaid and Medicare will continue to soar.

The high costs of medical care also directly affect the health care Americans receive. Put simply, if you don't have insurance and can't pay out of your own pocket, or if the cost of getting care is a significant threat to your economic well-being, you delay getting care or fail to get it at all. Despite Obamacare, many remain uninsured or underinsured. In the summer of 2015, after the second round of Affordable Care Act enrollments, almost 10 percent of U.S. citizens, some thirty million people, still remained without insurance.[5] In part this reflects the fact that even with Affordable Care Act subsidies, the cost of premiums remains a significant barrier for many. In part it reflects the ideologically driven refusal of many states to expand their Medicaid programs, despite the fact that the federal government picks up almost the entire bill.

The burden falls heaviest on people of color and the poor. As of early 2015, more than 15 percent of African Americans, 28 percent of Latinos, and almost 24 percent of those from poor families regardless of race or ethnicity had no insurance. Even many of those, white and nonwhite, who do have insurance are deterred from seeking needed medical care by soaring copayments (as much as 35–50 percent of the cost of each service) and deductibles (often several thousand dollars per family member), as their insurance companies try to cut the amount that they have to pay out for their enrollees' medical services.[6]

The results are predictable. A 2013 Commonwealth Fund study found that more than one in three Americans surveyed reported that they had skipped a recommended medical test, treatment, or follow-up due to cost, or had a medical problem but did not visit a doctor or clinic or had not filled a prescription in the previous two years for the same reason. Even for those who had health insurance throughout the year, more than one-quarter reported that their access to health care had been limited by cost over the preceding twelve months. By contrast, only 4–6 percent of British and Swedish subjects reported similar problems.[7]

The Quality of U.S. Health Care

The cost of health care and its consequences are familiar. But what do we get for that $2.9 trillion? The public conversation about health care seems to assume that the quality of U.S. health care is high, as good as it gets. Perhaps in this sense, bragging about the American health-care system as the "best in the world" might be justified. But this claim, too, fails to stand up to close examination.

First, the good news: By any reasonable standard, Americans are healthier now than in the past. Life expectancy at birth has gone up by five years since 1980 and more than ten years since 1950. The infant mortality rate is down 52 percent since 1980. Life expectancy at age twenty, age fifty, and age seventy has also lengthened dramatically, for both men and women and for both the white and the nonwhite population. Since 1991 alone, death rates from the leading forms of cancer—lung, colon, breast, and prostate—have fallen by more than 30 percent and age-adjusted mortality rates for coronary heart disease have declined steadily in the United States since the 1960s.[8]

Now the bad news: Though, in absolute terms, the health of Americans has improved, we live shorter lives and experience more injuries and illnesses than people in other high-income countries. In a National Research Council study, mortality rates in the United States were the worst among seventeen high-income countries, including Germany, Japan, Canada, France, Sweden, and the United Kingdom.

Americans die of higher rates of cardiovascular disease than citizens of all but two of the other wealthy countries. We have higher rates of respiratory diseases and infectious and parasitic diseases than citizens of all but one of the others, and we have higher rates of diabetes, endocrine diseases, genitourinary diseases, and perinatal conditions than any of the other sixteen wealthy countries studied. U.S. adolescents are more likely than their peers elsewhere to be obese or to have a chronic illness such as asthma. Older Americans report a higher level of arthritis and activity limitations than their counterparts. With respect to cancer deaths we are right in the middle of the pack.[9]

Despite forty years of spectacular medical progress, much of it based on made-in-the-USA research, we have actually lost ground compared to citizens of other industrial nations with respect to infant mortality and life expectancy at birth, in young adulthood, at midlife, and at age sixty. Before 1965, U.S. infant mortality rates were lower than those in other industrialized countries. Since 1975, however, U.S. performance has steadily deteriorated relative to other countries, and today the country has the highest infant mortality rate and the highest rate of low-birth-weight infants of any of the wealthy countries. A forty-to-fifty-year-old in Japan, France, or Sweden can expect to live two to three years longer than his or her equivalent in the United States.[10]

There remain enormous disparities in health status within the United States, as well. The mortality rate for African Americans in the first days of life is twice that for whites, and the disparities persist throughout the lifespan. Life expectancy at birth is more than four years shorter for black males than for white males, and the life expectancy of a sixty-five-year-old black man is 1.6 years shorter than that of a sixty-five-year-old white man. African-American men have a 27 percent higher death rate from cancer than white men and a 26 percent higher rate of death from heart disease. African American women have a 14 percent higher death rate from cancer than white women, despite having a lower rate of new cancer cases, and they have a 32 percent higher rate of death from heart disease.[11]

Socioeconomic status, education, and geographic location also matter. A white woman without a high school diploma lives on average 10.4 years shorter than a white woman with a college degree or more. For white men, the gap is even bigger—12.9 years. And although mortality rates have fallen in most of the United States, they have actually been rising in recent years for white men and women without a high school diploma, and female mortality rates (regardless of socioeconomic status) rose in almost 43 percent of U.S. counties between 1992 and 2006.[12]

It is tempting to blame the overall poor performance of the United States on aggregate measures of health status such as life expectancy on our having more poor people than other countries categorized as "affluent." But even white, insured, college-educated, upper-income Americans have higher rates of heart disease, diabetes, cancer, and other health impairments than their counterparts abroad.[13]

What does explains the health lag? By international standards, the United States does quite well in some aspects of medical care. We excel at the most advanced high-tech treatments, and U.S. doctors do better than their peers in other highly industrialized countries at talking with their patients about healthy lifestyle (e.g., the importance of good nutrition, exercise, and giving up smoking), encouraging patients to ask questions, and giving them clear instructions about care of chronic conditions or aftercare following surgery.

At least part of failure is on the part of the health-care system itself. By many indices, the quality of U.S. medical care is not up to world standards. Consider, for example, the almost sacred doctor-patient relationship. The mythology of the family doctor dies hard, but in fact one in ten Americans has no regular doctor at all, and only 57 percent of U.S. citizens have seen the same doctor for five years, rates much lower than those in almost all other industrialized countries. We are also less likely to get a same-day response when we call the doctor, and we are less likely to be able to get a same-day or next-day appointment with our doctor. Even for those with insurance, a 2013 survey of medical offices found that in cities such as Boston, the average wait time for a new patient to get an appointment for nonemergency care in five different specialties (cardiology, dermatology, obstetrics and gynecology, orthopedic surgery, and family practice) was almost five weeks.[14]

Many—perhaps most—U.S. doctors and hospitals maintain a high standard of knowledge and practice. But a patient here has a far greater likelihood than patients in other industrialized countries of being given a wrong medication or a wrong dosage at a pharmacy or while hospitalized or being given incorrect information about the results of a diagnostic or laboratory test. Hospital errors are the third-leading cause of death in the United States, and medical care not meeting current standards of best practice is all too common. One study of Medicare patients who had suffered heart attacks found that only 21 percent of eligible patients had received the optimal medication. Another analysis of hysterectomies performed in women in seven different health plans found that one in six operations was inappropriate. Many other studies have found that doctors prescribe antibiotics for children's ear infections far more frequently than indicated and that they often prescribe antibiotics for colds, which is never indicated. Inadequate treatment of other basic and common medical conditions such as hypertension is also common.[15]

If the purpose of our health-care system is to ensure the nation's health, it is hard to avoid the conclusion that the U.S. system is not doing a very good job. Yes, the health of Americans today is significantly better than it was decades ago, and that is certainly something to celebrate. But U.S. medical care is overly expensive and for far too many, often inaccessible. Even if one can get and afford care, it often falls below the standard of quality expected in other affluent countries. A 2007 *New York Times* editorial commented that "it is doubtful that many Americans, faced with a life-threatening illness, would rather be treated elsewhere." Yet it acknowledged that this might be as much "a cultural preference for the home team" as a realistic assessment. It is hard to disagree with this conclusion.[16]

A Short History

Disturbing though this critique of health care in the United States may be, it is also profoundly misleading. It diverts us from asking even more basic questions about American health care.

Let us go back to fundamentals. The goal of health care is better health—reduction of sickness, disability, suffering, and premature death, and increase in physical and mental well-being. What determines health? How could we make Americans healthier?

First, we can try to prevent health-related problems from developing. Much of the improvement in Americans' health over the past hundred years reflects a reduction of disease due to overall improvements in economic and social conditions and changes in the ways we go about our everyday lives. Better housing, improved sanitary facilities, cleaner water and air, reduced work hours, better education, reduced poverty, and the like have dramatically reduced disease independently of individual health care. The greatest impact of these changes was on infectious diseases. Deaths from tuberculosis, typhus, typhoid, scarlet fever, cholera, and other great nineteenth-century killers all declined sharply, long before specific vaccines or treatments became available.[17]

A more explicitly health-oriented approach is to change individual behaviors that are associated with poor health outcomes: encourage people to wash their hands after using the toilet, eat a healthier diet, smoke less, drive more safely, exercise more, drink less, cope better with stress, and engage in safer sex. Educational campaigns (e.g., "This is your brain on drugs"), laws and regulations (e.g., a ban on trans fats in foods), and incentives and disincentives (e.g., taxes on cigarettes) all can play a role in encouraging such behaviors.

Perhaps the best-known and most effective recent example of this approach has been the campaign to reduce smoking. Educational campaigns (starting with the Surgeon General's 1964 report, "Smoking and Health"), federal taxes on cigarettes (making them less affordable), laws banning cigarette advertising on TV and radio and sale of tobacco products to minors, and bans on smoking in public places all contributed to changing behavior and ultimately the nation's health. The percentage of people who smoke has dropped to less than half the 1950s level. As a result, deaths from lung cancer have declined 12 percent over the last three decades—a saving of over forty-five thousand lives a year.[18]

Another effective, explicitly health-oriented approach is concerted governmental actions to reduce environmental sources of health-related problems. Many environmental threats to health are obvious and remediable: raw sewage or industrial wastes dumped into the water supply, toxic substances released into the air in the course of manufacturing or in providing services such as dry cleaning, infectious materials in medical waste, particulate by-products of burning coal for energy, harmful bacteria in food or milk, safety hazards from poorly designed roads. Other hazards are embedded in products we use in everyday life and are harder to discern. We've just begun to understand the risks of "endocrine disrupters" such as some additives to plastics used for packing food and beverages, pesticides used in agriculture, fire retardants in upholstery, and prescription drugs disposed of by flushing down the toilet (and thence entering the public water supply). Other health threats, such as those from genetically modified foods, are more arguable but cannot be dismissed.[19]

This governmental approach to public health has been very effective. Our air and water are cleaner and our food supply and waste disposal techniques are safer than years ago, but the battle against known and unknown environmental, societal, and behavioral sources of illness is far from won. By one estimate, more than 60 percent of U.S. cancer deaths are caused by smoking and diet; other environmental causes, such as air pollution and contaminants in food packaging, also account for a significant percentage. The major causes of death from breast, lung, pancreatic, and colorectal cancers, heart disease, stroke, and diabetes remain preventable environmental, social, and behavioral factors. Variations in social determinants of health, such as poverty, poor nutrition, poor schooling, poor housing, living in polluted communities, and unemployment, account for a significant part of the disparities in health status. And climate change harbors potential new health threats, including prolonged heat waves and increases in weather-related natural disasters, exacerbation of respiratory disorders, increased food insecurity, and lengthened transmission seasons and expanded geographic distribution of insect-borne diseases.[20]

Sadly, many corporate and government behaviors actually undercut efforts to promote health. For example, nutritionists urge people to eat less sugar and less red meat. At the same time, however, the U.S. government subsidizes sugar, corn, and soybean producers, leading to cheaper sweetened foods and meat. Meanwhile, soft drink companies and fast food companies pour billions of dollars into advertising not just their products but what City University of New York public health professor Nicholas Freudenberg calls a lifestyle characterized by "hyperconsumption" and the belief that more consumption is the key to happiness.[21]

Some of this disregard for the nation's health is blatant. For example, a few years ago the Bush administration, pressured by sugar producers and the packaged food industry, threatened the World Health Organization to get it to tone down anti-obesity guidelines that called for reducing sugar intake and increasing consumption of fruits and vegetables. In 2015, the same actors are trying to block a Food and Drug Administration proposal to require that foods be labeled with the amount of added sugar they contain. But often, disregard for public health is unintentional, simply a by-product of the normal functioning of the economic system.[22]

Harvard public health professor Dariush Mozaffarian observes, "The main goal of food production through most of human history . . . was producing as many inexpensive calories as possible that were free from bacterial contamination and toxins. A whole system was built around creating, shipping, and storing a handful of products—rice, soy, wheat." In the United States, this goal has been met spectacularly. Agricultural subsidies made the raw products cheaper. Factory farming of cattle, pigs, and poultry, streamlined industrial processing of foods, and more efficient transportation and distribution systems made the final products cheaper. And development of mass markets through advertising brought unit costs down even more.[23]

As a result, U.S. consumption of animal protein and total calories is high and the variety of foods available has increased. Although too many Americans still experience food insecurity, outright starvation is rare. Most people obtain more than enough nutrients to maintain their bodies and public health has benefited tremendously. But in recent years, the problem has reversed. For many, the problem is that they eat too much, depend too much on processed foods, and do not eat enough whole grains, fruits, vegetables, fish, nuts, legumes, and vegetable oils such as olive oil.

What prevents people from adopting healthier diets? Mozaffarian's studies suggest one factor is cost. A healthy diet—one rich in fruits, vegetables, nuts, and fish—costs roughly $1.50 more per person per day than a diet rich in processed foods, red meat, refined starches, sugar, salt, and trans fats. That comes to about $2,200 a year for a family of four, a major barrier for most U.S. families. But there are no government subsidies for broccoli, and agribusiness and food companies have a major investment in the status quo. The healthy diet does not have the benefit of either government subsidy or a long history of corporate rationalization of production and distribution processes. In the absence of government subsidization of more healthy foods and reduction in subsidization of unhealthy foods, the cost-benefit barrier to healthy eating is not likely to change.[24]

Now inevitably, no matter how effective individual and social efforts to prevent illness are, sooner or later we will all develop health problems. It is at this point, and only at this point, that medical care becomes a relevant way of improving people's health. Preventive medicine (for example, immunizations and early detection programs), treatment, and rehabilitation all play an important role.

There is no doubt that advanced medical techniques have significantly cut mortality from heart disease, cancer, strokes, and acute trauma. A recent study found that better medical care is to thank for about half of the decline in mortality from coronary heart disease and an even larger part of the decline in breast cancer mortality.[25] But—and it is an important but—medicine *can't* take credit for the other half of the decline. In fact, study after study has found that, taken as a whole, variations in availability and quality of medical care account for only 10–15 percent of the variation in health outcomes. The remaining 85–90 percent of the improvement in our health is due to our improved standard of living, efforts to clean up our food, air, and water, and changes in individual behavior such as reduced smoking and drunk driving. By one estimate, preventive or therapeutic medical practice is responsible for only five of the additional thirty years we now expect to live compared to our forebears a century ago.[26]

Yet while we spend $2.7 trillion a year on personal health care (including public, insurance, and personal expenditures) and our debates about health care focus on medical care alone, we spend well under 3 percent of our health-care dollars on public health activities (including campaigns to change harmful individual behaviors). And the United States spends a far smaller percentage of its GDP on social services and economic well-being, including housing, nutrition, education, the environment, and unemployment support, than do countries such as France, Austria, Sweden, Denmark, and Italy.[27] Something is wrong here.

I am not suggesting that we should give up on modern medicine. That train has left the station. There is no doubt that advanced medical techniques have significantly cut mortality from heart disease, cancer, strokes, and acute trauma. And no matter how much we reduce the burden of disease through prevention, when we get sick, we want the best medical care for ourselves. When my father had tuberculosis, antibiotics did save his life.

The issue is one of balance, and if we don't understand how our health-care system became so unbalanced, we will not be able to figure out how to use our resources in the most effective way to improve our health.

Where Did We Go Wrong?

The conventional narrative of the progress of American health care focuses on what doctors do and on the technology that enabled them to do it. Until the late nineteenth century, the story goes, most health care was provided by the family and the community. If you got sick, there was little that doctors could do for you, other than bleeding, blistering, and emetics (which is more what doctors could do *to* you than what they could do *for* you). Opined Oliver Wendell Holmes, Sr., a distinguished nineteenth-century physician also known for his poetry, "If the whole *materia medica* [drugs and other substances used in the treatment of disease] as now used could be sunk to the bottom of the sea, it would be all the better for mankind—and all the worse for the fishes." In those days, people went to hospitals only if they were poor and had no family to support them. In an 1876 essay awarded a prize by Harvard University, Dr. W. Gill Wylie asserted that though hospitals were indispensable for the care of accident victims, people with contagious epidemic diseases, soldiers, homeless paupers, and "the insane," to extend their reach further would only encourage pauperism. Hospitals, he lamented, "tend to weaken the family tie by separating the sick from their homes and their relatives."[28]

Three scientific advances changed all that. First, chemists such as Humphrey Davy, experimenting with ether and nitrous oxide, two drugs previously popularly used for a recreational high, and chloroform, a drug discovered by accident in the course of efforts to develop a pesticide, noticed that they could be used to produce anesthesia. Physicians such as Crawford Jones and dentists such as William Morton and Horace Wells soon began using them to reduce pain. Second, dyes developed to color the newly abundant factory-made fabrics led to dramatic improvements in the ability to study living material under a microscope. Using these advances, chemist Louis Pasteur, who was trying to understand the spoilage of beer, wine, and milk and the silkworm diseases plaguing the silk industry, and physician and microbiologist Robert Koch proved that many illnesses were caused by microrganisms. Third, physicist Wilhelm Roentgen, experimenting with vacuum tubes provided by electrical engineering pioneers such as Heinrich Hertz, Nikola Tesla, and William Crookes, discovered X-rays. A scientific basis for both medical practice and public health activities finally became possible, based on preventing exposure to germs (e.g., through aseptic surgery and cleaning up water supplies and food), preventing germs from causing illness (e.g., by means of vaccines and antitoxins), and killing germs (e.g., with antibacterial sulfa drugs and, later, antibiotics) and on safer surgery, guided by X-rays and made painless by anesthetics.

The tools for using the new scientific understandings in medical practice took time to develop, and for a while there was still not all that much that doctors could do. The distinguished medical historian Lawrence Henderson once reflected that it was not until "somewhere between 1910 and 1912 in this country, that a random patient, with a random disease, consulting a doctor chosen at random had, for the first time in the history of mankind, a better than fifty-fifty chance of profiting from the encounter."[29] In those years before World War I, my own grandmother, reflecting the earlier skepticism of doctors' power over illness yet perhaps dimly cognizant of the changes brewing, alternated among three doctors based on cost. There was the "five-cent doctor" for minor colds and the like, the "ten-cent doctor" for more serious ailments, and the "twenty-five-cent doctor," to whom she turned only when life seemed threatened. Later medical historians have often judged Henderson overly optimistic about the exact date of the shift, but by the 1920s and 1930s things had clearly begun to change. Vaccines, sulfa drugs and then antibiotics to combat infection, insulin for the treatment of diabetes, and vitamins to head off a variety of nutritional deficiency diseases came into common use.

The Emergence of the Modern Medical Profession

Thus far, the history I have recounted is more of a history of medical technology than of medical practice. What about the doctors themselves? In the early and mid-nineteenth century, they were a disreputable lot, far from the exalted professionals of the modern era. Few had any formal medical education, but since little was known of practical medical value, it didn't really matter. Various medical sects vied for patients—lay practitioners, homeopaths, osteopaths, "eclectic" healers, and the "allopaths" or "regular doctors" who were the ancestors of today's physicians. Doctors complained about their reputation as quacks and snake oil dealers, bemoaned the cutthroat competition for patients, and decried their low incomes.

In the latter part of the nineteenth century, the allopaths went on the offensive. Their struggle for dominance on health care rested on three pillars. First, they sought to persuade state governments to establish licensing laws, giving doctors who had completed formal medical training a monopoly over the practice of medicine. Then came reforming medical schools themselves, to create the base of knowledge that any "real" doctor should have. (Never mind that we are talking about the 1890s, when there was still not all that much that doctors knew how to do with their knowledge.) Schools such as Johns Hopkins, the University of Chicago, and the University of Pennsylvania pioneered a new model of more scientific medical education.

All that remained to ensure allopathic domination over healing was to reduce the number of competing doctors by reducing the number of medical schools. Steel magnate Andrew Carnegie and oil baron John D. Rockefeller rode to the rescue. The Carnegie Foundation hired Abraham Flexner, a trustee of Rockefeller's General Education Board (later subsumed into the Rockefeller Foundation), to survey the nation's medical schools. His 1910 report *Medical Education in the United States and Canada* defined the characteristics of an acceptable medical school. With Rockefeller foundations providing millions of dollars for medical schools that complied with Flexner Report recommendations, and with the Carnegie Foundation supporting the Council on Medical Education's demand that attendance at an approved medical school be a precondition for licensing, by 1920 half of the pre-Flexner medical schools had closed, and the number of students graduating medical school annually dropped by 42 percent.[30]

With the supply of doctors under control, a legal monopoly in place, and finally the beginnings of some actual medical skills, doctors quickly rose in social class, income, prestige, and power within the health-care system. Almost all doctors practiced on their own or in small groups. Ever fearful of the threats to their independence from large groups, potential corporate employers, or governments, they vigorously opposed corporate medicine and governmental interference.

The doctors' professional organization, the American Medical Association (AMA), quickly became the "voice of American medicine." In that role, it effectively worked against reforms in the U.S. health-care system. In particular, from 1916 on, the AMA took the lead in opposing all proposals for national health insurance. In 1936, it successfully blocked inclusion of national health insurance in the Social Security Act. In 1947 it mobilized against President Truman's renewed efforts to develop a national health insurance program. In 1965, it suggested that subsidies to the elderly to buy private health insurance were preferable to the government-run Medicare program. In the wake of its failure to defeat Medicare and the benefits physicians actually gained from Medicare and Medicaid, the AMA's opposition to change diminished. It remained passive when President Nixon proposed a national health insurance scheme in 1973. After initially supporting President Clinton's 1993 Health Security Act, the AMA backed off and again joined the opposition. Only in 2009–10, when its membership was down so sharply that it represented only about 15 percent of the nation's practicing doctors, did it finally support reform, the Affordable Care Act, although even then its support was not unequivocal.[31]

The Triumph of the Hospitals

Meanwhile, hospitals were also assuming their modern form. Before 1890, they had little to offer patients beyond moral exhortation and prayer, and they were shunned by the middle and upper classes. With anesthesia, aseptic techniques, and X-rays opening the door to safer surgery, however, they became more respectable, and a wave of hospital construction followed.

Just as the nineteenth-century artisanal workshop and small factory gave way to the vast corporation, now the thousands of solo and small group practices were forced to cede power to large medical institutions. No one doctor could hope to stock an office with all the expensive new tools of the trade or hope to employ a full team of nurses, lab technicians, radiologists, respiratory therapists, and other highly skilled helpers. And as specialization in medicine grew, individual practitioners became more and more dependent on a stable set of associations with other doctors and on hospitals. By the 1960s, hospitals had achieved a dominant position in the U.S. health-care system.

If technology made hospitals important to doctors, it was the growth of health insurance plans and government financing—especially Medicare and Medicaid, which went into effect in 1966—that made hospitals independently viable institutions with a potential for growth. Essentially all of the means of financing health services that burgeoned after World

War II—Blue Cross, commercial health insurance, the federal Hill-Burton program for hospital construction, and later Medicare and Medicaid—were oriented toward financing hospitals. Increasingly hospitals could depend on a guaranteed income. They did not have to depend on individual patients' bank accounts or provide large amounts of free "charity" care. Better yet, most of the insurance plans paid hospitals on a "cost-plus" basis, so that the hospitals felt free to expand or buy new equipment, secure in the knowledge that their costs would be covered. By 2012, more money ($970 billion) was going to hospitals for acute patient care than to all of Social Security ($730 billion) or all of defense ($650 billion).[32]

No sooner had the hospital replaced the doctor as the center of modern medicine than a third phase of development began, characterized by hospital mergers and affiliations and by the absorption of the doctors. Chains of proprietary (profit-making) hospitals appeared, along with not-for-profit multihospital systems. In many cities, smaller hospitals and public hospitals formed affiliations with the big teaching hospitals. As early as the late 1960s, these medical empires—networks of affiliated institutions—had begun to replace the individual hospital as the basic units of modern medical practice in many cities. By 1980, about 30 percent of the nation's community hospital beds were in one or another form of multi-institutional system.[33]

This tendency has dramatically accelerated in the last two decades, as hospitals sought better bargaining positions with insurance companies over reimbursement rates. In addition to combining several hospitals into a larger system, regional hospital networks have absorbed nursing homes and rehabilitation centers and have spun off primary care, urgent care, dialysis, one-day surgery, and health-care centers. In New York City, for example, four private hospital systems (New York–Presbyterian Health Care System, North Shore–Long Island Jewish Health System, Mount Sinai Health System, and Montefiore Health System), together with the New York City–owned Health and Hospitals Corporation, collectively run almost fifty hospitals, a dozen nursing homes, and several hundred ambulatory care and primary care centers. In Chicago, Advocate North-Shore Health Partners alone runs sixteen hospitals, serving some three million patients.

Beset with rising costs and a large number of uninsured patients, many rural and community hospitals and public facilities serving minority and poor populations closed down altogether. In the late 1990s, Boston University researchers found that nearly 28 percent of acute care hospitals in fifty-two large and midsize American cities had closed over the preceding two decades, in a pattern that "may have had an adverse and disproportionate impact on minority Americans." Updated research in 2001 showed that of those hospitals that in the 1930s had served neighborhoods that were 80 percent or more minority, 70 percent had closed.[34]

Earlier, despite the growing dominance of hospitals in the health-care system, most doctors had remained independent of the hospitals. Whether in solo practice or small group practice, doctors had "admitting privileges" to the hospitals, which enabled them to admit and care for their own patients when they were hospitalized. The wave of hospital mergers and affiliations changed all that, and several patterns emerged. Sometimes physicians banded together to form medical practice organizations, which contracted with hospitals to provide services. In New York, for example, the Physician Affiliate Group now includes some three thousand doctors who provide medical services for the city's publically owned hospital network. Elsewhere, hospitals bought up doctors' practices, which continued to operate separately, though now owned by the hospital. Still other hospitals employed physicians directly. When a community physician admits a patient to these hospitals, the patient's care is transferred to a "hospitalist" and the independent physician no longer retains his or her direct relationship with the patient.

In the 1970s, the overwhelming majority of U.S. physicians were still in independent solo or small group practices. By 2010, more than half were directly employed by hospitals or by integrated systems, and more than two-thirds of young doctors with up to five years in practice were salaried.[35]

The Rise of the Medical-Industrial Complex

The history I have recounted—a tale of America's six hundred thousand doctors, its fifty-seven hundred hospitals, and its ever-improving medical technology—is a familiar one, but it also leaves a lot out. Government at all levels appears as a somewhat distant player, financing here, regulating there, but not central to the endeavor. Insurance companies appear as financers of health care but of little interest in their own right. The giant multinational corporations that produce drugs, durable medical equipment such as wheelchairs and eyeglasses, and medical devices appear only as the suppliers of the technology that drives health care. The professionalization of medicine is explained by technological developments, with no acknowledgement of the fact that lawyers, accountants, engineers, and other highly skilled occupational groups turn out to have been professionalizing at exactly the same time, in most cases, without benefit of significant technological changes, or that the advances such as X-rays, anesthesia, and the beginnings, at least, of germ theory were themselves products of the Industrial Revolution more than of medicine per se. And what of the 2.6 million nurses, 600,000 therapists, 2.9 million health technologists and technicians, and almost 4 million nurses' aides, orderlies, and others in health-care support occupations, most of whom are female and who come disproportionately from minority racial or ethnic groups, who provide most of what we call health care? What of the millions of clerical and custodial workers who keep the machinery of the hospitals, nursing homes, and doctors' offices running?[36]

The conventional narrative of the progress of U.S. health care focuses on doctors, hospitals, and technology, and on the path that leads from the old family doctor to the wonders of modern, high-tech, hospital-centered medicine. New drugs, high-tech equipment, and aggressive care by well-trained doctors have, of course, saved millions of lives. But the real story of post–World War II U.S. health care is not only the technological miracles but also the emergence of the "medical-industrial complex"—the tightly linked complex of government, drug companies, medical supply and equipment companies, health insurance companies, hospital networks, and the like—and the shift to a narrow, treatment-focused conceptualization of health care.[37]

The U.S. health care system of the 1960s and earlier, despite the emergence of large hospital systems and insurance companies, was still essentially a Corporate Capitalist system, built around an imperative of providing health care. But then things began to change rapidly. As early as 1969, Barbara Ehrenreich and I observed that the development of the medical-industrial complex "may have more impact on health services delivery than anything that happens in the next decade of medical research." The impact has been far greater than we imagined. Spanning the profit-making, not-for-profit, and governmental sectors of the economy, health care now accounts for more than 17 percent of our Gross Domestic Product and employs almost one out of every nine Americans. Health-care industry profits have grown even more rapidly, increasing fortyfold since 1970, an increase four times as great as that for overall health-care expenditures, and they now account for well over $100 billion a year.[38]

The medical-industrial complex is made up of four components. First, there are the *providers*—not-for-profit and for-profit hospitals, nursing homes, and rehabilitation centers; clinical laboratories; freestanding ambulatory care, dialysis, urgent care, MRI, and other centers; and, of course, doctors, dentists, and a host of other therapists, whether employed by hospitals or in private practice. Second come the *financers*—the health insurance companies. Third come the *manufacturers*—the companies that produce the materials used in modern medicine—drugs, medical supplies such as syringes, durable medical equipment such as wheelchairs and glasses, and medical devices ranging from MRI machines and dialysis equipment to pacemakers. Finally, there is the *government*—federal, state, and local—which is itself a major provider and financer but also regulates, subsidizes, and seeks to manage the whole enterprise.

I will not try to be encyclopedic but rather to focus on a few important aspects of each of the elements of this system.

Hospitals and Nursing Homes

Hospitals seem a friendly kind of business. Unlike big business corporations, most of them are nonprofit organizations. They present themselves as places that care for you. "The community providers you know and trust," proclaims Danbury (Connecticut) Hospital. "Quality and compassion," promises Manhattan's Mount Sinai. "We never forget that before you're a patient, you're a person," says Boston's Beth Israel Deaconess Medical Center.

Hospitals do provide essential human services, but they are much more than benevolent institutions. Consider the case of New York City's New York–Presbyterian Health Care System, one of the nation's largest hospital systems. It includes ten acute-care hospitals, three specialty and rehabilitation hospitals, and four nursing homes and is affiliated with two medical schools (Weill Cornell Medical College and Columbia University's College of Physicians and Surgeons). Its hospitals have 2,478 beds and 4,571 attending physicians. It employs 21,747 people. In 2013 it had total assets of $7.4 billion, total revenues of $4.3 billion (including $154 million in investment income), and total profits of $356 million. In 2011, its CEO, Herbert Pardes, then in his last year as chief executive, was paid $4.1 million, and at least ten other executives were paid over $1 million a year. In short, New York–Presbyterian is a big business. If it had been a for-profit enterprise, it would have appeared as number 556 on *Fortune*'s annual list of the largest companies in the United States.[39]

New York–Presbyterian is not a typical hospital, of course, but most hospitals share many of its attributes in scaled-down versions—an excess of revenues over expenses, high salaries for CEOs and other top officials, and status as one of the largest employers and one of the largest holders of real estate in the community.[40]

Most community hospitals, like New York–Presbyterian, are called "nonprofit" enterprises, but as I discussed in chapter 1, that term is grossly misleading. In reality, a nonprofit is just a peculiar form of business enterprise. In 2011, the nearly five thousand nonfederal, short-term, general community hospitals in the United States posted a cumulative profit (i.e., excess of revenues over expenses) of $53 billion. In some cases, they owned for-profit subsidiaries, which do pay taxes. They also served as conduits for traditionally profit-making companies to make money. For example, hospitals provided a $1.75 billion a year market for the privately held EPIC Systems Corporation, a Wisconsin-based provider of information technology services to hospitals, earning Judy Faulkner, EPIC's CEO, a fortune of almost $3 billion.[41]

The nation's nonprofit hospitals receive some $12 billion a year in tax breaks, but their follow-through on their supposed commitment to public service varies. A study in the *New England Journal of Medicine* found that although, taken as a whole, they claim to spend an average of 7.5 percent of their operating costs on charity care, many spend far less, and what they consider charity is often debatable. For example, the hospitals count as charity the money they lose because Medicaid reimburses them at rates below what they calculate as their costs. The supposed costs are often arbitrarily inflated to start with, however. As *New York Times* reporter Elisabeth Rosenthal wrote, "If a hospital forgives a $3,000 bill for three stitches for a poor patient, how much of that should be counted as charity if the charges are greatly inflated?" Similarly, expenses for educating health professionals (who provide a significant part of the professional services the hospital delivers, in return for getting educated) are considered a service to the community.[42]

"The standard nonprofit doesn't act like a charity any more than Microsoft does—they also give away some stuff for free," says University of Illinois tax law professor John D. Colombo. "Hospitals' primary purpose is to deliver high quality health care for a fee, and they're good at that. But don't try to tell me that's charity. They price like a business. They make acquisitions like a business. They are businesses."[43]

Like their for-profit counterparts, nonprofit hospitals may engage in a variety of business practices to increase their own bottom line that may not work to the benefit of their workers or their patients. For example, outsourcing and offshoring of medical tasks such as reading X-rays and MRIs, analyzing tissue samples, transcribing medical records, and providing business processes have increased in recent years, raising issues of both quality control and patient privacy.[44]

In addition to the nonprofits, about one in six hospitals are now "proprietary," or profit-making in the usual sense, and do not get tax exemptions. Proprietaries tend to operate in geographic areas with higher average incomes, lower poverty rates, and lower rates of the uninsured than those of the areas where nonprofits are located. Many of these for-profit hospitals are owned by large corporate hospital chains, and like the big nonprofit hospital systems, these chains are big businesses. The fifty biggest chains have a combined gross revenue of well over $100 billion a year. The biggest chain, Hospital Corporation of America, operates 162 hospitals and 113 surgical centers. Number 79 on the 2013 Fortune 500 list, it had profits of $1.6 billion.[45]

Drugs and Medical Appliances

Drugs, supplies, and equipment account for 13 percent of health-care spending. That drug and medical supply companies are big multinational businesses barely needs saying. In 2013, the top eleven global drug companies made $85 billion in net profits.[46] What does deserve emphasis is their predatory practices and their disregard for public health.

Like hospitals, pharmaceutical companies like to proclaim their benevolent purposes. "The desire of the people in our companies to make a difference has inspired every invention, every product, every breakthrough we've brought to human health," says Johnson and Johnson in its annual report. Access to medicines is "a cornerstone of Pfizer's commitment to health care," brags Pfizer's report. What they do not brag about are their pricing, research, and marketing strategies.

First, the prices Big Pharma charges are so inflated that it is hard to call them anything but price gouging. In most other industrialized countries, the government indirectly or directly sets an allowed price for drugs. In the United States, the government leaves drug companies free to charge whatever the market will bear, with no relation to the cost of developing and procuring them. One result: drug companies charge far more for the drugs they sell in the United States than for the identical drug sold elsewhere. The wholesale price for Merck's top-selling diabetes drug Januvia, for example, was $1.99 in Europe, $8.20 in the United States. A month's supply of Genentech's cancer medication Avastin costs about $8,800 in the United States, twice the $3,978 charged in the United Kingdom. Astra-Zeneca's Pulmicort, a steroid inhaler, generally retails for over $175 in the United States, while pharmacists in Britain buy the identical product from wholesalers for about $20. A 2011 European Parliament study found that the price in the United States for a standard basket of 150 pharmaceutical products was about double the level seen in European Union countries.[47]

Drug companies justify their high prices by explaining that they reflect the more than $1 billion it takes to develop and bring to market a single new drug (though how this explains the difference in what they charge in Europe compared to the United States is hard to understand). Many of the accounting assumptions the companies use to make their billion-dollars-a-drug estimate have been sharply questioned. Some analysts believe the cost per marketed drug is closer to $55 million, about one-twentieth the drug companies' claims. In any case, most of the basic research on which their drugs are based is either directly funded by the U.S. government or is heavily subsidized by favorable tax treatment.[48]

Take the case of Gilead Sciences' Hepatitis C drug, Solvaldi (sofosbuvir), a lifesaver for millions of people. Gilead set the price for a twelve-week treatment at $84,000, or $1,000 per pill. Outside researchers have estimated that the actual production costs are between $68 and $136 per pill. What about those research costs, though? The basic research, including the first set of clinical trials, was funded by the National Institutes of Health and other federal agencies. The original researcher patented the drug and formed a company to produce it, which he then sold to Gilead for $11.2 billion. Gilead and other private investors, by economist Jeffrey Sachs' estimate, put in no more than another $300 million in research and development. In 2014 alone, Gilead sold $12.4 *billion* worth of the drug.[49]

Despite their professed commitment to health care, drug companies' *raison d'être* is to make money for their shareholders. But the profit motive and the nation's health are not the same thing, and it is the former, not the latter, that drives research priorities. The companies do not seek to develop drugs, no matter how potentially useful, if they are not likely to produce huge profits. Much of their research expense is wasted on producing "me-too" drugs—minor modifications of already existing drugs that enable a company to compete with the products other drug companies have already made or to enable them to patent a drug (and so keep out competition from generic drug manufacturers) when their own patents expire. In one year alone, the Food and Drug Administration classified three-quarters of the 119 drugs it approved as similar in chemical makeup or therapeutic value to existing drugs.[50]

Which diseases drug development targets is also distorted by the drug companies' drive for profits. Drugs for chronic diseases, which patients will take for the rest of their lives, are profitable, and, appropriately, much effort is put into their development. But drugs that will be taken only for a short period, no matter how many lives they might save, are not.

For example, since World War II, death and illness from infectious diseases have been dramatically reduced. However, excessive prescription of antibiotics by doctors and widespread use of antibiotics in animals has created new generations of drug-resistant microorganisms. Methicillin-resistant staphylococcus (MRSA), vancomycin-resistant enterococcus, and other resistant bacteria have become major threats to public health. Every year resistant bacteria cause two million serious illnesses, twenty-three thousand deaths, and an estimated $20 billion in additional medical costs. But for decades most drug companies have abandoned research aimed at developing new antibiotics altogether. They simply do not generate revenue. A few companies have recently tiptoed back into antibiotic development, with government subsidies and reduced regulatory strictness encouraging the trend. Still, in the 1980s, thirty new antibiotic entities gained approval in the United States. Between 2010 and 2012, only one did.[51]

Another significant part of the price of medications reflects the enormous expenditures of the drug companies on marketing. Industry-wide, it has been estimated that drug companies spend 25 percent of their revenues on promoting their products. In one year, Warner Lambert claimed it spent no less than 47 percent of its revenues on sales and administration. In many cases, sales costs far exceed research and production costs. In 2013, Amgen spent $5.2 billion on selling, general, and administrative expenses (mainly advertising and marketing), compared to $4 billion on research and development and $3.35 billion to actually produce its drugs.[52]

A significant part of drug companies' marketing expenses appears to serve no socially useful function. Perhaps the best example is the drug companies' skirting of Food and Drug Administration regulations to promote so-called off-label use of medications and to fully disclose safety risks. When a drug is introduced, it must undergo extensive testing, not only to prove that it is safe but also to insure that it is effective for the conditions for which it will be marketed. Legally, however, once a drug is approved and on the market, a physician can prescribe it for anything, regardless of the evidence. Despite a few cases to the contrary, there is little evidence that this serves patients well. But drug companies persist in marketing their products to physicians for these off-label uses. Pfizer, Glaxo Smith Kline, Abbott Labs, Eli Lilly, and Johnson and Johnson, among others, have faced large fines and in some cases criminal charges over this practice in recent years.[53]

Most of the powerful remedies in modern medicine are available only by prescription. The training, experience, and legal authority of licensed physicians alone decides when they should be used and by whom. It would therefore seem entirely appropriate for drug companies to market their products to doctors (though some of their ways of doing so have been questioned). It is hard to see how the mass marketing of prescription medications to consumers is useful. In 1997, however, the Food and Drug Administration determined that advertising prescription drugs on television and in newspapers and magazines was okay. The drug companies rushed in, and we now have TV ads for drugs for diabetes, asthma, high blood pressure, erectile dysfunction, and the like, complete with rapid-fire bewildering lists of contraindications and complications. Ads are even directed to children. A few years ago, Pfizer sponsored a season of *Sesame Street*, featuring ads for its antibiotic Zithromax, used for children's ear infections, ending with "Pfizer brings you the letter Z—for zebra, and, of course, Zithromax." Federal health officials were already warning that Zithromax was not only more expensive than other antibiotics but less effective, a warning that has since been corroborated, but it remains a very popular drug. Many physicians blame patient pressure for their excess prescribing of antibiotics for colds and ear infections, but if so, it is hard not to conclude that drug company advertising has contributed to patient expectations.[54]

Health Insurance Companies

Everybody loves to bash health insurance companies—and with good reason. Giant corporations, always ready to raise premiums, until forbidden to do so by the Affordable Care Act they were quick to refuse coverage to those who had preexisting conditions (in other words, those who needed coverage) and to refuse policy renewals to those who used their policy too much. They continue to excel at creating a bewildering array of plans and copayments and deductibles and exclusions, cutting payments to providers, making errors in processing claims that somehow seem to always be in their favor, and scraping (to use Jaron Lanier's concept) every penny of profits they can get out of health-care consumers and providers. They are an easy target.

The beginning of health insurance was far more benign. The earliest forms of health insurance were provided by mutual benefit funds, established by many unions and fraternal organizations in the late nineteenth century. My grandfather, working in a Lower East Side shirt factory after his immigration from Russia, joined the *Arbeiter Ring*—the Workman's Circle, a Jewish mutual benefit society that provided unemployment, medical, and life insurance for its members (as well as militantly supporting social justice causes). The logic of such insurance was clearly mutual aid. Members paid a fixed amount on a regular basis, regardless of their individual immediate needs. If and when a member needed it, a pool of money was there to help. Over a lifetime, some members ended up putting in more than they would actually use. Others would take out far more than they contributed. Potential patients got peace of mind from knowing they would be able to pay for needed care, and providers got peace of mind from knowing that their services would be paid for.

During the 1930s, with the costs of health care rising and the Great Depression cutting into the ability of many to pay, hospitals found their revenues declining and themselves in competition with other nearby hospitals to fill their beds. Hospitals in many cities banded together to offer hospitalization insurance, branded with the Blue Cross symbol by the American Hospital Association. Many features of the old mutuality embodied by earlier experiments in insurance were retained. Most importantly, Blue Cross premiums were based on "community rating." They charged the same premiums to all patients regardless of health status, age, or sex. In return, the states offered them tax-exempt status and reduced the normal requirement that the insurance companies carry large reserves. The states themselves regulated the premiums that Blue Cross hospitals could charge, and hospitals guaranteed that they would provide insured people with beds and health-care services at a preferred rate. Soon physicians followed suit, forming the doctor-controlled Blue Shield plans.

Still, on the eve of World War II, most people did not have health insurance coverage. But with war production ramping up and millions of workers in the military, labor shortages loomed. Workers wanted higher wages, and employers wanted to be able to offer higher compensation to attract them, but wages and prices had been frozen nationwide as a war measure. The National War Labor Board, however, ruled that benefits such as health insurance would not be considered as wages or salaries, so unions were freed to bargain for employer-paid health insurance as part of workers' compensation. Postwar National Labor Relations Board and court decisions confirmed this position. Then, in 1954, the IRS declared that it would not consider health benefits as part of a worker's income for tax purposes. As a result, they were not considered in determining payroll or income taxes, a significant tax break for both worker and employer. The number of people with health insurance mushroomed.

Seeing the success of Blue Cross and Blue Shield, private insurance companies began competing for the health insurance dollar. Unlike the Blues, they charged different groups of consumers different rates and turned down the highest-risk patients altogether. This "experience rating" system of determining premiums reduced the total amount of care their overall mix of clients needed and enabled them to charge lower premiums, despite their lack of any tax exemption.

Faced with competition from the commercial companies, beginning in the late 1990s the previously nonprofit Blues began to convert themselves into publically held, for-profit companies, ridding themselves of the community rating restrictions on their premiums. Both ex-Blues and traditionally commercial health insurance companies continued to trumpet the old mutualistic ideals, however. "At Anthem Blue Cross and Blue Shield we understand our health connects us to each other," proclaims the formerly nonprofit Anthem. "Together all the way. . . . See how much healthier you can be when someone has your back," promises the always-for-profit Cigna in its annual report. But in reality, the commercial version of health insurance eroded what little was left of the mutual aspects of the earlier insurance.

The business model of a commercial insurance company is to maximize revenue (by keeping premiums high and by investing their reserves) and to minimize expenses (by doing its best to not pay for care). They implement the latter by keeping coinsurance and deductibles high, cutting payment rates to providers, excluding some medical procedures from coverage altogether, and, until the practice was limited by the Affordable Health Care Act, cherry-picking patients to eliminate those who might use more care than average.[55] They also try to pass administrative costs along to patients and providers—for example, by requiring them to navigate opaque automated telephone menus and spend endless minutes remaining on hold for a customer representative to take a call that they insist is "very important to us." They "manage" care, using a variety of mechanisms including providing economic incentives to patients to select less costly forms of care (generic rather than brand-name drugs, for example), reviewing the "medical necessity" of specific services, limiting which health care providers they will cover, and sometimes restricting the forms of service a provider can offer.

It is no surprise that many of these practices have created a widespread perception that health insurance companies are more interested in saving money and making profits than providing access to health care. They continue to seek ways to shift costs to the sick and to the providers and to get around the "no cherry picking" rules of the Affordable Care Act. For example, in late 2014, advocacy groups charged that some companies were raising copayments on drugs typically used by those with certain expensive ailments such as HIV and Parkinson's Disease. The effect would be to make the cost to the consumer with one of these diseases higher than for patients who did not have any of these diseases, perhaps persuading these patients to shift to another insurance carrier.[56]

Government

As with Eisenhower's military-industrial complex, the rise of the medical-industrial complex was not simply a testimony to the initiative of private enterprise. It was the passage of Medicare and Medicaid, in 1965, at the dawn of the Third Wave Capitalist era, that triggered its development, and today all U.S. health care depends on government spending. Medicare, Medicaid, and the Children's Health Insurance Program (CHIP) together directly pay for 40 percent of all medical services.[57] A quarter of all hospitals are directly government-owned and operated. Government-funded research subsidizes drug company products. Federal and state loans, grants, and bonds subsidize hospital construction. Medicare subsidizes hospitals' costs in providing graduate medical education. Tax deductions for corporations that pay for their employees' health insurance and Affordable Care Act mandates to buy insurance subsidize the insurance industry. Government tax deductions for individuals for their medical expenses subsidize all health-care providers and health products manufacturers and health-care financers by making the goods and services they provide cheaper for the consumer to purchase. Government tax exemptions boost the profits of nonprofit hospitals. Federal, state, and local governments also regulate various parts of the health-care industry, including controlling the release and safety of medications (the Food and Drug Administration), licensing medical professionals (a state government function), and monitoring workplace health and safety (the Occupational Safety and Health Administration).[58]

The lines between government and industry are further blurred by outsourcing and privatization of public-sector programs. At the public health end, the Food and Drug Administration saves money by allowing poultry producers to inspect themselves for evidence of sources of food-borne illnesses.[59] Within the medical-care system, a much larger program of privatization is the outsourcing of Medicare and Medicaid claims, payment processing, call center services, clinician enrollment, and fraud investigation to companies such as Ross Perot's Electronic Data Systems. And during the Clinton administration, a privately owned but publically funded system to parallel Medicare was vastly expanded. Under Medicare Advantage Plans (as they are now known), instead of the government providing health coverage for the elderly, it pays private health insurance plans to do so. The Medicare Advantage program costs more per enrollee than the traditional government-run Medicare and it is poorly controlled. A 2013 U.S. Government Accountability Office report charged that Medicare may have overpaid Medicare Advantage Plan companies to the tune of $3–$5 billion during 2010–12. A provision in the Affordable Care Act called for cutting the subsidies to these private, for-profit programs, but in the spring of 2014 and again in the spring of 2015, the Obama administration, bowing to industry pressure, rescinded the cuts and increased the subsidies instead.[60]

Even at the policy level, it is sometimes hard to tell where government ends and business begins. To take one example, Elizabeth Fowler, the Senate Finance Committee staffer who drafted most of the Affordable Care Act, was the vice president for public policy and external affairs (in other words, lobbying) at Wellpoint (now Anthem), one of the country's largest health insurance providers, before taking up her policy-writing role. She replaced Michelle Easton, who herself went on to lobby for Wellpoint. Eventually, after following up by playing a key role in implementing the ACA, Fowler moved to drug, medical equipment, and home health products company Johnson and Johnson as vice president for global health policy.[61]

The Impact of the Medical-Industrial Complex

If all were well in the U.S. health-care system, the concerns I have raised about the medical-industrial complex might seem overblown. But all is not well. The health-care system is too costly, often unavailable to many, and sometimes of questionable quality. Measured by its outcome, the health of Americans, its performance is mediocre by contemporary international standards.

The Impact on Health-Care Costs

Much of the excessive spending that characterizes the American health-care system is the direct result of the operations of the medical-industrial complex. It is not just a matter of excessive profits. Published figures on what are conventionally defined as "profits" vastly understate the take of the medical-industrial complex. Excessive costs are built into the system throughout. Not counted in profits are the excess of revenues over expenses in "not-for-profit" hospitals, or the inordinately high salaries claimed by top managers of insurance companies, drug companies, and hospital chains, or the high marketing costs of the drug companies, or the unnecessary and largely arbitrary fees paid to hospitals, rewarded by a cost-based reimbursement system for performing unnecessary tests and procedures. Not counted in profits are the insurance companies' enormous overhead costs for underwriting and administration or the inflated administrative costs incurred by hospitals to negotiate the complex world of insurance payments from dozens of different insurance companies, each with their own rules. Not counted in profits is the distortion of care, away from lower-cost solutions to health problems and toward high-tech higher cost solutions.

The magnitude of each of these costs looked at separately is hard to calculate precisely. One study compared administrative costs for doctors in the United States, with its multiplicity of insurance and other financing systems, with those in Canada, with its single-payer system. The U.S. costs were four times higher. If U.S. physicians had administrative costs similar to those of the Canadians, the study concluded, the total savings would be approximately $27.6 billion per year.[62] The average doctor, it has been estimated, spends three weeks a year and about 12 percent of his or her net revenue on billing and insurance. Other studies note that the costs of drugs and diagnostic procedures are not only high but are totally arbitrary. In Philadelphia alone, for example, the cost of an echocardiogram ranges from to $700 to $12,000. In Belgium, the same procedure costs $80, in Germany, $115.[63]

Looked at in aggregate, however, we know exactly how much of U.S. health care costs can be attributed to profits and unnecessary expenditures. As I noted earlier, Sweden, Germany, France, and Japan, all countries that provide health care whose quality matches or surpasses our own, spend less than half as much per capita on health care as we do. A properly organized system could cut spending by at least 50 percent without reducing quality.

The approaches to reducing the costs of medical care that have dominated recent discussions, including those contained in the Affordable

Care Act, all but ignore these facts. Some proposals call for administrative "simplification," but the real issue is not inefficient administration of the payment system but the inefficiency of the entire payment system itself. A system in which insurance companies spend billions of dollars to market their products and underwrite risks and in which providers spend more billions of dollars figuring out how to wend their way through the maze of multiple payment procedures and requirements is inherently inefficient. Others call for "prospective" systems of payment to replace fee-for-service reimbursement of doctors and cost-plus reimbursement of hospitals, or arbitrary "sustainable growth rate" limitations to payments for doctors' services or caps on overall hospital spending, or tort reform to reduce unnecessary spending on "defensive" medicine (treatment done to ward off potential malpractice suits). But without examining why costs are so high, none of these approaches can do more than reduce the rate of increase. Yet others suggest that shifting costs to the patients through high deductibles and high copayments will create a more efficient health-care marketplace. Patients, conscious of the real cost of services, will moderate their own spending. Never mind that all but the very affluent will fail to seek out necessary spending on prevention and early care of illnesses.

The Impact on Health Policy

The impact of the medical-industrial complex on U.S. medical care goes far beyond its taking a big cut every time we see a doctor or go to a hospital. Most immediately, the power of the medical-industrial complex restricts the range of health policies that are thinkable or realizable.

One might think that in return for massive subsidies and massive outsourcing of health programs, the government would be able to make demands on the health industry to be more responsive to people's needs. But in the America of Third Wave Capitalism, deregulation and governmental kowtowing to the needs of the private sector prevail.

I have already described how Medicare and Medicaid handed over the business end of their operations to private companies and how the Clinton and Bush administrations carved out what is now 30 percent of Medicare to be operated by private insurance companies, at a higher cost per enrollee than government-provided Medicare. I have already described the massive subsidies to drug and medical equipment companies, in the form of government-financed research, tax breaks, and weak regulation. Yet neither a "public option" (which would provide competition for the insurance companies), negotiated prices for pharmaceuticals (regulation of the drug industry), nor a requirement that hospitals and physicians accept much more economical prospective payment systems in place of fee-for-service compensation (regulation of providers) were ever real possibilities as part of the Affordable Care Act. And for well over a generation, the idea of a publically run single-payer system of national health insurance (for example, expanding Medicare or Medicaid to cover everyone) has been entirely off the table.

The Impact on Health Workers

The growth of the hospitals transformed the very definition of "medical professional." New technology in medicine, unlike in some other industries, increases the demand for labor rather than decreasing it. If you buy an MRI machine, you need someone to operate it. An army of new professionals—medical technologists, nurses, physical therapists, occupational therapists, lab techs, and the like—arose to operate the new technology and to take over many of the activities formerly carried out in more primitive versions by doctors. At the same time, the number of clerical workers, bookkeepers, accountants, lawyers, and the like, needed to deal with insurance companies and government regulations, grew. As the medical enterprise grew and as the need to keep revenues above ever-increasing costs rose (regardless of ownership—public, nonprofit, or proprietary), hospital management professionalized. Hospital managers were now trained in schools of business rather than medical or nursing school, and they were more attuned to the bottom line than to the complexities of patient care, more concerned with managerial techniques than with the human-to-human interaction at the core of health care.

Health care came to be largely organized along corporate lines, with business-trained managers; an elite corps of highly trained professional staff (physicians), analogous to engineers, who organize and direct production; and a working-class stratum, ranging from highly skilled nurses, technologists, and therapists, to clerical workers, nurses' aides, kitchen workers, laundry workers, and the like, who perform more routinized work. Historically, the latter stratum is overwhelmingly female and disproportionately made up of people of color.

Pressures from hospitals, from insurance companies, and the government to cut costs have grown. But the power of the medical-industrial complex puts the underlying cost structure for drugs, appliances, tests, and administration of insurance payments off limits, so it is health workers who are left to bear the burden of reducing costs. When inefficient community hospitals close or are absorbed into larger hospital networks, skilled and unskilled staff are displaced. For workers in all hospitals, workloads have gotten more burdensome, wages have stagnated, and demands that they work overtime have increased. Health care has come to look like work in other, less-service-oriented industries. "Everyone wants to cut the costs of health care—at any cost!" a staff member at a health workers' union told me.[64]

An embittered, alienated health-care worker is the enemy of quality. Decent treatment of staff is a necessary for high-quality care and in the interests of patients, despite its costs. But the interests of the medical-industrial complex in sustaining multimillion-dollar salaries for top hospital, drug industry, and insurance industry executives and *multibillion*-dollar profits for drug and insurance companies directly conflict with the interests of health-care workers and patients.

The Impact on the Concept of Health Care

Medical care plays only a relatively small role in determining the health of a population, but doctors and the medical-industrial complex have an enormous vested interest in promoting individual medical solutions as the primary approach to health problems. Treating heart disease, cancer, and diabetes yields enormous profits for health-care providers and companies. Strengthening controls on air and water pollution and disposal of toxic wastes, requiring safety devices in cars, restricting overuse of prescription drugs, reducing federal agricultural subsidies to sugar and tobacco producers, and investing in education and housing and income security do not yield financial profits. The well-being of the medical-industrial complex forces U.S. health-care expenditures to focus more on high-tech and pharmaceutical treatments, less on preventive care, and still less on public health measures. The imbalance in resources devoted to different approaches to improving the health of Americans is the result.

The medical-industrial complex even plays a role in defining what is or is not a disease. "In June 2013, millions of Americans contracted a disease," observed the *New York Times*, commenting on a decision of the American Medical Association to label obesity a "multi-metabolic and hormonal disease state."[65] Providing the label, among other things, means that insurance companies are likely to reimburse treatment. The decision can be seen as a way of focusing attention on an important health problem and as helping remove the shame of obesity as a moral failing. But it evades the questions: Is the epidemic of obesity, like other, less problematic "diseases," due to a biological cause? Is it due to practices of the food industry (marketing and promoting high-fat, high-sugar foods)? Is it due to the increased dependence of many time-stressed two-wage-earner families on fast food and processed food? Is it due to the limited opportunities for physical activity for most adults in cities designed for cars, not walking? And does calling obesity a disease disempower people, lead them to think that the only solution is passive dependence on their doctors? Each of these explanations of obesity implies different research priorities and suggests different social regulations and spending priorities. Calling obesity a disease, however, closes the discussion.

Health care is a probe of the quality of a society. It reveals how a society deals with such fundamental human experiences as birth and death, illness and disability, suffering, pain, and aging. It shapes how we feel about ourselves and our bodies. In American society, under the influence of the powerful health-care industry (with the professional self-interests of physicians playing a major role), normal stages of life and many social problems have increasingly been defined as diseases. Pregnancy and birth, death and bereavement, infertility and erectile dysfunction, menopause, baldness, obesity, small breasts, insomnia, sadness, aggression, boys acting "like boys," excessive alcohol or drug use, delinquency, and difficulty adjusting to a job loss or a marital breakup—all are diseases and must be treated by a physician.

What goes unsaid in debates about health-care spending is that we spend far more on treating these now-medicalized conditions than on responding to the social and cultural context in which they become problems. That creates a double problem: Health care costs go up. And resources available for addressing the social and cultural sources of problems and motivation to do so go down. That the burden falls disproportionately on poor people and on people of color should not go unremarked.

The Impact on the Community

Lou Margolis, my family's doctor when I was a child, was a friend as well as physician to many in my extended family. When I got sick, he paid a house call and stayed to have coffee with my parents. He lived not too far from us, and he and his family occasionally came for dinner. When I was ten, my mother had a near-fatal heart attack. In those days, children were not usually allowed to visit adult hospital wards, for fear of infection. Dr. Margolis, with the nurses colluding, broke hospital regulations and snuck me into the hospital, up a back staircase that connected with the receiving dock. My mother survived. Was it her medications? Or seeing her child, possibly for the last time? Or was it just what nature had planned for her? I suspect that the correct answer combines a bit of each.

In all societies before the modern era, health care was not only a technical transaction between a person and a physician (today, guided by "science") but an interpersonal and community function as well. Curing was linked to caring. Even in modern times, until perhaps the late 1950s, that was the case. Your doctor lived in your neighborhood. He or she (usually he) knew your family, knew your socioeconomic situation, knew your community, went to your church or other place of worship, and knew the people you knew. His children went to the school you or your children attended. When you were seriously ill and in need of hospitalization, you went to a hospital in your community. Because it was nearby, it was easy for your family and friends to visit. Many of the staff also lived in your neighborhood.

That system was inefficient. A doctor's time is not well used if he or she has to spend time going from one patient's house to another. Small community hospitals cannot achieve efficiencies of scale or afford to provide the highest of high-tech care. But efficiency and saving money are not ends in themselves. Human medicine is not the same as veterinary medicine. Medications and surgical interventions are powerful, but so are relationships with health practitioners and the healing touch of a doctor or nurse. The more distant, "professional" (and financial) relationships of recent years, between individuals and their healers and between healers and community, are themselves health issues.

Those old networks of healing relationships also contributed to maintaining a community. Social support and community integration are important predictors of population health. When Dr. Margolis made house calls or snuck me up the back stairs of the hospital, he was being inefficient in terms of the economics of individual treatment. His contribution to the aspects of my family's health that depended on maintaining a community is much harder to measure.

The Ideology of the Medical-Industrial Complex

Given the power of the medical-industrial complex and its allies throughout the economic system, responsibility for a person's health falls entirely on his or her own actions (stopping smoking, for example, or eating better) and on the ministrations of a physician. There is little choice. I can't reduce the amount of salt and sugar in processed foods through individual action or reduce the use of antibiotics in animals. I can't refuse to breath air polluted by fumes from the dry cleaner down the street, or refuse to digest endocrine-disrupting additives embedded in the plastic containers my food comes in, or refuse to sit on furniture impregnated with fire retardants, or refuse to drink water containing traces of prescription drugs others have flushed down toilets. I *can* adjust my own habits (often despite enormously powerful explicit and implicit societal messages urging me not to do so and despite added costs in time and money). And I can go to a doctor if I get sick.

Any idea of collective action to improve my health is hard to entertain. An individualistic ideology, one that sees the isolated individual as responsible for his or her own problems and responsible for solving them, becomes inescapable. We learn to blame the victim. Lung cancer is the fault of the victim because she smoked. Diabetes is the fault of the victim because he let himself get obese. We feel increasingly passive, powerless, and ever more dependent on the doctor (and the drug companies and the hospitals and the insurance companies) to take care of us.

If we conceptualize change in health status as exclusively and inevitably due to our individual behaviors, any governmental intervention to improve our individual health (as opposed to improving our health care) can only be seen as an intrusion on our liberty. When then New York mayor Michael Bloomberg proposed a ban on super-sized soft drinks, cries of "nanny state" went up, even from commentators on the Left, such as Jon

Stewart. It's a vicious cycle. The more the intrusions, the more hostility to government intervention of any kind grows and the less the likelihood of collective action. Efforts by government to control the behaviors of individuals contaminate efforts of government to suggest collective solutions to social problems. The medical-industrial complex both embodies and reinforces the hyper-individualistic, free-market-oriented ideology characteristic of Third Wave Capitalism, at the expense of a belief in public action for the public good.[66]

The Health Care System as a Third Wave System

The elements of the contemporary health care system—modern hospitals and other providers, insurance companies, and drug and medical supply and equipment companies, as well as government involvement in health care—took on their more-or-less current form in the era of Corporate Capitalism, certainly by the 1950s. It was the passage of Medicare and Medicaid in 1965, however, enormously expanding the role of government and providing a stable market for all of the other elements of the health-care system, that bound them together to form the modern medical-industrial complex. The lineaments of the complex came into view by the end of the sixties, but its maturation took place entirely during the following decades, the period of Third Wave Capitalism.

As one measure of the significance of the transition, in the 1940s, President Truman and Democrats in Congress proposed a universal, single-payer national health insurance system. As late as the early 1970s, a single-payer system was still one of the options widely discussed. (One was sponsored by the late senator Ted Kennedy.) It was the political weakness and eventual resignation of President Nixon after the Watergate scandal and President Ford's subsequent opposition to increased government spending in the face of the recession of 1973–75, as much as vigorous opposition from the health insurance industry, that doomed any form of universal insurance at that time. By two decades later, however, when discussions of how to finance health care finally resumed under President Clinton, the well-being of the private insurance companies took center stage. Single-payer systems were no longer even on the agenda. Similarly, a single-payer system was never seriously considered, fifteen-plus years later, as part of the relatively modest Affordable Care Act. Democrats and Republicans alike simply assumed that any proposal that would be opposed by the medical-industrial-complex would fail.

The health-care system that has evolved since the 1970s bears all of the hallmarks of the Third Wave Capitalist era. It is constructed around an individualistic, free-market-oriented ideology. It is the prototype of the intricately interacting system of relationships among businesses (multinational as well as local), the nonprofit sector, and government. And recall that the health systems of other affluent democracies provide more output (measured as the health of their population) at half the cost of our system. That unnecessary 50 percent of our annual $2.9 trillion in health-care costs constitutes spending that serves little purpose other than to enrich the masters of the health-care industries. It is purely the result of what I defined in chapter 1 as "rent-seeking." Our health-care system also accepts and reinforces preexisting inequities between black and white, rich and poor. And as the intense and concerted opposition to the Affordable Care Act has demonstrated so clearly, the health-care industries and their conservative allies have consistently sought to block efforts to use government to ensure the health of Americans, whether through public health measures, measures aimed at improvements in the social determinants of health care, or concerted actions to increase access, control costs and improve quality.

Getting Schooled

The health-care system matured into its present form over the last four or five decades and fully represents the essential characteristics of Third Wave Capitalism. By contrast, the U.S. school system had already reached the form in which we have known it (at least until the last few years) during the era of Corporate Capitalism.

In recent years public schools have come under heavy attack for their supposed failure to provide students with the education they need for the modern world. The school reform movement is less about fixing our schools to better meet the educational needs of students, however, than it is about turning the school system into a Third Wave Capitalist system.

The Manufactured "Crisis"

I attended a traditional neighborhood public school, which enrolled a very mixed group of students. Several children whose families were on welfare were in my class. So were the son of a top executive at a large industrial corporation and the daughter of the lieutenant governor of Pennsylvania. Classes were large (forty students) and discipline was strict, but no less than three of my forty classmates—all of them from lower-middle-class families—went on to win National Merit Scholarships.

Ah, the good old days when the public school system was the pride of America! Today we have become used to cries that American schools are failing. "This is our generation's Sputnik moment," proclaimed President Obama in his 2011 State of the Union message. Our schools are "fundamentally broken," says Melinda Gates, co-chair of the Bill and Melinda Gates Foundation. "We have a deep problem," CNN host and commentator Fareed Zakaria put it in a Peabody Award–winning special. "[W]e have slacked off and allowed our education system to get rigid and sclerotic." Fixing education, Zakaria's program headlined in its title, is essential for "restoring the American Dream."[1]

Complaints about the state of U.S. schools are nothing new. Rudolf Flesch's *Why Johnny Can't Read* was a best-seller in 1955. "Crisis in Education," trumpeted *Life Magazine's* cover story in March 1958, reflecting the nation's chagrin that the Russian *Sputnik* had beaten NASA into space. The nation's classrooms are "grim and joyless," complained Charles Silberman's 1971 *Crisis in the Classroom*. *"A Nation at Risk,"* headlined the report of President Reagan's 1983 National Commission on Excellence in Education, worrying that "the educational foundations of our society are presently being eroded by a rising tide of mediocrity that threatens our very future as a Nation and a people."

The current litany of criticisms of American schools is familiar. It goes like this: Our teachers and our schools are failing. Students' performance on tests of reading, writing, and math skills are a disaster, especially when compared to the performance of students from other industrialized nations. Individual students pay the price in reduced social mobility, and the country pays the price in reduced economic competitiveness.

The trouble is, every single one of these assertions is dead wrong.

The "Achievement Gap"

First, contrary to what most of us have heard from politicians and the media, the performance of our schools, at least as measured by the educational attainment of Americans and by the scores students get on standardized tests of reading, writing, and math, is improving, not declining.

Americans are getting more years of schooling than ever before. The percentage of those aged twenty-five to twenty-nine with a high school education (or a GED) has risen from 75 percent in 1970 to about 90 percent today. In 1967, 26 percent of all U.S. citizens aged eighteen to twenty-four were enrolled in two-year or four-year college. By 1990, the figure had grown to 33 percent, and by 2012 it had climbed to 41 percent. In 1970, 16 percent of citizens aged twenty-five to twenty-nine had a bachelor's degree or more. Today the percentage is more than twice that.[2]

As for skills learned by U.S. students, although Microsoft's Bill Gates insists that "over the past four decades . . . our student achievement has remained virtually flat," the facts do not bear him out.[3] The National Assessment of Educational Progress (NAEP) is the only measure of student academic achievement that has been administered consistently to a nationally representative sample of students over the last four decades. Average scores on the NAEP "long-term trend" reading and math assessments are dramatically higher today than when the tests were first administered more than forty years ago, and the gains have continued in recent decades. In 1990, only 13 percent of fourth graders and 15 percent of eighth graders met the NAEP criteria for math "proficiency" or better. In 2013 the figures were 42 percent and 36 percent, respectively. The rise in reading scores has been less dramatic but still steady and significant. The percentage of students achieving full reading proficiency went from 28 and 29 percent for fourth and eighth graders respectively in 1992 to 35 and 36 percent respectively in 2013. The gains were shared by black, Hispanic, and white students alike, although a significant gap still remains between the performance of white and black students and between white and Hispanic students.[4]

What about international comparisons? Current secretary of education Arne Duncan tells us that the failure of U.S. students in comparison to students from other countries is a "brutal truth" that "must serve as a wake-up call."[5] The most widely cited international comparison comes from the Program for International Student Assessment (PISA), a worldwide study of fifteen-year-old pupils' scholastic performance conducted by the Organization for Economic Co-operation and Development (OECD), which has been repeated every three years since 2000. In 2012, the United

States ranked seventeenth out of thirty-six OECD countries in reading, twenty-first in science, and twenty-sixth in math. Sounds terrible, but looked at slightly differently, in reading and science American students' scores were almost bang-on average for the OECD countries and they were above the OECD average in "problem solving." Only in math did American students score slightly below the OECD average, but their scores were still higher than those of students from such technologically proficient countries as Sweden and Israel.[6]

But looked at in isolation, the results are misleading. For one thing, the PISA tests have only been administered since 2000. While it's risky to compare results on very different test batteries, on standardized tests of basic skills administered fifty years ago U.S. students actually ranked well below that of other industrialized countries. In one measure of math skills, for example, the U.S. ranked eleventh out of twelve countries studied. With U.S. students now in the middle of the pack, we are possibly relatively better, certainly no worse than we were fifty years ago in the supposed heyday of America's schools.[7]

The PISA findings are also contradicted by U.S. students' performance in other recent international comparisons. On the Progress in International Reading Literacy Study (PIRLS) tests, U.S. fourth graders were tied for sixth place among fifty-seven education systems studied. On the Trends in International Mathematics and Science Study (TIMSS) tests, the United States was tied for ninth among forty-two systems studied in math, and it was tied for seventh among forty-seven systems studied in science. On all three PIRLS and TIMSS tests, the United States bested, among others, Australia, Germany, and Sweden and was ahead of or tied with England. We may not be number one, but we are certainly not seriously lagging.[8]

Even on the PISA tests, much of the disparity between the performance of U.S. students and students from other affluent countries reflects the high level of economic inequality in the United States more than unequal achievement levels or ineffective schools. Students from poor families fare worse educationally than their better-off peers in all of the affluent countries. The problem is that the United States has a higher percentage of students from poor families than other affluent countries have. Students from U.S. schools in which fewer than 25 percent of the pupils come from financially poor families actually score as high or higher as students from France, Germany, and the United Kingdom.[9]

The "Skills Gap"

The critique of U.S. education is not really about scores for their own sake, of course. It is about what the scores portend for students' own life chances and for the nation's economic competitiveness.

The conventional argument has been repeated so many times that it seems almost self-evident. Technology has increased the level of skill needed for many jobs. For an individual to get one of the new high-tech jobs, he or she needs an education. For the United States as a whole to be competitive, we must produce an adequate supply of highly trained workers. However, say the critics, there is a "skills gap"—a serious shortage of "qualified" Americans. "Eighty percent of manufacturers say . . . they cannot find enough workers with the skills necessary to fill open positions," worries President Obama. The Bill and Melinda Gates Foundation asserts, "The United States faces a growing economic challenge—a substantial and increasing shortage of individuals with the skills needed to fill the jobs the private sector is creating. . . . There is an urgent demand for workers trained in the STEM fields—science, technology, engineering and mathematics—yet there are not enough people with the necessary skills to meet that demand and help drive innovation." This skills gap "suppresses the productivity of our businesses and slows the overall economy," adds Mitt Romney.[10]

Once again, the facts contradict the critics. There may be labor shortages in some specific skills areas, but numerous studies have shown that there is no general shortage of highly trained or educated workers. An OECD study actually found the United States to be above the OECD average in the number of workers who are "over-skilled" for their jobs. That is, they are capable of handling more complex tasks, and their skills are underused. The same study found the United States to be below the OECD average in the number of workers who are "under-skilled." That is, they lack the skills normally needed for their job, exactly the opposite of what the school reformers claim.[11]

The Wharton School's Peter Capelli explains the disparity between what employers and educational reformers say and what actually exists: "The real issue is that employers' expectations—for the skills of new graduates, for what they must invest in training, and for how much they need to pay their employees—have grown increasingly out of step with reality." If there were a real across-the-board shortage of educated and trained workers, we would expect wages to be rising for skilled and educated tech workers, but wages have been stagnant for all but a few very particular skills since 2000, well before the Great Recession. As for lack of skills, in the past many employers expected that they would have to provide training for both new and continuing workers—an average of two and a half weeks of training a year in 1979. By 1995, the average amount of training workers received per year had dropped to less than eleven hours, with the most common topic workplace safety rather than skills. By 2011, one survey showed that only about one-fifth of employees reported getting *any* on-the-job training from their employers over the previous five years.[12]

The skills gap also appears invisible from the perspective of the individual student. Neither a high school diploma nor a college degree provide a clear road to employment. In late 2014, for instance, 48 percent of all high school graduates aged sixteen to twenty-four who were not in post-secondary educational programs were unemployed or out of the labor force. Although a high school diploma is a prerequisite to be hired for many jobs, most of these jobs do not require a high school education to actually do the work. Few minimum-wage jobs really require twelve years of schooling, but 72 percent of minimum-wage workers have at least a high school diploma (up from 37 percent in 1968), and 43 percent of today's minimum-wage workers actually have at least some college.[13]

The employment situation faced by recent college graduates is almost as bad. In early 2015, more than half of recent graduates were either underemployed, unemployed, or out of the labor force altogether. The rates are especially high for those who had liberal arts and social sciences majors, but even those with majors in science, technology, engineering, and mathematics (STEM fields) are not being grabbed up. Half of recent graduates with degrees in these fields were not working in STEM occupations, and, taken as a whole, wages are not going up in STEM fields. The reason? There is an *oversupply* of workers trained in STEM fields. The Center for Immigration Studies reports that between 2007 and 2012, about 105,000 new jobs in STEM fields were created in the United States each year. During those same years U.S. colleges and universities graduated about 115,000 students with majors in STEM fields annually. The country also admitted 129,000 immigrant workers with STEM expertise on H-1B work visas.[14]

Yet the high volume of complaints about shortages of adequately skilled workers continues, often accompanied by appeals to Congress to increase the number of H-1B visas so that well-trained foreign workers can fill the alleged gap. It is hard not to speculate that this has more to do with employers' desire for a pliable and lower-wage labor force than with any real concern about education.

As was the case with high school, many jobs for which a college education is generally required by employers do not really require a college education to do. Almost half of college degrees are in applied fields such as marketing, communications, and hotel and restaurant management, for which the need for a college degree is not obvious. Half of all employed U.S. college graduates under the age of twenty-five are in jobs that the Bureau of Labor Statistics describes as requiring less than a four-year college education, and 37 percent are in occupations that require no more than a high-school diploma. Despite the broad claims of so-called experts that one's future lies in fields that will require more education, the U.S. Bureau of Labor Statistics tells us that only six of the thirty fastest-growing occupations over the next ten years are expected to be in fields that require a bachelor's degree. Today, notes the *New York Times*, "Having a B.A. is less about obtaining access to high paying managerial and technology jobs and more about beating out less educated workers for a barista or clerical job." We have created a growing population of overeducated, underemployed young people.[15]

In any case, the supposed crisis in U.S. schools does not seem to be affecting the country's economic performance by world standards. Since the financial crisis of 2008, U.S. economic growth has far outpaced that of Europe. Despite decades of supposed crisis in our educational system, the United States still ranks third out of 144 countries on the World Economic Forum's measure of "Global Competitiveness." The United States is sixth out of 143 countries on the Cornell University and World Intellectual Property Organization's "Global Innovation Index." And the United States ranks second out of 82 countries on the Martin Prosperity Organization's measure of "Global Creativity," which ranks countries in terms of technology (research and development spending, R&D workforce, patents), talent (educational attainment and proportion of the work force in "the creative class"), and tolerance (openness to new ideas and people).[16]

The bottom line is simple. If U.S. schools are in crisis, they have been in the same crisis for well over fifty years, with little evidence of harm to individual mobility or national prosperity.

Lest I be misunderstood, there are certainly some seriously disquieting issues about U.S. schools. Although black students are now almost as likely to complete high school as white students, the same is far from true of Hispanic students, and the gap between college completion rates for whites on the one hand and for both blacks and Hispanics on the other remains large.[17] At all ages, the reading and math skills of children from poor families and children of color continue to lag significantly behind those of well-off families and whites. Although the gaps in academic achievement between white and black students and between white and Hispanic students narrowed sharply during the 1970s, they barely budged in the two decades following, and they have narrowed only very slowly in the fifteen years since passage of the No Child Left Behind Act (which was intended to improve educational equity for students from lower-income families).[18] As we have also seen, there is a significant mismatch between the education U.S. students get and the needs of the job market, though the problem is less one of a lack of adequately educated students for the available jobs than a lack of available jobs for the educated students.

Any serious effort to address these real problems would begin by asking why they occur, not by simply assuming without evidence that the primary source of the problems is with the schools attended by poor children and children of color, much less with U.S. schools in general. We will see below that, although there are far too many poor (and usually underfunded) schools, the educational lags of poor students and students of color and the deficits in the schools many of these children attend stem from poverty far more than they do from deficits in the schools themselves. And, as we have already seen, the education-jobs mismatch reflects lagging job growth more than failure of the schools to meet the needs of the labor market.

The reformers' claim that there is an acute general crisis in U.S. schools demanding sweeping changes in the entire educational system is, put simply, a fraud.

The Reformers' Vision for U.S. Schools

So now we have a puzzle. A consensus that the U.S. school system is in crisis has emerged across a broad swath of the political spectrum, across party lines, from conservative Republicans, such as Senators Ted Cruz and Rand Paul, to ostensibly more moderate Republicans, such as former Florida governor Jeb Bush and former New York City mayor Michael Bloomberg, to moderate Democrats, such as President Obama and New York governor Andrew Cuomo. Likewise the consensus ranges from conservative think tanks such as the Heritage Foundation, Americans for Prosperity, and the American Enterprise Institute, to more liberal foundations such as the Brookings Institution and the Center for American Progress, and from the conservative Koch brothers to the more liberal Bill Gates. U.S. schools and teachers are failing, they all say, with terrible consequences both for individual students and for the nation's economy as a whole. Yet as we have seen, the overwhelming weight of evidence says that they are wrong.

These are not stupid people, and while some of them may be demagogues, most of them mean well for the nation's children. What is going on here? We can find clues to the answer in the reformers' vision of what the U.S. school system should look like and from an examination of the problems in schools that the reformers fail to address.

The Vision of a Common Curriculum

The first major demand of the reformers is that there should be uniform and more rigorous standards for what is taught in American schools. In practice, that means requiring all schools throughout the country to adopt the Common Core Standards for reading, writing, and math. Whether the country really needs a set of common curricular standards, whether the Common Core Standards are any good, and whether spending the billions of dollars necessary to implement them is the best use of our education money are arguable. Here, however, I will focus less on the value of the Common Core Standards themselves than on how they were developed and imposed on schools.

The Common Core Standards were originally sponsored by the National Governors Association and the Council of Chief State School Officers, with the stated purpose of providing "a consistent, clear understanding of what students are expected to learn, so teachers and parents know what they need to do to help them." The standards themselves were developed in secrecy by work groups that were largely made up of representatives of the educational testing industry and of critics of the public schools. Few people with any actual experience as professors or teachers in the substantive areas covered by the curriculum, such as English or math, were involved. Development of the Common Core Standards was privately funded. The Bill and Melinda Gates Foundation invested nearly $250 million in developing and promoting the standards, and the Charles Stewart Mott Foundation and the Pearson publishing company threw in additional millions. The proposed standards were never pilot-tested and never opened to public scrutiny, much less debate. They were presented to states on a "take it or leave it" basis; no modifications to meet local needs or concerns were allowed. Although adoption of the Common Core was in principle voluntary, exemption from some of the more onerous provisions of President Bush's No Child Left Behind legislation depended on states adopting it, and the federal Race to the Top program, announced by President Obama in 2009, required states to adopt the Common Core Standards, to test students' mastery of the Common Core curriculum, and to evaluate teachers and schools based on these tests, under penalty of the loss of millions of dollars in federal aid if they did not comply. Under this pressure, forty-six states signed on, in many states without a single vote taken by an elected lawmaker. (Several states have subsequently withdrawn from adherence to the standards, as a result of massive public opposition).[19]

Schools are our major common effort to educate and socialize our children. One would think that, in a democracy, an effort to revamp what should be taught in our schools and how to teach it would be a topic for widespread discussion and input from many sectors of society. Instead, whatever their substantive merits or problems, the Common Core Standards were imposed through an end run around democracy. Yet when Bill Gates was confronted in an interview with the backlash against the Common Core, he responded angrily, "These are not *political* things [my emphasis]. These are where people are trying to apply expertise to say, 'Is this a way of making education better?'" (In fairness to Gates, he has repeatedly said that he does not see philanthropy as an appropriate substitute for the public role in education).[20]

The Vision of School Choice

The second major demand of the school reformers is to give parents "choices" about their children's education. One way to provide choice is to offer school vouchers or tax credits to enable parents to send their children to a private school or parochial school. Another way is to offer enrollment in a privately run (but publically funded) charter school rather than the traditional public school. Yet a third way is to permit parents to home-school their children. The theory is that market competition will then lead to improvements in all schools, traditional public schools as well as the alternatives.

Today, three hundred thousand students participate in private school voucher and scholarship tax-credit programs, 2.1 million children attend more than five thousand charter schools, and 1.8 million children are being homeschooled. However, research fails to show that these choices lead to a better education than that provided by traditional public schools. For example, a Center on Education Policy survey of six previous litera-ture reviews and twenty-one subsequent studies on the effectiveness of voucher programs concluded that there is "no clear advantage in academic achievement for students attending private schools with vouchers. . . . Achievement gains for voucher students are similar to those of their public school." A widely reported study of charter schools carried out by the gen-erally pro–charter school Center for Research on Educational Outcomes (CREDO) at Stanford University compared no less than 1.5 million stu-dents enrolled in 3,670 charter schools in twenty-seven states with a similar number of traditional public school students, matched student-by-student with respect to race and ethnicity, gender, English-language proficiency, special education status, grade level, and measures reflecting socioeco-nomic status. The National Education Policy Center summarized the re-sults: "In aggregate, charter schools are basically indistinguishable from traditional public schools in terms of their impact on academic test per-formance" Twenty-five percent of the charter schools CREDO examined did better than their local public school average in reading, but 19 percent did worse. Twenty-nine percent bested their local public schools in math, while 31 percent were worse. For both reading and math, the overall per-formance of the majority of charter schools was exactly the same as that of the public schools they competed against.[21]

It is tempting to conclude, "What's the harm? If voucher schools and charter schools are no better than traditional public schools, neither are they worse. Why not let parents decide?" But "parental choice" has con-sequences for all schoolchildren, those in traditional public schools as well as those in charters.

First, voucher schools and charter schools drain resources from the traditional public schools. State aid to local school districts usually is based on the total number of children attending school in the district. Money that goes to charter schools is subtracted from that going to the local school district. In Ohio, for example, in fiscal year 2012 the state deducted $774 million from traditional public school subsidies to fund charters. As a result, the remaining traditional public schools received on average $235 per child less state aid than in previous years, a cut of 6.5 percent.[22]

Second, charter schools remove a significant part of the nation's school system from public accountability. The image of a charter school is of a small, parent-initiated, locally run, nonprofit enterprise. While this is true of some charter schools, the reality is often quite different. The initiative to set up a nonprofit charter school often comes from a for-profit "educational management organization." The nonprofit school gets public dollars on a per-student basis. It then "sweeps" its publically provided dollars into the for-profit company that organized it. It pays the educational management organization to run the school—to rent it space (sometimes at well-above-market rates), to advertise the school, to run the lottery used to select students, and to perform services such as hiring and firing staff, developing curricula, and disciplining students.[23]

There is little public supervision of these arrangements. For example, the New York State legislature recently required New York City to provide charter schools with rent-free space in public school buildings or to pay their rent, even if doing so reduces space or funds available for its own schools. Although the public is providing the charter school's building and although the charter schools' funds come from the public, the state comptroller has no authority to audit them. In North Carolina, the salaries paid to employees of the for-profit management companies are not subject to public disclosure, although they are paid with public funds. A study of 2007–2008 school spending in Michigan found that publically funded charter schools spent $774 more per student on administration than traditional public schools, but $1,140 less on instruction, with no objection from the state.[24]

Charter schools also have negative consequences for teachers. Less than 10 percent of the nation's six thousand charter schoolteachers are unionized, compared to 50 to 98 percent of traditional public school teachers in all but a handful of states. Hardly coincidentally, long hours and low pay are typical. In Ohio, for example, the average charter school teacher is paid $34,714, almost 40 percent below the $57,310 average salary of traditional public school teachers in the state." It should come as little surprise that the rate of teacher turnover in charter schools, as much as 80 percent per year, is far higher than that in traditional public schools.[25]

The vision of paying lower salaries to inexperienced, non-union teachers provides a strong motive for school districts to convert traditional public schools to charters, regardless of the educational effects. In New Orleans, for example, the entire school system was closed after Hurricane Katrina. When it reopened, as a 100 percent charter system, the public system's older, unionized, predominately black teachers earning relatively decent salaries had been replaced by young, often white, non-union teachers earning much less. It didn't help educationally. In 2014, the New Orleans Recovery School District ranked number sixty-seventh of seventy-five school districts in the state. But Secretary of Education Arne Duncan bizarrely celebrated Hurricane Katrina as "the best thing that happened to the education system in New Orleans."[26]

While not exactly an argument for charter schools, it should be said that they are very good at one thing: using massive government subsidies to make money for private investors and school managers. Under the New Markets Tax Credit program, instituted by President Clinton, firms that invest in charter schools located in "underserved" areas can collect a generous tax credit of up to 39 percent to offset their costs. The message was not lost on the investment community. As David Brain, president and CEO of Entertainment Properties Trust (which according to its website "invests in properties in select market segments that require unique industry knowledge, and offer the potential for attractive returns") told CNBC interviewers, charter schools are "a high-demand product. There's [*sic*] 400,000 kids on waiting lists for charter schools . . . the industry's growing about 12–14 percent a year. So it's a high-growth, very stable, recession-resistant business." (See below).[27]

The flow of money into the private sector was not a pipe dream. Consider Imagine Schools, which operates seventy-one charter schools in eleven states and the District of Columbia and has had revenues of $227–$301 million a year since 2009. Or consider K12 Inc., which manages state-funded virtual charter schools (based entirely on distance learning, so they pay no rent at all) and hybrid schools in twenty-nine states and the District of Columbia. K12 had revenues of over $900 million in 2014, more than 86 percent of which came from the taxpayers. Executive Chairman Nathaniel A. Davis was paid $9.5 million in 2013. The aggregate salaries of the eight top K12 executives jumped from $10 million to over $21 million in one year, and four of them earned more than $1 million apiece in 2013. Village Academies Network CEO Deborah Kenny, who runs five New York City charter schools, earned $499,146 in 2011–12. Success Academy's CEO Eva Moskowitz, who ran nineteen schools, earned $475,000. Lest one think that such high salaries are the necessary price one must pay for a manager expert enough to manage such complex systems, then–New York City chancellor Dennis Walcott, who oversaw more than seventeen hundred public schools and a budget many times that of either Moskowitz or Kenny, scraped by on $212,614.[28]

Whatever the initial intentions of the promoters of school-choice programs, the only justification remaining for diverting resources to them is that, by definition, they provide parents with a choice. Like the development of the Common Core Standards, however, school choice is an end run around democracy, removing what should be societal decisions from collective discourse. It permits individual parents, to decide through their one-by-one decisions what the purpose of education is in the United States. It accepts the principle that education is purely for individual personal advancement as conceptualized by the child's parents, regardless of the cost to others.

Historically, the United States relied upon a public school system that was the envy of the world. The idea of a free common school, attended by children of all social origins, was central to the idea of democracy. It assumed that schools, in addition to teaching academic skills, prepared students for citizenship by teaching civic awareness and engagement, the value of cooperation with others, and a commitment to mutual defense of common values. It also assumed that in a democracy, decisions about education should be public, political decisions. This meant the choice as to whether children should get a broad education that included music, art, and history, or an education focused more narrowly on basic academic skills, or as to whether children should get an education to help them become responsible members of the community or solely to prepare them for a vocation should be based on open discussion and debate.

Today the call is heard to privatize education, as has already happened in New Orleans and in significant measure in cities ranging from Detroit to Kansas City to Washington, DC.[29] Says New York's governor Cuomo, one of the most vocal supporters of "choice," "I believe these kinds of changes are probably the single best thing that I can do as governor that's going to matter long-term to break what is in essence one of the only remaining public monopolies—and that's what this is, it's a public monopoly."[30]

The Vision of Accountability

The school reformers' third major demand is to increase the "accountability" of schools and teachers. It is hard to argue with the principle that when public money is spent, we should try to ensure that it is spent well (though it is odd that the reformers are concerned about accountability of traditional public schools and their teachers but not regarding charter school finances or the development of the Common Core Standards). But to hold schools and teachers accountable requires first that we agree on what we want them to do and then that we have a valid method for assessing whether or not they are doing this effectively.

Businessmen such as former New York City mayor Michael Bloomberg, an ardent supporter of school reform, made a quick jump to the "how," without ever thinking much about the "what." Schools had to be managed well, he argued, not unreasonably, but then added, "You can only manage what you can measure." Despite Bloomberg's impatience with those who dared question him, this adage is not a statement of self-evident principles but a value-laden conclusion. Even in business, "what can be measured" is not always "what should be measured." Short-term profits and high stock prices may seem obvious measures of how well a company is doing, but what about long-term competitiveness, worker well-being, product quality and safety, customer satisfaction, or impact on the environment? The latter are all much harder to measure. Does that mean they can't be legitimate goals? And if they are goals, how can success in reaching them be assessed?

In schools, the question of what to measure is especially value-laden. Does measurement of reading and math skills provide an adequate measure of the overall outcome of schooling? What about other student outcomes such as growth in creativity, curiosity, love of learning, appreciation of art or literature, understanding U.S. and world history, social and moral development, or assumption of civic responsibility? Even if there were agreement that some or all of these should be goals of schools, how would we assess the effectiveness of the school in meeting them? Among other problems, many of these are political minefields. What interpretations of the Civil War or of immigration would we all agree constitute understanding U.S. history? Even developing and assessing gains in reasoning ability, which would seem to be an unarguable purpose of education, are not uncontroversial. The Texas Republican Party's 2012 platform astonishingly stated: "We oppose the teaching of Higher Order Thinking Skills [and] critical thinking skills and similar programs that . . . have the purpose of challenging the student's fixed beliefs and undermining parental authority."[31]

Assessment: Taking the Easy Way Out Under political pressure to make schools accountable and influenced by business management models, school boards looked for the easy way out. They determined to measure what academics, school superintendents, and state education officials told them they *could* measure rather than think about what they *should* measure. That meant academic achievement—reading, math, and writing skills. Although occasionally other measures such as high school or college graduation rates are used as well, assessments of basic skills underlie essentially all recent criticisms of U.S. schools and teachers and have been used as the measure of the success or lack of success of alternative models such as charter schools. Specifically, the gain in a particular teacher's or a particular school's student achievement scores over the course of a year (the so-called value added by the teacher or school) has been widely adopted as a measure of the effectiveness of the teacher and the school. New York governor Cuomo justified it this way: "The test is really the only easy answer because it is objective numerical data." It is "objective" and it is "numerical." Never mind whether or not it measures what we are actually interested in.[32]

The belief that ineffective teachers are at the heart of our school's problems is based entirely on the use of these "value-added models" (VAMs). This is exemplified by a widely publicized study carried out by Harvard and Columbia professors Raj Chetty, John Friedman, and Jonah Rockoff. Students assigned to the most effective teachers as determined by

VAM evidence, they reported, were "more likely to attend college, attend higher-ranked colleges, earn higher salaries, live in higher SES [socioeconomic status] neighborhoods, and save more for retirement. They are also less likely to have children as teenagers . . . [Replacing a teacher] in the bottom 5% with an average teacher would increase the present value of students' lifetime income by more than $250,000." Concluded John Friedman, one of the study authors, "The message is to fire people sooner rather than later."[33]

The first problem with "value-added model" assessments of school and teacher quality, on which so much of the current discussion rests, is that they fail to give reliable information about school and teacher performance, even with respect to their effectiveness in improving students' reading, writing, and math skills, much less with respect to their ability to meet any other goals of schooling. In one study of data from five separate school districts, for instance, 25–45 percent of the teachers who were ranked in the bottom 20 percent in one year based on their student's average "value added" were ranked in the top 20 percent the next year. Likewise, those teachers whose students were initially at the top often fell to the bottom. In 2012, New York City rated eighteen thousand teachers, using their students' test scores. The statistical margin of error for each rating spanned 35 percentiles in math and 53 in English. That is, a teacher ranked as exactly average (50th percentile) could have had a real ability anywhere from the worst to the best in the city. Rankings also depend on the specific tests used. In one study using two different tests, one measuring basic skills, the other higher-order skills, 20 to 30 percent of the teachers who ranked in the top 25 percent based on their ability to produce changes in their students' scores on one measure ranked in the bottom half by the second measure.[34]

The use of value-added models for purposes such as determining whether or not a teacher is retained or a school is closed or whether we need radical reforms in our educational system has won almost universal condemnation from experts in assessment and statistics. For example, the Board on Testing and Assessment of the National Research Council of the National Academy of Sciences stated, "Student test scores alone are not sufficiently reliable and valid indicators of teacher effectiveness to be used in high-stakes personnel decisions, even when the most sophisticated statistical applications such as value-added modeling are employed. . . .

[A]nalyses of VAM results have led researchers to doubt whether the methodology can accurately identify more and less effective teachers." The Educational Testing Service agreed: "VAM estimates of teacher effectiveness should not be used to make operational decisions because such estimates are far too unstable to be considered fair or reliable."[35]

Yet, despite the condemnations, many school districts and states continue to use VAMs to assess schools, and many schools use them for assessing teachers. The U.S. Department of Education believes so strongly in this faulty procedure that it has threatened to punish states that have refused to use it to evaluate teachers and principals. A New York State court fined New York City $150 million for failing to agree on a VAM plan. The media, too, continue to uncritically accept studies using this mode of analysis.[36]

The VAM approach to assessing teachers and schools substitutes an illusion of meaningful assessment for reality. Worse, it has seriously negative consequences for schools. Let us assume that schools start out with at least some goals other than teaching the basics. If teachers are being evaluated primarily by their students' scores on tests of reading, writing, and math, they have an incentive to "teach to the test." The other goals of the school get neglected, because they don't count. Teachers ignore or reduce their focus on subjects such as the arts, music, and social studies and reduce their concern for eliciting student engagement, creativity, and social and moral development. By making reading, writing, and math the aspects of student learning that are tested, inculcation of basic skills becomes de facto the sole goal of the school. But the managerial imperative will not be denied. What began as a drive for accountability ends up as a drive to transform the schools to make them fit the seriously flawed measure of accountability.[37]

The zeal to reform education so that it meets national needs and provides measurable outcomes has undermined the traditional strengths of the American school system. The act of assessment itself forces schools to reform in ways that have never even been publicly discussed. A kindly interpretation would say that this is an unanticipated (and still usually unacknowledged) impact of the accountability movement. A less kind interpretation would say that the school reform movement was never about accountability. Narrowing the scope of education was the goal all along.

The Determinants of Student Achievement

There is an even more fundamental problem with using student scores on tests of academic skills such as reading, math, and writing as evidence that our teachers and our schools are failing. Underlying the use of test scores to judge teachers and schools is the assumption that variations in the effectiveness of teachers and the quality of schools are the primary factors determining levels of student achievement.

"There are a huge number of factors of [*sic*] whether a child succeeds in that school building," says Gates Foundation co-chair Melinda Gates, "but at the end of the day, it comes down to the teacher." The Hoover Institution's Eric Hanushek, one of the gurus of the school reform movement, ups the ante. The gaps in educational achievement between blacks and whites and between rich and poor can be *entirely explained* by the tendency of school districts to assign less experienced and less effective teachers to schools in poor and heavily minority neighborhoods, he argues. "Estimates of variations in teacher quality suggest that having a good teacher for three to five years would eliminate the average gap between children who do and do not receive free or reduced-price lunch, and between whites and blacks or Hispanics."[38]

Both Gates and Hanushek are dead wrong. The overwhelming majority of studies find that differences among schools themselves are not the principle determinant of student academic achievement, and, while teacher quality is the most important *in-school* factor affecting student performance, it is far from the most important *overall* factor. In a typical study, only about one-fifth of the variability in student achievement is associated with which school the students attend, and only about half of that has to do with differences in the quality of the teachers in the school.[39]

The studies do not say that school quality or teacher quality do not matter, only that they matter much less than we usually think. There can be no doubt that there are bad teachers and bad schools and that the latter, at least, are disproportionately found in poor communities. But the disparities in the school achievement of rich and poor students, white and nonwhite students, and U.S. students and students from other affluent countries are not primarily due to systematic failures on the part of U.S. teachers and schools. They are primarily due to factors outside of the school.

What are these out-of-school factors? In the United States, the poverty rate alone accounts for almost 60 percent of the variability in test scores from one state to another. Our high poverty rate by international standards also explains much of the mediocre performance of U.S. students in international comparisons of student achievement. A UNICEF survey found the United States to rank thirty-fourth out of thirty-five industrialized countries in rate of child poverty, just behind Latvia and just ahead of Romania. An American teacher is three times as likely as teachers in other OECD countries to teach in a school in which more than 30 percent of the students come from economically disadvantaged families.[40]

That schools and teachers do not make the chief difference in improving education seems counterintuitive. Many of us can recall the transformative impact a gifted teacher has had on us. It seems obvious: the teacher is the one who teaches you, so whether or not you learn depends on the ability of the teacher to inspire, motivate, instruct, and inculcate knowledge and skills. For many, the centrality of the teacher seems self-evident.

This may reflect a quintessentially middle-class experience. Assume for a moment that the outcomes of schooling are a product of both in-school factors (for example, teaching effectiveness, curriculum, class size, and school resources) and out-of-school factors (maternal and early childhood nutrition, child health, preschool experiences such as exposure to words and books, parental involvement, and extra-school learning opportunities such as trips to museums). In middle class communities, almost all children have high levels of the out-of-school factors. Little remains to affect children's learning save for the child's own ability and effort and school and teacher quality. It makes sense for middle-class parents to focus on in-school variables to improve their own child's chances in life. But in poorer communities, all the improvements one might desire in schools and in teaching can't make up for the adverse impact of the out-of-school problems. Are better schools for poor children a good thing? Of course. But they address the lesser part of the reasons for the educational disparities between poor and middle-class children.

The impact of poverty on academic achievement requires closer analysis. The gap in educational achievement between children from families in the bottom 10 percent of the income distribution (regardless of race or ethnicity) and those in the top 10 percent has risen dramatically since the early 1970s, closely tracking the increase in income inequality in the United States.[41] At the same time, the percentage of poor people and blacks and Latinos who live in neighborhoods that are predominantly poor has been increasing ever since the early 1970s. Poverty and race and ethnicity are not interchangeable, of course. But black and Latino Americans are more than twice as likely to be poor as white Americans. (For more on that, see chapter 4). In 2010, 23 percent of black schoolchildren lived in high-poverty neighborhoods, compared to 7 percent of white children. Sixty years after *Brown v. Board of Education* barred school segregation and fifty years after the Fair Housing Act of 1968 barred discrimination in housing, racial segregation in schools, now created and enforced by housing segregation rather than by Jim Crow laws, remains the rule, both North and South. In New Jersey, for example, more than a quarter of all black children now attend what some call "apartheid schools," schools with less than 1 percent non-minority students.[42]

Poor children, whether black or Hispanic or white, often do face dreadful schools. Writes *Salon's* Jeff Bryant, describing inner-city schools in Philadelphia,

> Imagine sending your child to a school with a leaky roof, busted windows and a rodent infestation. Or worrying whether the elementary school where you take your daughter every day is really a health hazard. Or telling your teenager to feel good about attending a school with no sports or athletic programs of any kind in winter or summer and no instrumental music classes. Imagine a school system where class sizes have gotten beyond ridiculous with one school so overcrowded that first, second and third graders are packed into a single classroom. In another school, classes overstuffed with 50 students or more are herded into the auditorium.

Others report similar findings: a sixth-grade math class with eleven textbooks for thirty-three students; a high school where the budget for extracurricular activities is zero; an elementary school with no full-time nurse, so the principal, with no training, plays the role; a high school biology class with sixty-two students.[43]

Schools in poor neighborhoods tend to have larger class sizes, less instructional time, less availability of learning specialists and tutors, less availability of after-school programs, fewer learning resources such as books, computers, and labs, fewer ancillary staff such as librarians, and worse building quality (no air conditioning in warm weather, for example). Teachers in schools in poor neighborhoods are less likely to have training that included coursework in their content area and field-based learning as well as courses in pedagogy. They receive less ongoing professional development and support, and they typically have less experience. High turnover of staff, a hallmark of schools in poor neighborhoods, reduces student and parent trust in teachers, undercuts professional development, interferes with teacher collaboration, makes the instructional program less consistent, and makes the school less desirable for more qualified teachers.[44]

The importance of addressing these problems is well known, but they require that cities and states commit adequate resources to the schools. In recent years, however, cities and states have slashed school budgets. At least thirty-four states provided less funding per student for the 2013–14 school year than they did in 2007, before the Great Recession. Emergency fiscal relief from the federal government helped offset state cuts at first, but this aid expired at the end of the 2011 fiscal year. Since 2010, spending in the major federal assistance program for high-poverty schools is down 12 percent after adjusting for inflation, and federal spending on education for those with disabilities is down 11 percent.[45]

Regardless of overall funding levels, more than half of all states (including New York and Michigan) provide less funding for poor school districts than for richer ones. In many states, recent cuts have made matters worse. In Virginia, to take one example, since 2009 school districts with the highest poverty rates have seen their state funding drop at a rate three times greater per student than the wealthiest districts.[46] In the face of the financial assault they have faced, to blame the schools for their failure to be effective is hypocrisy.

But poverty doesn't just lead to poor schools. It has a direct impact on students. Poor mothers are more likely to have received substandard prenatal care, resulting in higher rates of prematurity and difficult births. In turn, these are associated with higher rates of developmental delays, vision and hearing deficits, attention disorders, and specific learning disabilities in their children. Subsequent lack of medical attention and poorer living conditions means poor children are more likely to have asthma, dental problems, visual and hearing problems, lead poisoning, anemia, and other health problems that both produce more absenteeism and directly impact learning.

Poor children change schools much more frequently than those from families in more stable living situations and are absent or late much more, so teachers have to spend more time repeating lessons. In a middle-income school, the range of student skills based on past instruction is more varied and teachers can focus attention on those who are lagging. In a lower-income school, with lower achievement levels overall, all or most of the children need "extra" attention, which means that no one gets the individual support they need. And because students are less prepared for learning, more time must be devoted to dealing with discipline, and less time is available for instruction.

Poor parents, having to work multiple jobs to survive, are less likely to have available time or the knowledge and education to be involved with their child's school or to supervise homework. Their children are likely to have been exposed to fewer books and are less likely to have attended preschool and to have been read to as a toddler. The child enters school with a smaller and less complex vocabulary. He or she is less likely to have after-school art or dance or music or sports activities, which build self-reliance, discipline, and conceptual breadth and depth. The child of poverty is less likely to have a room of his or her own or a private place to study and do homework.

Living in a less safe neighborhood and more exposed to violence, the child from a poor family experiences more stress, and the time spent by the teacher in providing the support necessary for learning is taken from classroom instruction. The child from a poor family has fewer role models of economic or educational success, and it is hard for the child not to be aware of the limited economic opportunities adults in his or her neighborhood experience, resulting in lower expectations of success and a realistic devaluing of school.

Would Hanushek's three to five years of a good teacher solve these problems?

The Debate over Tenure

The sources of the lags in educational achievement for many black, Latino, and poor students are no mystery. Yes, it is legitimate to want to improve teaching effectiveness in schools serving children from poor or minority families. Yes, it is legitimate to want to bring the schools in poor neighborhoods up to the standards of more affluent neighborhoods. But to focus on the supposed failings of schools and teachers alone is to direct our attention away from the chronic underfunding of the schools serving poor children and from the poverty, racial and ethnic discrimination, and economic inequality that are the real culprits. And despite the fantasies of reformers that improving the schools attended by poor children will provide them with a route out of poverty, recall the lack of demand even for those with skills. It is easier to blame low academic achievement on "bad" schools than on the social system, easier to blame bad schools on "bad" teachers than to put resources into improving the schools, and easier to blame poverty on the failings of the schools than on the workings of the job market. The teachers and the schools have become the scapegoats.

The great barrier to getting rid of ineffective teachers and improving schools, say the reformers, is the tenure system and the unions that enforce it. Republicans such as Wisconsin governor Scott Walker and New Jersey governor Chris Christie, and Democrats such as Chicago mayor Rahm Emmanuel and New York governor Mario Cuomo join in calls to get rid of tenure protections for teachers.

Let us start with the basics. Tenure is not a guarantee of a lifelong sinecure or about unions protecting incompetent teachers. It merely requires due process for a teacher if a school district wants to terminate him or her for cause. In the days before tenure laws, teachers could be fired for expressing an opinion differing from their principal's. Hiring and firing decisions were often based on nepotism. Discrimination against nonwhite faculty was common. Sexual harassment was rampant, and women teachers were sometimes dismissed for offenses such as getting married, becoming pregnant, wearing pants, or being out too late in the evenings. Today, tenure notwithstanding, *in every state* a teacher can be dismissed for inadequate performance as well as for conduct, immorality, insubordination, neglect of duty, failure to comply with the reasonable requirements of as school board, or use of alcohol or drugs, among other things.

Is the tenure system abused, used by the union to "protect" incompetent teachers? Anecdotal horror stories abound. Reliable figures are not available, but the existing data, though imperfect, indicate that tenured teachers are dismissed for cause at rates comparable the rates at which physicians lose their licenses or lawyers are disbarred. No figures exist to compare the ease of firing a teacher with the ease of firing a corporate employee, but in 2012, large private-sector firms, which are comparable in size to many public school systems, lost only 2 percent of their workforce to firings, resignations, relocations, and layoffs combined. The comparable combined figure for teachers was about 14 percent. It seems hard to conclude that teachers are disproportionately protected by their due process protections.[47]

In any case, there is no reason to eliminate tenure altogether. it is easy to reform the tenure system to lessen the potential for the abuses that may occur. Conditions for getting tenure can be made more rigorous and procedures for adjudicating dismissals of tenured teachers for cause can be streamlined.[48]

The demand to abolish tenure has little to do with ensuring teacher quality. It is a stalking horse for an attack on teachers' unions. The unions are nothing more than "political thugs" who have become the main obstacles to improving children's education, says New Jersey governor Chris Christie. The intrinsic conflict between high rates of union membership and school quality is another myth of school reformers. In countries such as Singapore and Finland, whose educational systems are greatly admired by the school reform movement for their students' outstanding performance on internationally administered tests, 100 percent of teachers are unionized. Closer to home, states that have higher rates of unionization, such as Maryland, New York, and Massachusetts, tend to have schools that perform better (as measured by student achievement test scores) than those in states that have little union participation, such as Mississippi and Louisiana.[49]

The real reason for the reformers' attacks on teachers' unions is that the unions have opposed many of the changes demanded by the educational reformers. The attack on unions is an effort to make teachers more compliant with the demands of their principals and school boards. It is also the spearhead of an attack on public-sector unionism in general. And for some, it is an unapologetic attempt to weaken one of the major organizational supports for the liberal wing of the Democratic Party.

Again, the bottom line is that the claims of the critics of U.S. schools have absolutely no basis in fact. Their supposed solutions to the crisis in education are as wrongheaded as their claims that there is a crisis.

The First Conundrum: What Drives the Reformers?

The first great puzzle is why the reformers ignore or misrepresent the enormous body of evidence suggesting that their core critique is simply wrong and that their proposed reforms have little value. Why do they turn the growing disparity between American students' educational attainment and the demand for labor into complaints about supposed shortages of educated workers? Why do they bash teachers and unions rather than focusing on the central role of poverty in limiting the effectiveness of schools?

The most charitable interpretation is that the facts are sufficiently ambiguous to justify alternate interpretations. Research on the effectiveness of schools and the impact of schooling on the economy is complex, and the studies are full of "noise." There are many, many studies, and the conclusions of some contradict the conclusions of others. One could argue that people of good will could read the evidence differently and that interpretation of "the facts" is not an entirely objective process.

But the charitable interpretation is discredited by the tendency of the reformers to distort the significance of information or to blatantly misrepresent the facts. Bill Gates worries that "[Our] percentage of college graduates has dropped compared to other countries," but surely he is aware that, in absolute terms, the percentage of the adult population who are college graduates in the United States has actually doubled over the last four decades, and that the decline compared to other countries is because the latter, starting at a much lower level, have gained more rapidly. U.S. Secretary of Education Arne Duncan complains that "forty percent of your high school graduates are taking remedial classes when they go to four year universities," when the actual proportion of entering college students taking such classes in 2007–2008 was half that, 20 percent, and the numbers have been dropping since the mid-1990s. Surely he knows the actual figure: their source is the Department of Education itself. When researchers at the Stanford-based Center for Research on Educational Outcomes issue a press release trumpeting their study's conclusion that "charter school students now have greater learning gains in reading than their peers in traditional public schools," surely they know that their study found that the charter school students' advantage in reading was 0.01 standard deviations, a difference of absolutely no real world significance whatsoever.[50]

It is hard to know what to make of the reformers' persistent disregard or misrepresentation of the evidence. Their statements have an aura of what Stephen Colbert famously called "truthiness"—preferring concepts and facts that "feel right" over concepts and facts supported by logic, evidence, and intellectual examination. Or maybe there is something about schools themselves that, to use singer Nancy Griffith's memorable phrase, "brings out the stupids" in otherwise well-meaning people. But whether the reformers deliberately deceive or simply cannot see past their own desires, we are still left with the question: Why?[51]

The Role of Ideology

The first answer comes from what cognitive psychologists call "confirmation bias," which is the tendency to search for, recognize, interpret, or weight information in a way that confirms one's beliefs, hypotheses, or ideologies. Perhaps it is ideology that explains the reformers' overconfidence in making claims that support their contentions of "crisis" in the schools.

The central clue to the ideology of the school reformers is who the reformers are. As Haley Sweetland Edwards put it in a widely cited 2014 *Time* article,

> The [school] reform movement today is led not by grassroots activists or union leaders but by Silicon Valley business types and billionaires. It is fought not through ballot boxes or on the floors of hamstrung state legislatures but in closed-door meetings and at courthouses. And it will not be won incrementally, through painstaking compromise with multiple stakeholders, but through sweeping decisions—judicial and otherwise—made possible by the tactical application of vast personal fortunes. . . . It is a reflection of our politics that no one elected these men to take on the knotty problem of fixing our public schools, but here they are anyway, fighting for what they firmly believe is in the public interest.[52]

While many politicians, Democrats as well as Republicans, pundits, and "ordinary people" believe in school reform, much of the energy and most of the funds for the reform movement has come from hedge funds, corporation executives, and the foundations and think tanks created from their wealth. The Bill and Melinda Gates Foundation (Microsoft), Walton Family Foundation (Walmart), W. K. Kellogg Foundation (cereal manufacturer Kellogg), Michael and Susan Dell Foundation (Dell Computers), Robertson Foundation (Tiger Management, a hedge fund), William and Flora Hewlett Foundation (Hewlett Packard), Broad Foundation (KB Home, the nation's fifth-largest home building company, and Sun Life, now part of AIG), and Democrats for Education Reform (hedge funds) top the list.

Among the central elements of corporate ideology are belief in the sanctity and wisdom of the marketplace; suspicion of the role of government and of social demands on private enterprise; the belief that consumer choice always leads to meeting public needs; the desire to maximize control over the workforce (which implies, at best, grudging acceptance of unions); the belief that better management techniques are all that is necessary to improve public services; the desire to shift costs (including training costs) to the public wherever possible; the belief that public policy decisions are better left to experts beholden to corporations than to the democratic process; and the belief that the privileged position in society of wealthy people is a well-deserved reward for their own merit and their own contributions to society.

All of these beliefs are directly reflected in the actions of individual school reformers, as well as in the program of school reform itself. In 2014, for example, Facebook's Mark Zuckerberg offered $120 million to San Francisco area schools, but his support was absent when California considered a ballot measure to increase funding for its schools. Hedge funds gleefully welcome the opportunity to invest in charter schools but their managers lobby against the higher taxes that would generate new revenue for public education. The Walton Family Foundation parades its efforts to remake our schools, while Walmart, the source of its money, pays low wages and vigorously opposes unionization of its employees. The Eli and Edyth Broad Foundation gives millions to the school reform effort, while Eli Broad, its founder, himself donates $1 million to a nonprofit that helps defeat higher taxes and opposes the power of labor unions to raise political cash. The Gates Foundation worries about the impact of poor teaching on employment prospects for U.S. workers, but Microsoft's Bill Gates worries that raising the minimum wage will "cause job destruction." The same contradictions are evident in the actions of politicians who support school reform. For example, in New York, Governor Cuomo repeatedly insists that "inequity in education is probably the civil rights issue of our time," but during the first five years of his administration, the gap in funding between the richest one hundred school districts and the poorest hundred rose from $8,024 per student to $8,733 per student.[53]

As University of Oregon political economist Gordon Lafer put it,

> When you look at the agenda of the biggest and richest corporate lobbies in the country, it's impossible to conclude that they want to see the full flowering of the potential of each little kid in poor cities. To say "I want to cut the minimum wage, I want to prevent cities from passing laws raising wages or requiring sick time, I want to cut food stamps, I want to cut the earned income tax credit, I want to cut home heating assistance. Oh but, by the way, I'm really concerned about the quality of education that poor kids are getting"—it's just not credible. You're creating the problem that you now claim to want to solve.[54]

Reinforcing the belief that deeper social solutions are unnecessary is the widely held American belief that we live in a meritocratic society. An individual's success is determined by his or her determination, we insist, by hard work, in combination, of course, with innate ability. This belief is especially alluring to those at the top of the social ladder, for whom meritocratic ideology seems to justify their outsize share of the societal wealth.[55]

Absent the will to expand government-based programs to address poverty and segregation, and absent the willingness to provide more public resources to schools, the only alternative left to deal with social problems is a shift to compensatory policies aimed at making up for the social disadvantages conferred by poverty or race (see chapter 4). What shall we do about the stubborn persistence of poverty? Give the children of the poor better schools, so that those who have the ability and grit can better make their way in the labor market and escape poverty.

But schools do not actually provide a level playing field. Regardless of individual ability or determination, poor children are locked into lower-income neighborhoods by their families' lack of income, by the lack of affordable housing in more affluent neighborhoods, and, too often, by racial discrimination. They are plagued with poorer health and a multiplicity of problems diverting them from school success. They must attend schools with fewer resources, fewer well-trained teachers, fewer after-school programs, and lower teacher expectations. And even if they succeed at school despite all of the obstacles, they face the unavailability of jobs and the unaffordability of college. With failure inevitable for all but a very few, what is left other than to assert that teacher incompetence is at the root of school problems and that the free market will solve all the problems of the educational system?

The claim that grit and good teaching can trump poverty is embraced by the reformers. Journalist Stephen Brill, himself an enthusiastic supporter of the reform efforts, reports, "Charters like KIPP or Harlem Success . . . proved that intense, effective teaching could overcome poverty and other obstacles and that, as [former New York City schools chancellor Joel] Klein liked to say, demography does not have to be destiny."[56]

So let us consider the claims of the KIPP and Success Academy chains of charter schools, widely regarded by reformers as models for the country. Both chains, like many other charter schools, embrace a "no excuses" model, characterized by long days, large amounts of homework, a test-preparation-based curriculum, uniforms, group chants, strict military style, and "zero tolerance" discipline.

KIPP and Success Academy administrators claim that their students get high scores on tests of student achievement, and they report very high rates of college attendance by their graduates. What they do not explain is that their students are not a completely random selection or that they suspend or expel a much larger percentage of their students than traditional public schools. The very students who have the most difficulty in traditional public schools—the students with attention disorders or learning or physical disparities, the students who are English-language learners, the students who come from chaotic families—are precisely the ones who are less likely to attend charter schools like KIPP and Success Academy in the first place and who are more likely to drop out or be thrown out. The high attrition rate means that the measures of student scores and college matriculation rates are all but meaningless. Independent evidence as to KIPP's and Success Academy's actual performance, taking into account non-random selection of students and their high attrition rates does not exist, as far as I know. Yet KIPP and Success Academy administrators insist that their example shows that *any* student will succeed academically if he or she attends a school that adheres to their model. The keys to success, they insist, are zest, grit, and effort, and all that distinguishes those that succeed from those who fail is optimism, a strong work ethic, and unquestioning respect for authority.[57]

The Role of Self-Interest

A second source of the school reformers' ideas is direct self-interest, whether conscious or not. While the school reformers may honestly believe that their struggle to reform the nation's schools is in the public interest, what is their own self-interest, as individuals and as heads of corporations and foundations?[58]

The school reform movement has masked an attempt by private business to extract profits from what has historically been a governmental function. More than $1 trillion is spent in the United States each year on education at all levels, some 7.2 percent of GDP.[59] Historically it has been hard for the private sector to grab a piece of this, save in the old-fashioned form of selling textbooks and supplies and constructing school buildings. The potential profits from "mining" the public sector (to use economist Duncan Foley's phrase) are enormous. Capital Roundtable, which describes itself as "America's leading conference company for the middle-market private equity community," held a "master class" called Private Equity Investing in For-Profit Education Companies, noting that "for-profit education is one of the largest U.S. investment markets, currently topping $1.3 trillion in value." As consultant Rob Lytle of the Parthenon Group told investors at a conference on private equity investing in for-profit education companies, "You start to see entire ecosystems of investment lining up."

Sure enough, venture capital transactions in the K–12 education sector soared from $13 million in 2005 to almost $400 million by 2011.[60] Educational technology, charter schools, standardized tests, and programs for special needs children have been especially popular as investment opportunities. Rupert Murdoch's News Corporation has invested well over $500 million in the education sector, largely in all-digital curricula. Textbook and curriculum creation, dominated by Pearson, Cengage, and McGraw Hill, who collectively control over three quarters of the market, is a $7.8 billion a year industry. A business partner of former tennis star Andre Agassi seeks to raise $1 billion in capital for education system investments.[61]

Big foundations have worked hand-in-hand with big corporations and local, state, and federal government officials to create a new "educational-industrial complex." Recall the controversial Common Core Standards, initially sponsored by state governments, developed privately with massive private foundation funding, vigorously promoted by high-tech and hedge fund moguls, and adopted by the states under heavy federal government pressure. And then come the rewards: Pearson, which already makes billions of dollars from its sales of textbooks, landed a contract from a consortium of states to develop and administer exams to match the standards and to set performance standards for students on the exams. Gates's Microsoft then teamed with Pearson to produce a Windows tablet containing the Common Core curriculum, providing schools with a "single coherent ecosystem of teaching and learning." Google and the News Corporation have joined in with other tablet–Common Core pairings. Gates forthrightly justified his foundation's work on the Common Core to the American Enterprise Institute: "When the tests are aligned to the common standards, the curriculum will line up as well—and that will unleash powerful market forces in the service of better teaching." He added, "Scale is good for free market competition. Individual state regulatory capture is not good for competition."[62]

The Second Conundrum: Why Do We Believe the Reformers?

The second great puzzle is why the flawed arguments of the school critics have met such uncritical acceptance. If our schools were actually failing disastrously, the appeal of the school reform movement would be understandable. But given the inability of the reformers to show this or to show that their solutions would make anything much better, it is puzzling that they have managed to convince much of the media and millions of Americans of the urgency of gutting the public school system.

The success of the school reform movement seems to reflect a convergence of history, ideology, social anxieties, and self-interest. Throughout U.S. history, mistrust of public schools periodically surfaces. Writing about our schools has been "to a remarkable degree a literature of acid criticism and bitter complaint," noted historian Richard Hofstadter more than fifty years ago. The many past claims that our schools were inadequate, however, were always accompanied by a belief that they could be fixed through one or another curricular reform. Today the belief is more in the inherent inadequacy of public education.[63]

To those on the right, mistrust of the public sector in general plays an important role. Schools are the third-largest arena for government spending in the United States (trailing only health care and Social Security and ahead of defense). Following President Reagan's mantra that "Government is not the solution to our problem, government is the problem," conservatives have welcomed private-sector, free market solutions for schools, as for everything else. At the far right edge, more than a few Tea Party adherents denounce public schools as "socialist." The school reformers' message of public school failure was met with open hearts.[64]

Over recent decades, as the country has shifted to the right (in electoral terms, at least), many Democrats, too, have moved away from their traditional allegiance to government as the source of solution to social problems. To centrist factions in the Democratic Party, such as the Democratic Leadership Council and the New Democratic Coalition, deregulation, balanced budgets, rejection of traditional Democratic positions on issues such as welfare and free trade, and a move away from overly close ties to public-sector unions have seemed a winning strategy. The rejection of the more sweeping approach to societal reform characteristic of FDR's New Deal and LBJ's Great Society and the preference for the piecemeal, compensatory schemes of the school reformers are in keeping with this strategy.[65]

At a less politically sophisticated level, suspicion of schools has deep roots in many Americans. Some recall their own school experience as boring, dreary, and full of daily experiences of inadequacy and humiliation. Almost all of us have had the experience of teachers we loved and teachers we disliked. As a result, the narratives of "schools are failing" and "teachers are at fault" are easily understandable.

Schools tap into deeper sources of anxiety as well. Schools are not merely neutral places, imparting skills and information and holding out the hope of upward mobility. They are where people from a professional class (teachers, principals, educational "experts") control and help socialize children of all classes. Children are taught to accept the rigid time schedules characteristic of the adult work world, to exercise self-control and defer gratification, to accept the approval of adults other than their parents as sufficient reward for "good" behavior, and to control their own aggression and sexuality. But all of this requires blocking and harnessing their instincts, and so school may be experienced by children as alien and hostile, even if as adults, they recognize its necessity.[66]

Schools also teach, explicitly and implicitly, ideologically loaded information, theories, and values. This places them squarely into the political and ideological arenas. Insofar as the values or information inculcated at school deviate from those of parents or from those of powerful people in the wider community, schools are scrutinized. Anger at schools and teachers, though often mixed with respect, lurks just under the surface. In the fifties, fears of communism led some schools to censor books and fire the "reds" who had led 1930s teachers' unions. More recently, fears that schools might teach "deviant" social values (such as non-traditional views of sexual morality) have surfaced. So have fears that children might be taught material that conflicts with religious doctrine (on evolution and climate change, for example) or that contradicts conservative views of the Civil War, the history of race, the immigrant experience, or the role of the United States in the world. These fears may add to the hostility to schools.

For many black and Latino parents, the experience of the inadequacies of their own children's schools combines with awareness of the failure of schools to eliminate the disparities between white students and black and Latino students. Small wonder that black and Latino parents and some (though by no means all) civil rights organizations are more welcoming of school choice and of repeated administration of standardized tests than white parents.[67] Similarly, for working-class students and their families, regardless of race or ethnicity, frustration over the lack of economic opportunity in the United States in recent decades, combined with the widespread, if mistaken, belief that it is the schools alone that create the possibility of upward mobility, leads to easy blame of the schools.[68]

Anxiety about schools is not limited to those suffering the burdens of racial or ethnic or economic inequality. In the United States, for all save the very wealthy, social class is achieved, not inherited.[69] Professionals and managers, who have made it into the upper part of the middle class, know that their children will retain their family's social status only through school achievement. Pressure on children to succeed at school is intense, and, especially in a time when the income and autonomy of many professionals is threatened, what Barbara Ehrenreich called "fear of falling" is readily attributed to supposed inadequacies of the schools.[70]

Finally, fears of foreign economic and ideological competition are often projected onto the schools. In the fifties, it was the post-Sputnik fears of the Russians. In the nineties, it was fears that Japan would overtake the United

States economically. Today the economic performance and test scores of students from China, South Korea, Singapore, and other lands whose economic growth rate far surpassed ours over the last two or three decades, seems the threat. In this context, the terrifying, if superficial, international comparisons ("Our schools are lagging internationally") find a ready audience, and the subtleties of analyzing the results are lost in the uproar.

Conclusion

The "school wars" of recent decades have little to do with education but much to do with promoting a conception of school as little more than narrowly prevocational training, with an assault on public-sector unions aimed at forcing teachers to comply passively with administrative demands, with transferring resources from the public sector to the private sector, with a deliberate undermining of democratic decision-making, and with an attack on the very notion that schools should meet social, as opposed to individual, needs.

The American school system, as we have known it until very recently, developed over the course of the nineteenth and early twentieth century. It reflected the needs and culture of the eras of Industrial Capitalism and Corporate Capitalism. Based on the "common school" tradition, it assumed schools were intended to create good citizens (and, at its best, educated men and women), as well as to provide prevocational preparation. It was certainly not without terrible flaws, most notably in its discrimination against racial minorities and the unequal opportunities it provided for poor children, but Americans had what Richard Hofstadter described as a "persistent, intense, and sometimes touching faith in the efficacy of public education," and the U.S. educational system was the envy of the world.[71]

The current school reform movement is at its heart an effort to bring our schools into conformity with the imperatives and style of Third Wave Capitalism. If the reformers have their way, our school system will come to resemble our health-care system. The newly emerging educational-industrial complex will feature a mix of public, private, and hybrid providers of services, with the latter two as well as the former largely financed by taxpayer money. The entire system, public and nominally nonprofit as well as for-profit, will provide a rich market for suppliers of goods and services and serve as a conduit for transferring massive profits to private investors, with no improvement in educational outcomes. That is, like the health-care system, it will provide abundant opportunities for rent-seeking. Despite the public funding, there will be little public accountability. The ability of local school boards (whether elected or selected by elected officials) to ensure the well-being of all students will be eroded by the whims of the wealthy. Teachers' autonomy and professionalism will be degraded, and education will become increasingly uniform in content, routinized in methods, and subjected to narrowly managerial conceptions of quality. The schools will give priority to serving individually determined goals rather than publically agreed upon ones. The disconnect between labor market needs and students' expectations will grow, further reinforcing a narrative of self-blame for the structural inequities of the larger system. And the idea that all of us collectively determine how the next generation is educated will be abandoned.

4

RACE AND POVERTY: THE BETRAYAL
OF THE AMERICAN DREAM

For a brief moment in the 1960s and early 1970s, eliminating poverty
and racial inequities seemed realistic goals. But it was not to be. The
productivity of the American economy and our national wealth have
skyrocketed, yet poverty levels remain well above their early 1970s
lows. Legalized discrimination in schools, housing, jobs, and other
areas of daily life is no more, the economic and social gains for people
of color have been substantial, and open racism among whites has
become less acceptable. But disparities in income, wealth, schooling,
and health persist, progress in eliminating housing and school segregation is at a standstill, and one out of every three black males born
in the United States today can expect to go to prison in his lifetime.

Growing poverty amid growing wealth, persistent racial disparities
despite declining racism—these seem like contradictions. But given the
pervasive drive of Third Wave Capitalism toward inequality and given
its determined withdrawal from public action to address social ills,
they are entirely predictable.

Turning to poverty and especially to race, I feel more than a little trepidation. Health and education are worlds I have lived in, as a provider of services and as a receiver of services, my entire life. Race, however, I have not experienced from the inside. More accurately, I *have* experienced race, but from the privileged white position of being free to "not feel" race. I have the luxury of being able to cut myself off from the realities and even the awareness of racial inequities and of the privileges that being a white, middle class male convey.

I am equally aware that, even among those firmly committed to progressive social change, racial justice discussions and efforts can be contentious. Political correctness is a mirage. No matter my sympathies, I am aware of treading on thin ice, caught between a commitment to social justice, a fear of understating or misunderstanding the issues, and the ease of retreating into facts and analysis.

My own direct experience of race began as a small child, sitting beside my father in the front seat of the car, driving our part-time housekeeper, Ever, home at the end of the day. (She was a follower of the black spiritual leader and civil rights movement precursor Father Divine and had taken the name Everlasting Life.) Ever sat in the back seat, forbidden by Divine's International Peace Mission movement to permit any greater physical intimacy with a white man. I also painfully recall Mandy, another African American woman who later worked for us as a housekeeper, sitting dutifully but awkwardly with the family in the living room after my left-wing mother (whom "Mandy" called "Mrs." Ehrenreich) invited her to join us in watching the television news of the Montgomery bus boycott. And I recall myself as a boy barely in my teens, brimming with fury over lynchings and other atrocities committed against blacks in the South in the mid and late fifties.

Later I found ways to act on my rage, though never in ways that assuaged the guilt. I picketed Woolworth's in support of the first sit-ins. I was arrested at a sit-in to desegregate an amusement park outside of Baltimore. I tutored black children in support of community control of schools during the New York City teachers' strike of 1968. I chose to spend my entire academic career at a public college that was a pioneer in opening the door to college for poor people, people of color, Vietnam veterans, and women returning to school after raising families ("those traditionally bypassed by higher education," as the college administration euphemistically described them). Over the years, faculty and students repeatedly struggled to get the college to admit more poor and minority students, to develop curricula responsive to their needs and learning styles, to provide the academic and non-academic support services they often needed, and to hire more minority faculty and administrators. Today the College at Old Westbury is repeatedly rated one of the three or four "most diverse colleges in the United States" by *U.S. News and World Report*. But diversity in itself is not enough, and I am only too aware of the ways in which our dreams of an educational revolution fell short.

My own confusion and guilt undoubtedly find their way into this chapter. Can bare facts and numbers capture the rage with which the facts and numbers should be spoken? Do facts and analysis do justice to understanding how America treats its poor people and its people of color, whether poor or not? But expressing moral outrage is not a solution, and the short-term emotional relief it creates quickly turns to ashes in the face of its real-world impotence. So let me retreat into facts and analysis, but let not the analytical tone disguise all that's left out.

The Tangled Web of Race, Ethnicity, Poverty, and Class

Untangling the interrelationships among race, ethnicity, poverty, and class is filled with pitfalls.

First, poverty: Current estimates are that forty-five million people (about 15 percent of the U.S. population) fall below the poverty line (defined as an income of $24,250 for a family of four in 2015, which is adjusted for other family sizes and configurations). But to talk about poverty as if it is a clear category and about "the poor" as if the word "poor" describes a specific group of people is deeply misleading. The official definition of poverty is arbitrary and is widely believed to underestimate the income needed to support a family at a minimal standard of living. By many estimates, families need an income about twice the federal poverty level just to meet basic expenses. That less strict definition implies that more than one-third of Americans are poor at any given time.[1]

In any case, being poor (using the Census Bureau definition) is not a fixed status. People move in and out of poverty. Becoming poor is most commonly triggered by losing a job or taking a cut in pay. About one-third of those families who are below the poverty threshold in any given year are no longer below it the following year, and fully three-quarters remain "poor" for less than four years. About half of those who escape will fall below the poverty line again at some time over the following five years, however. Conversely, some 51 percent of the U.S. population experience some period of time before the age of sixty-five in which they fall below the poverty level.[2]

At best, "below the poverty line" provides a snapshot of the most desperate part of the population, for whom getting food and other immediate necessities is severely problematic at a specific moment. But looked at over a period of even a few years, poverty is far from being the lot of a distinct and relatively small group. It is the experience of a large proportion of the U.S. population. If we use the commonly employed term "lower-middle-class" to describe the bottom half of the U.S. income distribution, then "poor" and "lower-middle-class" are not far from coextensive. The continued use of the words "poverty" and "the poor" as if they describe a distinct category serves more to prevent people in the much larger group from identifying with one another than it does to provide any real conceptual clarity.

Then there is "race." The Census Bureau lists some forty-two million U.S. citizens as "black or African American" But race too is a fuzzy, heterogeneous, and sometimes contested concept, defined socially, politically, and personally more than by any objective characteristics such as skin color. A person who has one black grandparent and three white grandparents is usually considered and considers himself or herself as black, not white, and a light-skinned person with some African ancestry, pale enough to "pass," may nevertheless choose to define himself or herself as black. Race is also inseparable from history. Both in the personal identity of black Americans and in the perceptions and reactions of whites, it reflects America's long history of slavery, the defeat of post–Civil War Reconstruction, the violent creation of the Jim Crow system, and the Great Migration of some six million African Americans from the rural South to the urban Northeast, Midwest, and West between 1910 and 1970. Race is a label that contains bigotry, discrimination, and violence by whites against blacks, as well as sometimes-romanticized or sanitized stories of black resistance against oppression. Race also contains a history and an ongoing present-day reality of structural and institutional racism, the sometimes explicit, more often implicit policies and practices engaged in by public and private institutions that systematically treat black and white differently, to the disadvantage of the former.

Further complicating our notion of race are ethnicity and immigration. Today there are some seventy-six million or so Americans who are not black or African American but who are "people of color."[3] America has a long history of discrimination against recent waves of immigrants, often using racial categories to define them regardless of their actual skin color. Even the Irish were sometimes regarded as not "white" in the early nineteenth century, and at the turn of the twentieth century, Jews, Italians, Greeks, Slavs, and other immigrants from eastern and southern Europe were often described as "colored" races.[4]

Today's immigrants from Latin America, North Africa, the Middle East, South and East Asia, and the Pacific, and their children, even when born in the United States, are often conflated with blacks by whites, who may attribute to them characteristics stereotypically attributed to blacks. They also are targets, in varying degree, of the same kinds of individual and structural discrimination that affect blacks. And like blacks, many of these groups are at the bottom of the social ladder with respect to income, wealth, education, health, housing, and power.[5]

The fate of any of these groups over the long run is unknowable. A generation or two hence, will they, like the Irish, Jews, Italians, and others before them, be largely indistinguishable from white America as a whole, or will they remain discriminated against and stuck at the bottom of the U.S. class structure? One ominous sign: the relatively stable and high-wage industrial jobs that enabled many from earlier generations of immigrants to ascend into the middle class exist no more, and, since the 1970s, Americans other than the top 20 percent of income earners have benefited little from the nation's economic growth and gains in productivity.

Regardless, the current situation of various ethnic minorities is mingled with and in many ways similar to that of blacks, but it is impossible to simply fold the story of black America into the story of immigration. Blacks do not have to assimilate. They have been an integral part of the American story from the very beginnings, but for centuries they have been systematically locked in to a subordinate position in society. Today white Americans' perceptions of blacks are heavily confounded with their perceptions of "the poor" and vice versa, in a way that is much less true of their perceptions of other racial and ethnic minorities.[6]

The media often conflate race and poverty, using "the poor" or "residents of the inner city" as code words for "black." But poverty and race are not interchangeable. Almost half of the poor are white. Only about one-quarter are black and roughly another quarter are Latino. Conversely, three-quarters of black Americans and three-quarters of Latinos are *not* poor, using the standard, if flawed, official poverty levels as our measure. Nor are the poor predominately residents of the "ghetto" or the "inner city" of major metropolises. Fewer than half of the poor live in large or medium-sized cities, and one-sixth live in non-urban areas.

That said, race, ethnicity, and class in the United States are inextricably intertwined. Black Americans are almost three times as likely to be poor as white Americans, and Latinos more than twice as likely. Many of the problems faced by poor black communities with respect to schooling, health, housing, employment, crime, and emotional distress reflect low economic status as well as race. It is impossible to address poverty without addressing race or to address race without addressing poverty.[7]

But conflating the two is also problematic. As President Johnson said in his 1965 commencement address at Howard University, "Negro poverty is not white poverty. Many of its causes and many of its cures are the same. But there are differences—deep, corrosive, obstinate differences—radiating painful roots into the community, and into the family, and the nature of the individual." What makes black poverty different is not merely the scars "of long years of slavery and a century of oppression, hatred, and injustice" (Johnson's words) but the systematic ways in which blacks have continued to face discrimination and violence and racism in the United States in the years since the civil rights revolution of the 1960s.[8]

Economic opportunity and security, the right to get a good education, the right to good health care, a sense of well-being, the right to have one's voice heard politically, "liberty and justice for all"—these are our expectations of our birthright as Americans. If particular groups are systematically denied opportunity, political equality, liberty, and equal justice under law, if government fails to secure the rights of some and fails to "promote the general welfare," then the American Dream has been betrayed. Has America met its own standards? Or was the 1963 cry of Martin Luther King Jr. that America had "defaulted" on the "promissory note to which every American was to fall heir" not merely a statement about the past but a foretelling of the future?[9]

It is now sixty years since *Brown v. Board of Education*. Fifty years ago, President Johnson admonished America that millions of Americans were deprived of the blessings of liberty "not because of their own failures, but because of the color of their skin. . . . It cannot continue. Let us close the springs of racial poison." "The time of justice has now come," he added. "No force can hold it back." Fifty years ago President Johnson also declared "unconditional war" on poverty, promising, "We shall not rest until that war is won." In response, Congress passed the Economic Opportunity Act, declaring, "It is . . . the policy of the United States to eliminate the paradox of poverty in the midst of plenty . . . by opening to everyone the opportunity for education and training, the opportunity to work, and the opportunity to live in decency and dignity."[10]

So how have Americans of African descent fared in the years since then, and what happened to the hopes of eliminating racism and poverty in a single generation?

The State of Black America

For black Americans, the positive changes have been dramatic. The world has changed dramatically since the early 1960s. Jim Crow is no more. Legalized racial segregation in housing, schools, and transportation is gone. Discrimination in hiring is illegal. The armed forces and most businesses are integrated. The percentage of black families with incomes below the poverty level has been cut in half. A large black middle class has emerged. The gap in the high school completion rate between Americans of African descent and those of European descent has all but disappeared. Open expressions of racism can cost a millionaire his basketball team and a politician his election. Black men and women vote for president at a higher rate than whites. We have had many black mayors and congressmen and judges and secretaries of state, and we now have a black president. Looking at these changes, together with changes in racial attitudes on the part of many younger people, many whites feel the battle for racial justice is over, that we live in a post-racial society.

But the sense of progress is partly illusory. Looked at over the span of fifty years, the gains are obvious, but most of the gains were made in the sixties and seventies. Since then, progress has slowed or stalled altogether. As a result, the average black household today still earns less than two-thirds as much as the average white household and has only 6 percent of the assets. Twenty-seven percent of black Americans—more than two and one half times the percentage of whites—remain below the poverty line, and another 10 percent or more are stuck just above the official poverty line. The black unemployment rate has remained twice that of whites, regardless of education, gender, geographic area, or the state of the national economy. Black children are more likely than white children to attend schools with inadequately prepared teachers, and major gaps in students' scores on tests of basic academic skills and in college completion rates remain. Blacks own their own homes at a rate only 60 percent of that of whites. Blacks are more likely to live in areas threatened by environmental pollution. Although life expectancy is up for all, black life expectancy at birth remains four years less than that for whites, and although infant mortality rates are down for all, the infant mortality rate for black babies is double that of comparably educated whites.[11]

What is puzzling to many white Americans is the persistence of these disparities in the context of apparent reductions in the acceptability of overt racism on the part of whites (what comedian Chris Rock has called "white progress").[12] All too readily, white politicians and the media conclude that the fault must lie in some characteristics of blacks themselves, such as overdependence on welfare, or the inevitable consequences of families that have no father present. The real explanation, however, lies in the distinction between individual racism and structural racism. Racialized outcomes do not necessarily require racist actors. More and more, it is the persistence of structural racism—disparities that are embedded in systemic institutional policies and practices—that place blacks and other people of color at a disadvantage.[13]

Let me give a few scattered examples:

- For many years, poor black communities have received less investment and fewer services from local governments. Lack of medical facilities, inadequate parks and recreational facilities, poor public transportation, and infrequent trash pickup quickly turn black neighborhoods into "slums." Poverty, continued discrimination in housing and lack of affordable housing elsewhere locks blacks into those communities.

- School budgets depend on property taxes. The lower value of homes in largely black communities mean that school budgets are lower in these areas. As a result, black children systematically attend poorer schools with fewer resources.
- For three decades tobacco companies, recognizing the overall decline in their consumer base, have targeted black communities. Predictably, blacks suffer higher rates of lung cancer than whites.
- Banks, after years of restricting mortgage loans to black customers, in the early 2000s deliberately targeted minority communities for the sale of "sub-prime" mortgages. As a result, black homeowners were more likely than whites to lose their homes in the housing bust of 2008 and the years that followed.
- One and one half million black men are incarcerated or prematurely dead. For every one hundred black women aged twenty-five to fifty-four and not in jail, there are only eighty-three black men. For black women, potential mates are relatively scarce, and family formation and stability are disrupted.
- Many white parents want their children to attend a nearby neighborhood school and not be bussed to a distant neighborhood. Many financially stretched white taxpayers oppose tax hikes to pay for services that will be not directly benefit them. In neither case are they necessarily motivated by explicit racism. Yet the result of their actions is to preserve school segregation and poorer services to black communities.[14]

The energy and commitment behind the effort to realize the goal at the very heart of the civil rights revolution, school desegregation, have also declined. In the wake of *Brown v. Board of Education*, school segregation declined rapidly in the South, largely as a result of federal court orders. Over the last three decades, however, courts have relinquished their supervision of southern school districts, and, predictably, segregation of public schools has crept up again. Nationwide, 38 percent of black students and 43 percent of Latinos are in schools that are more than 90 percent nonwhite. The typical black student now attends a school where only 29 percent of the students are white, down from the 36 percent of 1980. The worst problem now is in the North. New York State, where two-thirds of all black children attend schools that are more than 90 percent nonwhite, now claims the most segregated schools in the country, followed closely by Illinois. In New Jersey more than a quarter of all black children now attend what some call "apartheid schools," schools that have less than 1 percent non-minority students.[15]

School segregation today is largely driven by residential segregation, which in turn is based on both income and on race and ethnicity. Neighborhood segregation is not an accident, and it is not simply due to the inability of poorer people to afford better housing or due to "white flight" or to resistance on the part of whites to integration of their neighborhoods, although these factors certainly play a role. Current patterns of neighborhood segregation were initially created as a result of intentional government-created or government-tolerated or government-enforced policies, including local zoning restrictions, urban renewal programs, federal subsidies for suburban development conditioned on exclusion of blacks, bank refusal to give mortgages for home purchases in minority neighborhoods, restrictive covenants, and real estate brokers steering black and white clients to different neighborhoods and encouraging white flight.[16]

Although court decisions and the Fair Housing Act of 1968 outlawed many of these practices, policies that maintain residential segregation continue, often in the form of discrimination that on the surface is blind to race. These include disproportionate use of federal subsidies for low-income housing to build housing in neighborhoods that are already low-income, local zoning rules in white neighborhoods that prevent construction of affordable low-income and middle-income housing, continued discriminatory lending practices by banks and mortgage companies, and poor funding of the federal housing voucher program. Today racial and ethnic and economic segregation go hand-in-hand. The percentage of poor people who live in neighborhoods that are predominantly poor has been increasing ever since the early 1970s, and especially so for black and Latino families.[17]

The retreat from governmental policies to end housing segregation was deliberate. Nixon administration secretary of housing and urban development George Romney, Mitt Romney's father, believed that the 1968 Fair Housing Act's mandate to "affirmatively further" fair housing gave him the authority to pressure predominantly white communities to build more affordable housing and to end discriminatory zoning practices. As a 2012 ProPublica report described the events, he ordered HUD officials to reject applications for water, sewer, and highway projects from cities and states whose local policies fostered segregated housing. President Nixon, in "southern strategy" mode, forced Romney to back off and finally drove him from the cabinet. Nixon understood what he was doing: "I realize that this position will lead us to a situation in which blacks will continue to live for the most part in black neighborhoods and where there will be predominately black schools and predominately white schools." Ever since, Democratic and Republican presidents alike have refused to use the leverage of HUD's billions to fight segregation.[18]

The Poor You Shall Always Have with You

The story is similar with respect to poverty. Again, the good news first. In the early sixties, one in five Americans had incomes below the poverty level, but by mid-decade a broad attack on poverty was underway. Under President Johnson there were Medicaid and Medicare, Head Start, the Community Action Program, expansion of access to higher education, housing subsidies, improved unemployment benefits, affirmative action in hiring, expansion of access to welfare, and civil rights acts providing protections against discrimination in schools, workplaces, and housing. President Nixon's legacy was more ambiguous, with cuts in many existing programs, but it still included a vast expansion of the food stamp program, indexing of Social Security pensions to the cost of living, Supplemental Security Income, and proposing the Earned Income Tax Credit. Despite budgetary competition from the war in Vietnam and ideological opposition, the War on Poverty (in the broad sense of all of the Great Society initiatives, not just the Economic Opportunity Act per se) was a resounding success. By 1973, the poverty rate had been cut almost in half, to 11 percent.[19]

But then progress in fighting poverty came to an abrupt halt. The poverty rate began to rise again, and it has wobbled between 11 and 15 percent ever since. Today it stands at about 15 percent. More than forty-six million Americans, including more than one in five children, live in families with incomes below the poverty line. Almost half of these are in "deep poverty"—that is, have incomes less than half the already austere poverty level.

"Poverty" is a pallid word. Most immediately, of course, it refers to a lack of money. But lack of money has many specific consequences. In the United States 8.5 million children live in "food insecure" households in which at times during the year they are uncertain of having enough food to meet their needs. Over the course of a year, 2.5 million U.S. children are homeless. Poor people are five times more likely than their more affluent peers to report being in "poor" or "fair" health, and those over age sixty-five will live five fewer years than their richer counterparts. One out of seven poor families lives in severely physically inadequate housing, with inadequate heat or hot water or infestations of vermin. In polls, poor people are eight times as likely to report experiencing "severe" emotional distress over the preceding month. And while the black-white and Latino-white gaps in educational achievement have narrowed significantly since the 1960s, the class gap—between children from families in the bottom 10 percent of the income distribution and those in the top 10 percent—rose dramatically.[20]

The immediate reason for the persistence of poverty is simple: since the early 1970s poor people have not shared in the benefits of U.S. prosperity. In the quarter century following World War II, it may have been true that "a rising tide lifts all boats." The incomes of the poorest 20 percent of Americans actually grew more rapidly than the incomes of the top 20 percent. But in the last four decades, despite a tide of economic growth, it has been mainly the yachts of the already wealthy that have risen. Between 1979 and 2007, real per capita Gross Domestic Product doubled, but while the average income for the top 1 percent of U.S. households rose 156 percent and the average income for the top 0.1 percent rose 362 percent, income for most Americans in the middle barely moved. As for poor people, income for the bottom 20 percent actually fell.[21]

Putting it at its simplest, poverty has been sustained by what the Economic Policy Institute's Josh Bivens has called the "inequality tax." In the early seventies the richest 1 percent of Americans collected about 10 percent of national aggregate wages; today they collect more than 20 percent. Had incomes for the bottom 20 percent of U.S. workers kept up with productivity instead of lagging behind, by the mid-eighties there would have been *no* (you read it right, *no*) Americans below the poverty line. In effect, the money that could have gone to eliminate poverty was seized by the wealthiest 1 percent.[22]

Consider a single mother with one child who worked in late 2014 as a Walmart cashier. Even if she worked full time, her family would have remained below the poverty level. Like thousands of other Walmart workers, she would have survived by supplementing her income with support from public programs such as Medicaid, food stamps, and housing subsidies. In 2014, taxpayers subsidized Walmart's payroll costs to the tune of $4,500 per worker per year—more than $6 billion in all in 2014. That same year, Walmart made $16 billion in profits. A little arithmetic suggests that if Walmart had raised the wages of every single one of its workers to above the poverty line instead of asking the taxpayers to pick up the tab, it would still have left $10 billion in profits for the stockholders. The other $6 billion in Walmart profits were a direct gift from the taxpayers. As a result of their profits over the years, the six Walton heirs, the wealthiest family in the United States, now have assets of almost $150 billion, more than the combined assets of all of the poorest 49 million Americans—that is, more than all the people in the United States below the poverty line.[23]

The bottom line is simple. Growth is not enough.

The Retreat from Social Justice

Many of the social problems that lead to fears that America is in decline are in large measure tied to poverty and to race. Being poor and/or not being white leads to lower educational achievement, poorer health, higher rates of crime, and higher rates of mental illness. But as was the case with efforts to end segregation, as a nation we have retreated from any systematic and sustained effort to end poverty. In the late 1960s and early 1970s, hope arose that we could address these problems at their root. Said President Lyndon Johnson, in his 1964 State of the Union address,

> Let this session of Congress be known as the session . . . which declared all-out war on human poverty and unemployment in these United States; as the session which finally recognized the health needs of all our older citizens; as the session which reformed our tangled transportation and transit policies . . . and as the session which helped to build more homes, more schools, more libraries, and more hospitals than any single session of Congress in the history of our Republic.

The many Great Society programs followed. The centerpiece of Johnson's War on Poverty was the Economic Opportunity Act. The act included among its major programs the Job Corps and the Neighborhood Youth

Corps to provide work, basic education, and training for young people; the Federal Work-Study program to enable colleges to offer part-time employment for students from low-income families; the Adult Basic Education program to provide English-language literacy programs; and programs of loans for rural families and assistance for needy children.

The most innovative part of the act was the program for urban and rural community action. A "Community Action Program" was defined as a program "which provides services, assistance, and other activities of sufficient scope and size to give promise of progress toward elimination of poverty or a cause or causes of poverty through developing employment opportunities, improving human performance, motivation, and productivity, or bettering the conditions under which people live, learn, and work." Money was provided for community organizations to set up a "Community Action Agency" to develop, coordinate, and mobilize a whole range of programs, services, and community development projects to reduce poverty. Community health centers, Head Start, Neighborhood Legal Services, family planning services, and addiction services were among the activities sponsored.[24]

The local Community Action Agency was also supposed to prod existing service providers to become more comprehensive, more integrated, and more responsive to the needs of the poor. To ensure the latter, it was required that the Community Action Program encourage the "maximum feasible participation" of the poor. This was later interpreted to mean that at least one-third of the board of directors of the local Community Action Agency should be chosen by and come from the community targeted by the Agency.

Taken at face value, "maximum feasible participation" meant not simply helping poor people but empowering poor people to help themselves and to challenge anyone who got in their way. According to Office of Economic Opportunity director Sargent Shriver, the Economic Opportunity Act was intended to be "for the poor what the National Labor Relations Act was for unions. . . . It establishes a new relationship and new grievance procedure between the poor and the rest of society." Perhaps needless to say, increasing the power of poor people generated enormous opposition from those whose previously undisputed power was to be challenged, including mayors, agency heads, local business owners, and local union leaders.[25]

The hope soon faded that the War on Poverty and other Great Society measures would "eliminate the paradox of poverty in the midst of plenty" (to use the words of the "declaration of purpose" prefacing the Economic Opportunity Act). By the late 1960s, political backlash, budgetary competition from the war in Vietnam, and economic downturn led to cutbacks in funding for antipoverty efforts. By 1972, Richard Nixon, under less pressure from the rapidly fading community and left movements of the previous decade, proclaimed that the era of small government was at hand and made further cuts. By the Reagan era, the much-weakened efforts that remained came under further attack.

The mechanisms for rolling back the concerted effort to end poverty were many. Tax cuts, especially for the wealthy, reduced funds available for services and for the social safety net. Racially coded politics led to attacks on programs such as welfare. Supreme Court decisions handcuffed affirmative action programs aimed at ending disparities in employment and education. The executive branch pulled back on direct efforts to reduce housing and school segregation, on enforcement of existing antidiscrimination laws, and on enforcement of occupational health laws. The Office of Economic Opportunity was chronically underfunded, and after 1967, under pressure from big-city mayors, the idea of "maximum feasible participation" was reduced to the fuzzy idea that the community should give advice.[26]

The social safety net eroded or was directly dismantled. Inflation ate away at the minimum wage, which in real purchasing power is now 33 percent lower than in it was in 1968 (see chapter 1).[27] Over the twenty-five years before its ultimate repeal in 1996, cash benefits under the Aid for Families with Dependent Children program ("AFDC," commonly simply called "welfare") declined even more sharply. Whatever its deficits, AFDC, originally established as part of Roosevelt's New Deal, helped support two-thirds of children living in poor families in the mid-seventies and eighties, but the 1996 Clinton welfare "reforms" slashed the protections offered. Today only about one-quarter of the children of the poor are reached by welfare's successor, the Temporary Assistance for Needy Families program, and the inflation-adjusted benefits provided are now 20 percent lower than even the 1996 level. From 1980 to 2003, federal support for low-income housing also dropped 49 percent. Cuts in food stamps, in Pell grants for college students, in funds for public school systems, and in unemployment insurance also took their toll.[28]

In 1987, President Reagan famously remarked, "In the sixties we waged a war on poverty, and poverty won." It was an outright lie. What really happened was that conservatives, exemplified above all by Reagan himself, persuaded frightened middle-class Americans to ally themselves with the rich and defeat the poor.

After the mid-1970s, concerted efforts to *address* poverty and discrimination were no more. Instead, if poverty was a concern at all, we got programs aimed at merely trying to *compensate for* poverty, economic insecurity, and racial inequities and at "helping" individuals who were poor. Poor because you don't have a job? Your lack of education is to blame, so we'll improve the schools. (Never mind the increasing level of segregation in schools or that the demand for labor has lagged behind the supply of educated students or that even in "good" schools, children from families living in poverty are handicapped.) Unhealthy because you are poor? Your poor health habits are to blame (too much sugar and fats, too much smoking); at best, you need better access to medical care. (Never mind that substandard housing conditions adversely affect health or that environmental threats to health tend to be concentrated in poor areas or that the government subsidizes production of sugar and animal fats and tobacco and not production of healthier foods.) Living in substandard housing in an inner city neighborhood because you are poor? We'll provide rent subsidies or build low-income housing (though not enough to meet the need and certainly not in a middle-income white neighborhood). Providing opportunities to help a few people escape poverty replaced structural changes to help the many.

Criminalizing Poverty

Less benignly, in the absence of efforts to end poverty and discriminating, we expanded the criminal justice system. Rigorous policing, harsh sentencing policies, and long prison terms replaced antipoverty programs and policies aimed at reducing structural racism.

The overall incarceration rate in the United States began to rise in the mid-seventies. Today more than six times as many Americans are in jail or prison as in 1970. The rate of increase is greater for women than for men, although women are imprisoned at a much lower absolute rate. Today, more than two million people are imprisoned, more than half of them non-white. An additional five million people are on probation or parole. The United States has a rate of incarceration far higher than that of any other country in the world.[29]

The criminal justice system is ostensibly concerned with deterring or punishing crime, but increases in crime do not explain why the American rate of imprisonment is so high. Studies carried out by criminologists Allen Beck and Alfred Blumstein of imprisonment for murder, sexual assault, robbery, assault, burglary, and drug offenses indicate that changes in the crime rate in the United States explain essentially none of the 220 percent increase in the rate of incarceration in state prisons for these crimes between 1980 and 2010. Increased police effectiveness (that is, arresting a larger fraction of those who commit crimes) played only a small part in the period before 1990, and has played no part since. Almost the entire increase was due to the fact that persons arrested for a felony became far more likely to be sentenced to prison and that convicted felons were given much longer sentences. Most other Western countries also experienced rising crime rates beginning in the 1960s or 1970s, but they did not respond to increased crime by adopting markedly harsher policies and laws, and their incarceration rates did not soar the way it did in the United States.[30]

Another factor that helps explain the difference in incarceration rates between the United States and the rest of the industrialized world was the release of hundreds of thousands of patients from state mental hospitals in the years from the late 1960s on. "Deinstitutionalization," as it was called, was driven by the availability of then-new anti-psychotic drugs, by states' desire to lessen the financial burden of sustaining patients in long-term hospitals, and by the availability of Medicaid money to treat those with mental illnesses. The "community mental health centers" established by the 1963 Community Mental Health Act were expected to take over the care of most of the patients released from the hospitals, but only half of the proposed centers were ever built. None were fully funded, and money was not provided to operate them long-term. Many ex-patients became homeless or semi-homeless. Still more were swept up into the nation's jails and prisons. There are now ten times more people with severe mental illness in prison than in all of the psychiatric hospitals in the United States.[31]

The big source of rising incarceration rates, however, was the changes in laws and sentencing policy. But such changes do not occur in a vacuum.

The exceptionally high proportion of the population that is imprisoned in the United States is rooted in the collapse of efforts to directly address poverty and segregation. The 1960s and early 1970s were tumultuous times, characterized by the demonstrations and sit-ins of the civil rights movement, urban riots, "community control" movements sparked by the Community Action Projects' insistence on "maximum feasible participation" of the poor, other militant movements of urban poor people such as the Black Panther Party and the Latino Young Lords Organization, anti–Vietnam War demonstrations, campus unrest and the rise of the New Left, and, at the end of the period, the emergence of militant feminist, gay, and environmentalist movements. Encouraged by the Civil Rights Act, the Economic Opportunity Act, and other Great Society programs, poor people, blacks, ethnic minorities, and others came to believe that they had political and marketplace rights that must be respected and that it was the responsibility of the government to protect them.

The unrest created widespread anxiety, not only among the business owners, union leaders, and local politicians whose traditional power and positions were threatened, but also among large numbers of white Americans who found it easier to be angry at poor people and nonwhites than at the system that sustained inequality. Richard Nixon's "southern strategy" embraced the anxiety and propelled a historical shift to the right in American politics. The FBI's COINTELPRO infiltrated, discredited, and disrupted left-wing domestic political organizations and black and other community movements (see chapter 1). The rise of the Christian right and the intensely waged "culture wars" of the period were other major elements of the backlash.

But how could the unrest be controlled? The social safety net was unraveling, and the Johnson administration's concerted, if flawed, attack on poverty, segregation, and discrimination had been taken off the table. The criminal justice system stepped in as a mechanism for controlling public spaces as well as for preventing or punishing crime. The drive for law and order (that is, getting tough on crime), President Nixon's "war on drugs" (which was waged almost exclusively in black and Latino communities), New York governor Nelson Rockefeller's draconian drug laws (which were imitated across the country), and state gubernatorial candidates' demands to "build more prisons" all were racially coded ways of getting tough with unruly blacks, Latinos, and poor people.

The criminal justice system became, in the words of Harvard sociologist Devah Pager, "the only effective institution that could bring order and manage urban communities." Toward the end of the 1900s and in the early 2000s, even as the crime rate fell to historic lows, arrest rates and incarceration rates continued to rise. Police in many cities adopted the "broken window" (or "zero tolerance") theory of policing, aggressively focusing on minor offenses and misdemeanor arrests. Racially targeted "stop-and-frisk" programs in the absence of any real suspicion of wrong-doing, arrests for offenses such as dancing on subway trains, standing on the sidewalk with a group, or playing basketball in the park after hours, demands by police to show an ID when standing outside one's own apartment, and breaking up by police of groups of young men accused of "lingering," all in effect criminalized everyday activity. Although the police defended these practices as reducing serious crime, research on the effectiveness of "broken windows" and similar policies has failed to produce any consensus that the model actually reduces serious crime and has failed to show any link between disorder and crime. For poor urban communities, however, the policies created an atmosphere of fear, damaging the fabric of those communities.[32]

Yet another factor that did not initiate the current incarceration regimen but that does help maintain its inequities is the emergence of what has been called the "prison-industrial complex." (It might more accurately be called the "justice system–industrial complex"). Today about 6 percent of state prisoners, 16 percent of federal prisoners, and by some estimates half of all Immigration and Naturalization Service detainees are held in privately owned, for-profit prisons. The prison system mobilizes more than one million prisoners to work for wages of less than dollars a day, often for large private corporations. (Dell, Starbucks, Macy's, Boeing, Victoria's Secret, JC Penney, and the U.S. Army are among those who reportedly have used the products of prison labor, either directly or through suppliers.) A private system of so-called alternatives to incarceration, including private halfway houses, probation supervision agencies, electronic monitoring systems, and "rehabilitation" services has also arisen. The justice system employs over 1.5 million workers, including almost 800,000 police, almost 500,000 corrections officers, and several hundred thousand judges and court employees. Police unions resist subordination to social demands such as ending "stop and frisk" policies; prison guards' unions resist programs to release prisoners early; and, in some cases, contracts between for-profit prisons and governments require the state to fill a quota of cell spaces.[33]

There is a real disconnect between the increase in the rigor of law enforcement, including increases in the number of police, instituting innovative policing techniques, and putting more people in prison, and the fall in the crime rate. Superficially, it might seem obvious: if you are in jail, you can't commit a crime. The conclusion: being tough on crime reduced the crime rate. But obvious though this conclusion might seem, it is incorrect.

Most studies have concluded that the increased intensity of law enforcement accounts at most for a part of the reduction in crime before the mid-1990s and none of the drop in crime in the twenty years since. A 2015 report from the Brennan Center for Justice at New York University School of Law, for instance, concluded that when other variables are controlled, increasing incarceration had a minimal effect on reducing both property crime and violent crime, during and since the 1990s. Another study concluded, "We delved deep into over 30 years of data collected from all 50 states and the 50 largest cities. The results are sharply etched: We do not know with precision what caused the crime decline, but the growth in incarceration played only a minor role, and now has a negligible impact." Incarceration, the study continued, may have been responsible for approximately 5 percent of the drop in crime in the 1990s. "Since then, however, increases in incarceration have had essentially *zero* effect on crime" [emphasis in original].[34]

Whatever the conscious motives, and however much we may appreciate the role of the justice system in combating crime, it is hard not to see the police and the courts as a system of direct control of the black population and, more broadly, of poor people. Today almost half of all black men under the age of twenty-three have been arrested at least once, and, at present rates of incarceration, one-third of all black men can expect to be imprisoned at some point during their lives. Fully one-quarter of black children will see a parent imprisoned by the time they reach fourteen.

Although a wide body of research supports a causal relationship between urban economic decline and individual economic distress and crime, the racial patterns are not explainable by differences in the rate at which blacks and whites actually commit crimes. For example, although actual rates of overall drug use and sales are not substantially higher for blacks than for whites, blacks are arrested for drug offenses at a three to four times higher rate. Young black men are more likely than whites to be stopped on the street, and, if arrested, they are more likely to be held in jail pending trial, more likely to be offered plea bargains that include jail time rather than community service or probation, and more likely to be convicted. If convicted, they are given sentences on average 19 percent longer than whites for possession of drugs, 13 percent longer for convictions on charges of robbery, 22 percent longer for burglary, and 14 percent longer for aggravated assault. In the end, black men are imprisoned at more than five times the rate of white men.[35]

Regardless of race or ethnicity, it is the less educated and less stably employed who are most likely to be caught up in the prison net. High school dropouts, black and white alike, are five times more likely to be incarcerated than those with a high school degree.[36]

If race and poverty lead to higher incarceration, incarceration contributes to maintaining poverty and to maintaining the link between poverty and race. By one estimate, the high rates of incarceration increase the national poverty rate by 10 to 20 percent. A family in which the father is imprisoned suffers on average a 22 percent drop in income, higher rates of housing insecurity (including child homelessness), and higher rates of dependency on public assistance. Imprisonment of a family member disrupts family relationships, and, even after release from prison, ex-inmates have greater difficulty forming stable marriages or relationships. Children separated from one of their parents show higher rates of aggression and delinquency and lower school achievement, which in turn locks them into poverty. Poor communities, too, are damaged. High rates of imprisonment disrupt social networks and destroy community cohesion and solidarity—the "social capital" that helps people get out of poverty.[37]

Once a juvenile prisoner is released, he or she is much less likely to finish high school. Once an adult prisoner is released, he or she faces much greater difficulty in gaining stable employment and lower wages if a job is obtained. He or she may be excluded from publically subsidized low-income housing or from eligibility for federal aid for higher education. The ability of poor and black communities to use the political process to get government to address their needs is also undercut by state laws barring those with felony convictions from voting, even after their release from prison. In 2012, almost six million men and women who had served their time were disenfranchised, including no less than 8 percent of potential African American voters.[38]

It is poor people and people of color who bear the biggest burden of violent crime and community disorder. That is one more way in which they are the victims of society's abandonment of efforts to end poverty and racial discrimination. They, too, are concerned about safety in their communities. In one survey of over a thousand residents of a poor neighborhood in the Bronx, more than two-thirds of the respondents reported having been stopped by the police over the previous year, over a third reported being asked to move by the police when they were standing right outside their own building, and over half said that police abused their power. Nevertheless, asked whether being stopped by police is "the price we have to pay for a safer neighborhood," one-third said "yes" and another quarter were "in the middle"; only 43 percent unequivocally said "no." In a Milwaukee survey, again despite awareness of inequitable treatment, 63 percent of black residents surveyed reported that overall they were "very satisfied" or "somewhat satisfied" with the police department; only 15 percent replied that they were "not at all satisfied."[39]

But the fact that poor and black neighborhoods have higher crime rates than richer and whiter neighborhoods and, like white neighborhoods, need police protection is not a defense of unequal treatment at the hands of the law. In another poll, 70 percent of blacks (compared to only 17 percent of whites) considered that police targeting of blacks was a serious problem, and more than 60 percent of blacks, compared to 25 percent of whites, did not feel that the courts give everybody a fair trial. In a Gallup survey, 50 percent of blacks blamed the higher black male incarceration rate on discrimination, compared to only 19 percent of non-Latino whites.[40]

In any case, reforms in police tactics, court procedures, and sentencing guidelines, today increasingly supported by Democrats and Republicans alike, are long overdue. But reforms limited to the criminal justice system alone are not enough. As the Black Lives Matter movement that has emerged in response to repeated instances of police killings of black men has pointed out, police harassment and excessive use of force are just the tips of the iceberg. To quote their website, "When we say Black Lives Matter, we are broadening the conversation around state violence to include *all of the ways* in which Black people are intentionally left powerless at the hands of the state" [emphasis added].[41]

Unless the social control functions of policing are distinguished from the control of serious crime, and unless the underlying causes of the disproportionately high crime rates found in many poor communities are addressed, the boundaries between legitimate law enforcement and maintenance of public order and a program of social control through terrorization of a community will remain hard to maintain and the excesses of the latter will be impossible to overcome.

On Fighting Poverty and Racism

The bottom line is simple: poverty and segregation will not disappear by themselves. Conservatives such as Paul Ryan may fantasize that "the best anti-poverty program is economic growth," but growth has consistently failed to budge the poverty rate for forty years. Pro–Wall Street liberals such as New York's Andrew Cuomo may proclaim that improving the schools attended by poor children and children of color is "the civil rights issue of our time," but the increase in the inequities in funding between rich and poor school districts—a major example of structural racism—during his administration as governor make his words a mockery. Supreme Court chief justice John Roberts may opine that "the way to stop discrimination on the basis of race, is to stop discriminating on the basis of race," but gutting the Voting Rights Act, gutting affirmative action, limiting discrimination claims in employment cases, and relying on the justice system to preserve order tells us that he has no intention of confronting discrimination.

There is no real mystery about how to fight poverty and discrimination. What's required is to systematically and coherently address their sources. Ending poverty and discrimination requires concerted action to produce jobs, raise minimum wages, provide income security when a job is lost, and enable parents of small children to work by providing paid parental leave and paid sick leave and day care. Ending poverty and discrimination requires funding schools equitably and adequately, providing universal low-cost health insurance, making affordable housing available (and not just in already poor communities), strengthening and fully enforcing antidiscrimination laws, ending discriminatory and overly harsh practices in the criminal justice system, and reforming an electoral system that raises barriers to voting and gerrymanders away equal representation. And, lifting a page from the Great Society playbook, ending poverty and discrimination requires re-empowering poor and working people by removing obstacles to unionization, supporting community organization, and removing the power of big money from elections.

These programs, of course, require resources, but the costs would be largely if not entirely offset by the stimulation of the economy and the increases in productivity they would produce. Most of them would directly and substantially benefit Americans at all income levels and of all races.

But in the end, there is no way around it: "poverty" means lack of money. It is impossible to reduce poverty without a redistribution of wealth. The funds for programs to reduce poverty can't come from the middle class. The middle class doesn't have them. The great majority of middle-class Americans themselves struggle to keep their families above the poverty or near-poverty level. In practical terms, ending poverty means transferring wealth from the wealthy.

The cost on top of what we are already spending on programs to assist poor people is not that great. I am certainly not suggesting that poverty should be ended by literally transferring cash to the poor, but as a purely heuristic demonstration, $175 billion, distributed to the forty-five million Americans who were below the poverty line in 2012, would have raised every single one of them above the official poverty line. That is barely one percent of the country's GDP, less than one-fifth of the $925 billion we spend on our military budget, and less than half the annual income of the richest 1 percent of Americans. And if we took that amount of money entirely from the richest 1 percent, it would still leave the latter with an average of more than $350,000 a year to live on. Two or three times that amount—hardly excessive, given the vast monies accumulated by the wealthy over the last four decades—would not only pull everyone now below the poverty line well above it, but would rescue a good part of the lower middle class from the chronic insecurity of recent decades.[42]

Conservatives rail against "redistributionist" schemes but have silently cheered while we redistributed wealth from the poor and working class to the rich. Conservatives denounce proposals to redistribute income downward as "class warfare" but have celebrated the class warfare waged by the rich against everyone else for forty years. Conservatives say that the war on poverty failed to end poverty, but they have also insisted that Americans, working collectively through government, not even try to do that. Poor people and people of color have paid a heavy price for the triumph of Third Wave Capitalism.

5

THE CRISIS OF THE LIBERAL AND CREATIVE PROFESSIONS

The greatest victims of Third Wave Capitalism have been the poor and people of color, but the upper parts of the American middle class have also come under pressure. The modern professions were called into existence by the needs of Corporate Capitalism. Professionals played a key mediating role between the needs of corporations, on the one hand, and the workers and consumers on the other. For years they functioned with a relatively high degree of autonomy, as solo practitioners, in small nonprofit agencies, and even within large corporate enterprises. Their roles sometimes brought them into conflict with their employers, however, and by the late 1960s, students (professionals in training) and young professionals were often resisting the corporate system itself. During that turbulent decade, they joined black Americans as the drivers of progressive social change far more than

This chapter is adapted from Barbara Ehrenreich and John Ehrenreich, "Death of a Yuppie Dream: The Rise and Fall of the Professional-Managerial Class," published and © by the Rosa Luxemburg Stiftung—New York Office, 2013, http://www.rosalux-nyc.org.

did the working class that had propelled New Deal reforms. Third Wave Capitalism, however, brought the professionals to heel. The social movements of earlier years were defeated, and the combination of new technologies, outsourcing, corporate reorganization, and decline in commitment to public spending have made professionals' experience much like that of other parts of the American working classes.

Every would-be populist in American politics wants to defend the middle class, although there is no agreement on what it is. In the last few years, "middle class" has variously been defined as everybody, as everybody minus the 15 percent living below the federal poverty level, as everybody minus the very richest Americans, or as a sort of default group—what you are left with after you subtract the very rich and the very poor. Mitt Romney famously excluded "those in the low end" but included himself (2010 income $21.6 million) along with "80 to 90 percent" of Americans. President Obama's 2012 effort to extend the Bush-era "middle-class tax cuts" excluded only families earning over $250,000 a year (the top 2 percent), while Occupy Wall Street excluded only the richest 1 percent. The Department of Commerce has given up on income-based definitions, announcing in a 2010 report that "middle class families" are defined "by their aspirations more than their income. . . . Middle class families aspire to home ownership, a car, college education for their children, health and retirement security and occasional family vacations"—which excludes almost no one.[1]

Though using the term "middle class" is common, even the slightest implication that the word "class" has any meaning separately from "middle" or to the possibly different interests of different occupational and income groups is likely to draw charges of "class warfare." Insisted former Pennsylvania senator and presidential hopeful Rick Santorum, "middle class" is a term "that I don't think we should be using as Republicans. . . . There are no classes in America."[2]

Short of that, everyone intuitively recognizes various distinctions even within the vague "middle class" of political discourse (working class, lower middle class, upper middle class), but we have no consensus about how to talk about them. Is it useful to distinguish by occupational category, separating industrial workers ("old working class") from clerical and retail sales workers ("new working class") and small business owners and self-employed professionals ("old middle class") from salaried professionals ("new middle class"), for example? Or is income the key? Or should we slice up the U.S. population using some index of socioeconomic status, involving income, occupation, education, and perhaps other criteria? And is class purely an economic category, or does status, power, or even ethnicity enter into it?[3]

Regardless of nomenclature, one group that has been particularly interesting to many social theorists in recent decades includes service professionals (e.g., doctors, lawyers, teachers and professors), creative professionals (e.g., writers, journalists, artists, and entertainers), technical professionals (e.g., electrical and civil engineers, software engineers, and accountants), and mid-level and upper-level managers.

Corporate Capitalism and the Rise of the Professional-Managerial Class

There was little need for large numbers of professionals in the Industrial Capitalism of the nineteenth century. In the simplest case, the owner raised the funds to finance the enterprise and directed the production process (and in many early cases had himself contributed to the design and development of the machinery of production). He was simultaneously financer, owner, chief engineer, and chief manager.

By the time Corporate Capitalism began to emerge at the end of the nineteenth century, this do-it-yourself business model was becoming increasingly obsolete. The growing size of capitalist enterprises required more capital than an individual could supply, more varied and complex technology than a single person could master, more complex management than one or a few owners could provide, more stability in labor relations than police and hired thugs could offer, and ultimately more stability in markets than chance alone would provide. But it was also increasingly possible to meet these needs, because the new centralization and concentration of markets meant that business owners could afford to hire "experts" to do the work of management, long-term planning, and rationalizing the production process.

By the early twentieth century, American capitalism had also come to depend on the development of a national consumer goods market. Items like clothing, which had previously been produced at home, were replaced by the uniform products of mass production. The management of consumption came to be as important as the management of production.

Creating a culture of consumption required the efforts of legions of trained people in addition to engineers and managers: teachers, professors, journalists, entertainers, social workers, doctors, lawyers, "ad men," "domestic scientists," and "experts" in child-rearing, marriage, and practically all other aspects of daily life.[4]

Professional and managerial employment grew rapidly. In the infancy of the Corporate Capitalist era, from 1870 to 1920, the number of people in professional and managerial jobs grew more than tenfold to about 1 percent of total employment. In the years that followed, that growth accelerated dramatically. Although a variety of practical and theoretical obstacles prevent making any precise analysis, by 1972, about one-quarter of all American jobs were in professional and managerial occupations.[5]

The relationship between emerging professionals and managers on the one hand and the traditional working class on the other was riven with tensions from the start. It was the occupational role of managers, engineers, and many other professionals to manage and regulate and control the life of the working class. They designed the division of labor and the machines that controlled workers' minute-by-minute existence on the factory floor, manipulated their desire for commodities and their opinions, socialized their children, and even mediated their relationship with their own bodies. As experienced day-to-day, contacts between teacher and student, manager and worker, doctor and patient, and social worker and client featured a complex mixture of deference and hostility on the part of working-class people, paternalism and contempt on the part of the professional-managerial class. At the same time, the role of professionals and managers as "rationalizers" of society often placed them in direct conflict with the capitalist class. Like the workers, the professionals and managers were themselves employees and subordinate to the owners, but since what was truly rational in the productive process was not always identical to what was most immediately profitable, they often sought autonomy and freedom from their own bosses. It was just these potential antagonisms and links that led Barbara Ehrenreich and me to argue that professionals and managers formed a distinct "professional-managerial *class*," situated between labor and capital.[6]

Some, such as economist and social scientist Thorstein Veblen and Edward A. Ross, a Progressive ideologue who is often considered the founder of American sociology, proposed that professionals and managers were the only group capable of impartial leadership of society, based on science rather than on any narrow class interest. In 1907, for instance, Ross argued, "Social defense is coming to be a matter for the expert. The rearing of dikes against faithlessness and fraud calls for intelligent social engineering. If in this strait the public does not speedily become far shrewder . . . there is nothing for it but to turn over the defense of society to professionals."[7]

In their own defense, but with considerable encouragement from the capitalist class, the professionals and managers organized themselves, creating in the process the modern conception of a "profession." The Carnegie Foundation, based on steel money, funded the reports that launched the medical, legal, and engineering professions in the early twentieth century. Railroad, Wall Street, and oil money underwrote the development of the social work profession. State licensing boards defined the new professions and limited practitioners to those who professed to uphold a set of ethical standards and could demonstrate that they had mastered a specialized body of knowledge, accessible only through lengthy training.

The claim to specialized knowledge as the basis for claiming professional status now seems obvious and necessary, but at the time the emerging professions had little such knowledge to call their own. Even today it is not clear why an accountant or engineer is required to take liberal arts courses as part of his or her education, or why a pre-law student needs to master trigonometry. Advertised as "reforms," such requirements served largely to limit access to the professions and to justify a broad claim to autonomy from outside interference in the practice of the profession—particularly from business interests.[8]

By mid-twentieth century, professional and managerial jobs were proliferating. Corporations, with their legions of managers, had come to dominate the economy; public education was expanding; the modern university had come into being; national, state, and local governments were growing in size and role; charitable and social service agencies emerged; hospitals began to take on their modern form; newspaper circulation soared; traditional forms of recreation gave way to the popular culture and entertainment industries (including sports)—and all of these developments created jobs for highly educated managers, engineers, and other professionals, including journalists, social workers, professors, doctors, lawyers, artists, and writers.

The Professional-Managerial Class at Its Peak

Although a handful of managers and engineers preserved some independence as "consultants," the overwhelming majority were fully integrated into corporate operations right from the start. Completely dependent on the corporation, they increasingly identified with the goals of their employers. Many of those in the service professions managed to retain a measure of autonomy, however, and with it the possibility of opposition to business domination.

Most doctors, many nurses, and the majority of lawyers worked in independent, private, often solo practices. In the case of doctors, as late as 1940 there was still little medical technology in use and no significant economies of scale were possible. Even much professional nursing could be done outside the hospital by nurses who were self-employed or who worked for small, local agencies. Some lawyers did work directly for corporations or in large law firms serving corporations, but the majority remained in local, solo practices serving nearby small businesses and individuals and using little technology.

Other service professionals, such as teachers, professors, and social workers, were employed in the nonprofit or governmental sectors where there was little incentive for corporations to intrude. Universities, for example, were still relatively small and elite. In 1929–30, only about 7 percent of the "college-aged" population was enrolled in colleges and universities nationwide; the numbers did not pass 15 percent until the early 1950s.[9] Many universities could trace their origins to churches and other nonprofit groups and remained in the nonprofit sector. Others, the land-grant universities, were in the public sector. Educational work was highly labor intensive, and there was no obvious way to automate or streamline the student-teacher interaction and make universities a profitable undertaking. Social service agencies, which employed a third of a million or so social workers and therapists, were even less tempting to entrepreneurs and corporations because their services, which were mainly directed at the poor, offered no opportunity for profits. So the social workers were pretty much left to run their own agencies.

The most historically fractious group among the professionals—those in the "creative" professions, including journalists and editors, artists, musicians and architects—also retained considerable autonomy well into the late twentieth century. Although many of these were employed by for-profit corporations (such as newspapers, book publishers, movie studios, ad agencies), a substantial and very visible minority remained self-employed. And insofar as fulfilling their occupational roles required a degree of autonomy, even top corporate management often recognized and tolerated their eccentricities, at least to an extent.

In the 1960s, for the first time since the Progressive Era, a segment of the professional-managerial class—more those in the service and creative professions than the managers and engineers—had the self-confidence to take on a critical, even oppositional, political role. Jobs and grants were plentiful, a college education did not yet lead to a lifetime of debt, and materialism was briefly out of style. College students—professionals and managers in training—quickly moved from supporting the civil rights movement in the South and opposing the war in Vietnam to confronting the raw fact of corporate power throughout American society, from the pro-war inclinations of the weapons industry to the governance of the university. The revolt soon spread beyond students. By the end of the sixties, almost all of the liberal professions had so-called "radical caucuses" demanding that access to the professions be opened up to those traditionally excluded (such as women and minorities) and that the service ethic the professions claimed to uphold be actually applied in practice. The "second-wave" feminism of the late sixties and early seventies, too, was largely rooted in the professional-managerial class, and the first Earth Day, staged in 1970, opened yet another front in the attack on corporate domination and priorities.[10]

The Professional-Managerial Class Meets Third Wave Capitalism

As Third Wave Capitalism began to emerge in the 1970s, corporate leaders and those immediately beholden to them decisively reasserted their own interests and began to raise the alarm: College students, young professionals in all fields, and urban blacks and other people of color, inspired by third world nationalist movements, were talking openly about revolution. The traditional working class was engaged in the most intense wave of strikes and work actions since the 1940s. Profit rates were falling and foreign competition rising in key industries like auto and steel. Business leaders who could see beyond the confines of their own enterprises declared that capitalism itself—or, in perhaps more attractive terms, "free enterprise"—was under attack.

The ensuing capitalist offensive was geographically widespread and thorough. Thatcher in the United Kingdom, Pinochet in Chile, and Reagan in the United States all upheld the ideal of unfettered and expanded free enterprise. They pushed for reductions in welfare, deregulation of business, privatization, free trade, and the elimination of unions. Within the United States, elite organizations like the Business Roundtable sprang up to promote pro-business policies, assisted by the efforts of a growing number of foundations and think tanks to provide an intellectual undergirding for free market ideology.

At the level of the individual corporation, the new management strategy was to raise profits by reducing labor costs by moving manufacturing offshore where labor was cheaper or, more directly, by using automation to eliminate the need for employees altogether. Those workers who remained employed in the United States faced a series of initiatives designed to discipline and control them ever more tightly: intensified supervision in the workplace, drug tests to eliminate slackers, and increasingly determined efforts to prevent unionization. Cuts in the social safety net also had a disciplining function, making it harder for workers to imagine surviving job loss.

Most of these measures also had an effect, directly or indirectly, on elements of the professional-managerial class. Government spending cuts hurt the job prospects of social workers, teachers, and others in the helping professions. The decimation of the U.S.-based industrial working class reduced the need for mid-level professional managers, who found themselves increasingly targeted for downsizing. Technological innovation undercut demand for industrial, mechanical, and electrical engineers while stimulating employment of computer specialists.

But there was a special animus against the troublemaking "liberal" professions. (I will use this term broadly to include both service professions such as medicine, law, teaching, and social work, and creative professions such as art, writing, and architecture.) The awakening capitalist class had begun to nurture its own intelligentsia, based in the new think tanks and the proliferating right-wing media, and it was they who promoted the ostensibly populist idea of a "liberal elite"—what a 2004 conservative Club for

Growth ad called the "tax-hiking, government-expanding, latte-drinking, sushi-eating, Volvo-driving, New-York-Times-reading, body-piercing, Hollywood-loving, left-wing freak show."[11] Crushing this liberal elite—by "defunding the Left," by attacking liberal-leaning nonprofit organizations such as National Public Radio, and by demonizing the very word "liberal"—became a major conservative project.

Of course, not all of the forces undermining the liberal professions from the 1970s on can be traced to conscious conservative policies. Technological changes combined with ruthless corporate profit-taking to create an increasingly challenging environment for the liberal professions, including the creative ones.

In medicine, new technologies such as MRI, which were too expensive for solo practitioners, and the need to bargain more effectively with insurance companies over reimbursement rates, pulled physicians into ever-growing dependence on hospitals. By 2010, more than half of practicing U.S. physicians were directly employed by hospitals or by integrated delivery systems, compared to the 24 percent of doctors who were salaried employees in 1983. Many others worked for group practices that were themselves often owned or controlled by hospitals (see chapter 2).[12]

The transformation of the legal profession resulted from a great expansion in the demand for legal services, driven by the expansion in the number of government regulations, the rapid growth of the legal-services-hungry financial sector, the emergence of new practice areas such as environmental law, intellectual property law, pension and benefits law, and health law, and shifts in legal practices making it easier to use the legal system (for example, reductions in obstacles to class action litigation). Rapid expansion and the growth in the number of lawyers led to increased competition for legal business, which in turn led to mergers and consolidation of law firms. The number of lawyers working in corporate-like settings soared. Around 1960, there were fewer than forty law firms employing as many as fifty or more lawyers. Today there are many hundreds, twenty-one of which employ more than one thousand lawyers each. Currently 42 percent of all practicing lawyers work in one of the biggest 250 firms or in other institutional settings (corporations, government, or the nonprofit sector).[13]

The sheer size of high-tech hospitals and mega law firms seemed to require increasingly bureaucratic forms of organization. Hospitals hired professional managers to take a role once played by doctors. Law firms came under the sway of senior partners specializing in management. Similarly, universities, which had been undergoing a parallel growth spurt since the 1960s, began to depend on the managerial leadership of business school graduates rather than old professors. The pressure in all of these institutions—profit-making and nonprofit—is to cut costs and drive up revenues, whether these came from the number of procedures performed, the number of billable hours, or class size. As a result, the work experience of the liberal professions has been coming to resemble that of engineers, managers, and others in the business service professions—more like a cog in a machine and less like an autonomous practitioner.

For the plight of journalists, writers, art directors, and editors, the Internet is often blamed, but the transformation of journalism and publishing long preceded the Internet. Years before the Internet was a factor, a wave of corporate consolidation and aggressive profit-seeking swept through the publishing industry. A Federal Communications Commission report noted, "Editors at papers across the country became increasingly frustrated that editorial decisions were being made not in order to keep the papers afloat, but to propel profit levels ever higher." Journalism jobs began to disappear, as corporations, responding in part to Wall Street investors, tried to squeeze higher profit margins out of newspapers and TV news programs. By 1980, the number of daily newspapers began dropping precipitously.[14] Mergers simultaneously transformed the book publishing industry, as new corporate managers, whether from Bertelsmann or Viacom or the News Corporation, pressed for higher rates of return, meaning blockbusters rather than works of literature or scholarship.

A new, even more potent challenge arrived with the millennium—the Internet. Craigslist, eBay, and other Internet services took much of the classified ad business away from newspapers. Many papers tried to compensate for declining revenues by diversifying into non-journalistic areas. The *Washington Post*, for example, bought a for-profit university (Kaplan), radio stations, a cable television station, and the online magazine *Slate*. The *New York Times* took over the *International Herald Tribune*, the *Boston Globe*, fifteen other daily newspapers, and more than fifty websites, and is now a minority stakeholder in the Boston Red Sox. But for many papers it was too late. Even profitable papers, such as the *Philadelphia Inquirer* and the Minneapolis *Star Tribune*, faced with a massive burden of debt, were forced into bankruptcy. Faced with these pressures, more than 25 percent of newsroom staff alone have been laid off since 2001.

The book publishing industry too was transformed by mergers, long before it was hit by Amazon and e-books. Historically, publishing was characterized by many small publishers. Competition for market share focused more on taste (who the publishing house's authors were) than on reducing costs and finding other efficiencies. Beginning in the sixties, a series of mergers increased the size of the major players. Knopf, Pantheon, and Doubleday, among others, were gobbled up by Random House, which then itself was bought by RCA and later sold to the German publishing company Bertelsmann. Simon and Schuster (and for a while, Prentice Hall and Macmillan) were bought by Gulf and Western and later sold to CBS. Rupert Murdoch's News Corp swallowed Harper Collins. At the other end of the publishing business, bookselling was also transformed by consolidation. Big chains such as Barnes and Noble, B. Dalton, and Borders drove many small bookstores out of business. Then along came Amazon, gobbling an increasing share of the market, a share increased further by the subsequent arrival of e-books. By 2004, 80 percent of the retail book market was in the hands of eight big chains plus Amazon.[15]

Along with consolidation came a change in management. The old author-oriented publishers, dominated by editors such as Max Perkins (Scribners), Bennett Cerf (Random House), and Alfred Knopf (Alfred A. Knopf, Inc.) were no more. The new corporate managers, whether finding their home at Bertelsmann or Viacom or News Corp., wanted a higher rate of return. Pressures on profits from the enlarged retailers increased the need to cut costs and increase efficiency. Cutbacks in advances to authors, and outsourcing of editing, proofreading, graphic design, and for textbooks, even parts of content creation, have increased the pressures on writers and editors alike.

With minor variations, the same story could be told of much of the media, including magazine publishing, academic publishing, television, and radio. Corporations that had in earlier days remained somewhat aloof from the more rapacious behavior characteristic of other sectors of the economy merged and grew. Staff writers, editors, photographers, announcers, and the like faced massive layoffs, increased workloads, salary cuts, and a loss of their sense that publishing was a different kind of industry, one concerned with its product as much as with revenues. From the perspective of freelance writers and artists, this has meant a constriction of opportunities. While the Internet itself provides a growing set of outlets for writers, it has yet to develop a financial model that provides compensation.

Then, in the last fifteen years, professionals and managers of all sorts began to suffer the fate of the industrial working class in the 1980s: replacement by cheap foreign labor. Earlier, business analysts had promised a new global division of labor in which low income countries would provide the "hands" for manufacturing while the United States and other wealthy countries would continue to provide the "brains." So it came as a shock to many when, in the first years of the new millennium, businesses began to avail themselves of new high-speed communications technologies to outsource professional and technical functions. Hospitals sent a growing variety of tasks abroad, including reading X-rays, MRI scans, and echocardiograms, analyzing pathology specimens, monitoring ICU patients, operating nurse call centers, performing orthopedic procedures such as preparing digital prosthetic templates, and keeping and manipulating medical records. Law firms outsourced legal transcription, document review, review of litigation emails, legal research, contract-related services, and legal publishing services. The publishing industry sent out editing, proofreading, graphic design, and, for textbooks, even parts of content creation. For engineers and computer professionals, it was product design, development of phone apps and mobile phone chips, systems programming, and network design. Even the business professionals and managers were hit by outsourcing of activities such as processing mortgage applications and preparing corporate financial analyses and industry reports.[16]

By the time of the financial meltdown and deep recession of the post-2008 period, the pain inflicted by conservative policies, both public and corporate, extended well beyond the industrial working class and into core segments of the old professional-managerial class. Unemployed and underemployed professional workers—from information technology workers and electrical engineers to journalists, academics, and lawyers—became a regular feature of the social landscape. Young people did not lose faith in the value of an education, but they learned quickly that it makes more sense to study finance rather than physics or "communications" rather than literature. The old professional-managerial class dream of a society rule by impartial experts gave way to the reality of inescapable corporate domination.

But the professional-managerial class was not only a victim of more powerful groups. It had also fallen into a trap of its own making. Acquiring the credentials demanded for professional employment, which required a prolonged, expensive, and specialized education, had always been a challenge to professional-managerial-class families—as well, of course, as an insuperable barrier to the working class. If the children of the professional-managerial class were to achieve the same class status as their parents, they had to be accustomed to obedience in the classroom and long hours of study yet able to function with a great deal of autonomy. They had to be disciplined students while remaining capable of critical and creative thinking. Thus the reproduction of the class required a considerable parental (usually maternal) investment—encouraging good study habits, helping with homework, arranging tutoring (and SAT preparation), and stimulating curiosity about academically approved subjects—and this aroused a considerable amount of parental anxiety (see chapter 6).

Up until the sixties, at least, the professional-managerial class was generally successful in reproducing itself. Access to college was growing, tuitions were still relatively low. But then the cost of college skyrocketed. To take one example, in-state tuition at the publically funded University of California, Berkeley, rose from about $320 a year back in 1970 to $12,240 a year today, a rate of increase almost seven times greater than in the cost of living. Since 1970, college tuition at four-year institutions has increased three times faster than consumer prices in general, far more rapidly than middle-class salaries.[17] Part of the rise, especially in the larger universities, is directly attributable to the corporatization of the university—the proliferation of multiple layers of administration, the growth of real estate holdings, and aggressive efforts to court star professors, superstar coaches, and paying students. As tuition rose, parents from the professional-managerial class often found themselves too rich for their children to qualify for needs-based scholarships but too poor to pay for their children's education themselves.

The solution, of course, was to have the students themselves rely on loans, backed by the federal government. Today the average undergraduate student graduates with some $29,000 in outstanding debts and little likelihood of finding a good job. By 2014, aggregate student loan debt was considerably greater than either aggregate car loan debt or aggregate credit card debt. Graduate students are even worse off. For example, the median tuition at private law schools rose from $7,385 in 1985 to over $42,570 in 2013–14. The average debt of recent graduates is over $84,000 for students attending public law schools, $122,000 for those attending private law schools, although only barely over half of recent law school graduates are actually finding stable, full-time jobs requiring passing the bar exam.

Higher degrees and licenses are no longer a guarantee of professional-managerial class status. Hence the iconic figure of the Occupy Wall Street movement: the college graduate with tens of thousands of dollars in student loan debts and a job paying about ten dollars an hour or no job at all.[18]

The Legacy of the Professional-Managerial Class

College-educated workers continue to thrive as a demographic category. But a demographic category is not a class with coherent interests. Decades ago, the college-educated population and the professional-managerial class were almost coextensive. But now a college education has become the new norm, with employers in a growing number of occupations favoring degree-holders not so much because of any specialized knowledge or skills they possess, but because they have demonstrated the discipline to get through college.

Whatever its apparent potential in 1920 or 1968 to act independently, the professional-managerial class has not managed to hold its own as a class. At its wealthier end, skilled professionals continue to jump ship for more lucrative posts in direct service to capital. Scientists give up their research to become "quants" (quantitative analysts) on Wall Street. Physicians can double their incomes by finding work as investment analysts for the finance industry or by setting up "concierge" practices serving the wealthy. At the less fortunate end of the spectrum, journalists and PhDs in sociology or literature spiral down into the retail workforce. The center has not held.

The professional-managerial class's old dream of a society led by public-spirited professionals and ruled by reason is no more. The movements for social justice it engendered have collapsed. The professional-managerial class has also managed to discredit itself as an advocate for the common good. Consider our gleaming towers of medical research and high-technology care, all too often abutting urban neighborhoods characterized by extreme poverty and shortened life spans.

Should we mourn the fate of the professional-managerial class or rejoice that there is one less smug, self-styled elite to stand in the way of a more egalitarian future? A case can be made for both responses. Professionals and managers played a significant role in the disempowering of the old working class. They have offered little resistance to the Right's campaign against any measure that might ease the lives of the poor and the working class. Some, in fact, supplied the intellectual firepower for that campaign. On the other hand, service and creative professionals, if not the managers and engineers, have also at times been a liberal force, defending the values of scholarship and service in the face of the relentless corporate pursuit of profit and the all-encompassing imperatives of rent-seeking which have characterized recent years. In this respect, their role in the last century bears some analogy to the role of monasteries in Europe in late antiquity, which kept literacy and at least some form of inquiry alive while the barbarians raged outside.

Who will uphold those values today? And is there any way to salvage the dream of reason—or at least the idea of a society in which reasonableness can occasionally prevail—from the accretion of elitism it acquired from the professional-managerial class?

6

ANXIETY AND RAGE: THE AGE OF DISCONTENT

I have chronicled the impact of Third Wave Capitalism on the U.S. economy, government, the health-care and school systems, social problems such as the persistence of poverty and racial disparities, and on the roles and autonomy of the professions. The transition to the Third Wave has been felt in everyday life as well.

Stagnant wages, a deteriorating social safety net, jobs shipped overseas or lost to automation, the growing use of temporary and contract workers, and the appropriation by the wealthy of a disproportionate share of the national wealth have produced chronic financial and job insecurity. Declining responsiveness of government to the needs of all but the wealthy and the collapse of unions and other countervailing forces that once provided a voice for ordinary people at work and in the halls of government have created a growing sense of disempowerment. Americans' historic belief in social and governmental solutions to societal problems has given way to individualism and an ethos of "every man for himself and the devil take the hindmost."

Traditional communities and relationships have been torn apart by the never-ending corporate search for new aspects of everyday life that can be monetized. The impact of these changes is felt in popular culture, in patterns of personality, in interpersonal relations, in our inner emotional experience, and in our political beliefs.

The Age of Anxiety

America is in a gloomy, anxious, and dyspeptic mood. A recent *Wall Street Journal/NBC News* poll reported that almost 70 percent of Americans polled believe that the United States is "headed in the wrong direction," with respondents endorsing words such as "divided," "troubled," "deteriorating," and "broken" to describe the country today. Other polls report that our lack of confidence in government is rivaled only by our lack of confidence in business and that 70 percent either hate or are disengaged from their jobs.[1]

What's going on here? Is our grumpy mood a response to specific current problems, such as economic stagnation and political gridlock? Or does the national malaise have a deeper origin in longer-term societal processes? Is there any connection between the personal discontent and the ugly turn our politics have taken?

One clue is that, judging by the statistics, we've become a nation of the mentally ill. Today, in any given week, about 7 percent of Americans are suffering from major depression and almost twice that many from an anxiety disorder. Over the course of a lifetime, nearly half of all Americans will at some point meet standard diagnostic criteria for a mental illness, accounting for more disability in the United States than any other group of illnesses, including cancer and heart disease.[2]

The prevalence of mental illness has rapidly increased. Levels of Major Depressive Disorder in the United States have more than doubled in the last fifty years. More than 15 percent of boys are now diagnosed with Attention Deficit Hyperactivity Disorder (more than twice the rate of only twenty-five years ago). Levels of self-reported anxiety and panic attacks among young people have also doubled, and complaints of general physical malaise are up more than 50 percent. College counseling centers report that there has been a rapid increase in the number of students seeking help for mental health problems, since the 1990s, with depression, anxiety, suicidal ideation, drug and alcohol abuse, eating disorders, and feelings of hopelessness, helplessness, boredom, and social isolation all common. The number of people so disabled by mental illness that they qualify for Supplemental Security Income or Social Security Disability Insurance has increased nearly two and one half times over the last two decades alone.[3]

It is tempting to dismiss the statistics as an illusion. The increase in enrollment in Social Security Disability programs, for example, may not reflect increases in mental illness so much as the fact that the programs have become alternatives to welfare for poor and unemployed individuals who have any kind of psychiatric problem. The increasing number of students seeking help from counselors may reflect lessening levels of stigma in acknowledging emotional distress and growing awareness that help is available. The rise in ADHD diagnoses may reflect efforts by school districts, anxious to meet increased federal standards for school performance, to take children who have academic difficulties out of the pool required to take standardized tests. It is hard to account for more than a small fraction of the very rapid increase in distress by these factors alone, however, and, in any case, emotional distress reaching the level where it is diagnosed as a "mental illness" is the tip of a much larger iceberg of unhappiness.[4]

So where does this epidemic of emotional distress come from? I was trained as a clinical psychologist. In the course of my training, I was taught theories about the causes of depression, anxiety, and other mental disorders. Today, as a college psychology professor, I have students revisit these explanations in their textbooks. There are various perspectives on normal and abnormal behavior—biomedical, psychodynamic, behaviorist, and cognitive, among others. While these psychological theories may be useful in understanding and treating anxiety, depression, and other disorders in *individuals*, none of them can make any sense of the rapid rise in the *rates* of mental illness and emotional distress in America. To understand the latter demands that we take broader, societal factors into account.

There are several possibilities. Perhaps the rising levels of some illnesses reflect changes in the physical environment (for example, increased fetal exposure to environmental toxins or to psychoactive drugs taken by the mother) that affect brain development in fetuses and young children. Or perhaps long-term pharmacological treatment of emotional distress paradoxically converts acute illnesses into chronic ones. However, there is little more than scanty circumstantial evidence to support these hypotheses.[5]

Another possibility is that it is not the prevalence of depression and other mental disorders that is rising but rather the willingness of people to acknowledge personal misery to others (for example, to those conducting surveys of the prevalence of symptoms of distress) or to seek treatment. There is some evidence that the stigma associated with mental illness has declined somewhat in recent years. The magnitude of the decline in stigmatization is modest, however, and at best can only account for a part of the increase in prevalence.[6]

Or perhaps the rise in the apparent frequency of mental illness is merely the result of over-diagnosis. Have we turned ordinary sadness into "Depressive Disorder" and the high energy of normal boyhood into "ADHD"? But that explanation just creates a new puzzle: Why have we increasingly pathologized normal behavior? Is this simply the psychiatric version of the "medicalizing" of human and social problems discussed in chapter 2?

Part of the answer comes from the history of psychiatry. Former *New England Journal of Medicine* editor-in-chief Marcia Angell recalls the 1960s and 1970s, when psychiatrists "were seen as less scientific than other [medical] specialists, and their incomes were lower." In the face of growing public disrespect and rising competition from other non-physician mental health practitioners, it was necessary, in the words of Melvin Sashin, then director of the American Psychiatric Association, to "remedicalize" psychiatry.[7]

The result was DSM-III—the new edition of the previously largely ignored *Diagnostic and Statistical Manual of Mental Disorders*, explicitly designed by its principle developer Robert Spitzer to be "a defense of the medical model as applied to psychiatric problems." DSM-III defined more than two hundred distinct patterns of emotional and behavioral abnormality as "mental disorders." ("Mental disorder," "mental illness," and "mental disease" are generally used as synonyms). Then psychiatrists, alone among mental health providers in their legal authority to prescribe medication, embraced a biological explanation of these mental illnesses, despite the absence of much evidence for this at the time. This gave them the decisive role in treatment of mentally ill people and relegated the other mental health professions to an ancillary role. Needless to say, the pharmaceutical companies were only too happy to add their influence to the drug-obsessed American Psychiatric Association's ensuing all-out campaign to restore the authority of the psychiatrists. From that day forth, psychiatrists and drug companies have had a powerful incentive to expand the patient population by defining ever-new categories of behavior as evidence of mental illness.[8]

The Rise of the Me-Directed Individual

But greater willingness to acknowledge symptoms and over-diagnosis alone cannot explain the trends. The problem is that it is not only the number of people who meet the DSM criteria for specific mental illnesses that have increased. The frequency of broader measures of emotional distress—*of* anxiety, of depression, of loneliness—has risen as well. This increase in emotional distress may be related to broader social changes and broader changes in what is usually considered "normal" personality.

In the early 1950s, sociologist David Riesman chronicled a shift in the typical American personality pattern from the "inner-directed" individual, guided by an inner set of goals and principles, to the "other-directed" individual, sensitive to the preferences and expectations of others and wanting to be loved rather than esteemed. If the former pattern was well suited to the age of the frontiersman and the industrial entrepreneur, the latter pattern was better fitted to the age of the "corporation man."[9]

Since the 1970s, psychologists have documented what seems to be yet another shift in personality patterns. Compared to earlier generations, the typical American of the era of Third Wave Capitalism is characterized by greater narcissism and unrealistically high self-appraisal. There is an increased focus on immediate gratification and external goals such as money, image, and status rather than on an internalized sense of self-acceptance, competence at work, or affiliation with others. Young people today are more likely to feel misunderstood. They are less trusting, show less concern for others, show less dispositional empathy, and are less likely to contribute to charity, express interest in community action programs, or think about social problems. Although they are more accepting of individual differences in race, gender, and sexual orientation, this may reflect greater individualism rather than any increase in empathy. They are more likely to be engaged in community service, but this reflects, at least in part, increasingly common high school requirements to engage in such projects or efforts to buff up resumes. "Inner-directed" and "other-directed" have given way to "me-directed."[10]

The time course of increases in self-reported anxiety and depression parallels the shift in personality patterns. Perhaps our increased anxiety and depression are caused by high rates of narcissistic fixation on the superficial and on goals that, though they may be reachable for a few, are out of reach for most of us. To a psychologist, unrealistically high expectations, an exaggerated sense of one's own competency, difficulty delaying gratification, gratification from achieving external goals, a reduced sense of affiliation, and ungratified narcissism seem a recipe for anxiety and depression.

Where might these changes in personality have come from? One immediate factor driving them may be changes in the expectations and behavior of parents over the last four decades. Observers have noted two superficially contradictory tendencies. First, parenting and schools have become more permissive and relentlessly affirming. Mom and Dad are friends, not authorities. Parental authority declines, and parenting is oriented to building the child's "self-esteem." For the child, once grown up and faced with the less malleable demands of the real world, it is a short step to anxiety and depression. "Good eye!" shout ten-year-old Tommy's parents, as he restrains himself from swinging at a pitch that is two feet high and two feet outside the strike zone, and at the end of the season there are trophies for all, regardless of performance or whether or not the team has won a single game. Small wonder that ten years later, Tommy, now a college junior, comes to me distraught because he has gotten a B– on an exam: "But I *deserve* a better grade," he says, angry and near tears. "I didn't miss a single class and I got all of the assignments in."

At the same time, we have seen the emergence of the "helicopter" parent, hyper-vigilant, over-involved, shuttling the child from one activity to another without cease. But as psychologist Ron Taffel has observed, over-involvement is not the same as real connection. Parents may look at the child but not really see the child. The parent's own attention is often fragmented by the demands of work and by the ever-present smart phone, and the parent-child relationship itself comes to serve ends beyond the moment. Too often, writes Taffel, "parental behavior isn't really about what it seems to be about, but is in service of a whole other agenda.... 'I give my child a hug when he does something well because kudos build self-esteem' or 'When she bumped herself, once I realized she wasn't really hurt, I let her cry because she needs to develop grit' or 'We're strict about keeping schedules because rituals instill emotional security.'" For the child, diminished empathy and weakened connections to others result.[11]

Third Wave Capitalism and the Me-Directed Individual

At a deeper level, the changes in personality and the changes in patterns of parenting that produce them reflect changes in the functioning of American society and in the demands and opportunities it presents to individuals. For many of us, our relationship to the world of work and our place in society have become less secure in recent decades. Wages have stagnated and social mobility has declined. Americans can no longer look forward to a steadily rising standard of living or have confidence that life for their children will be better than it has been for them.[12]

Underlying this growing insecurity is a sea change in the behavior of American corporate leaders over recent decades, from an orientation toward "stakeholders" to an orientation toward "shareholders" (see chapter 1). Until the early 1970s, although corporate executives were certainly not immune from engaging in behaviors that harmed the public, there was a widespread consensus that profits were inseparable from broader social goals and obligations. In the decades that followed, social obligations came to be seen as barriers to market efficiency, to be minimized. Companies shifted toward a relentless search for short-term profits, no matter the cost to their workers, their consumers, or the communities in which they were located.[13]

One immediate impact was a decline in the predictability and control over work life. Corporate raiders and activist shareholders pushed companies to undertake novel measures to increase share price, including downsizing operations, drastically cutting the workforce or even liquidating the company. Rapid automation displaced millions of workers; outsourcing, offshoring, and importing skilled workers from abroad displaced others. Companies increasingly preferred temporary workers, workers on short-duration contracts, freelancers, independent consultants, and foreign workers with special visa statuses, to long-term employees to whom they had an obligation. Many workers found themselves hired for limited-term "projects" rather than long-term jobs, much less careers. The typical baby boomer already had had more than eleven different jobs before reaching the age of forty-six.[14]

The shift from a long-term to a short-term perspective and the weakened connection to a particular job or to a particular set of workmates undercut the social relationships of the workplace. Friendships came to take on what Richard Sennett has called a "fugitive" quality, characterized by detachment, superficial cooperativeness, the corrosion of loyalty, trust, and mutual commitment, and an underlying belief in the necessity of looking out for oneself. With the skill sets needed to do a job constantly changing, the value of experience and of institutional knowledge diminished. Instead of age implying wisdom, it meant obsolescence. Long-term planning and stable expectations of the future were devalued. It is only *now* that matters.[15]

A sense of powerlessness in other spheres of life appeared as well. Institutions and other societal mechanisms that in earlier decades had provided some protection were on the decline. Unions, under relentless corporate and government attack, lost members and power. U.S. politics shifted from a "participatory" model, driven by grassroots activism (often organized by unions) to a "mass communications" model, based on television, robocalls, social media, and other technologically sophisticated approaches and driven by money. As we saw in chapter 3, education no longer provided a reliable way out.

Other changes in society were also affecting the daily lives of Americans. A media culture of shallow, sexualized celebrity equated success with glamour and possessions and inculcated a feeling of "I must be entertained at all times." Easy credit, readily available in the form of credit cards since the 1970s and home equity loans since 1980s, led to what psychologist Jean Twenge has called a "repeal of the reality principle." No longer did gratification need to be delayed. The Internet's offer of instantly available information and a 24/7 news cycle further removed incentives to tolerate delay. And the rise of social media, allowing communicating to the world one's most fleeting thoughts and activities (often accompanied by photos), encouraged a preoccupation with self-expression.[16]

In the new world of the late twentieth century and early twenty-first century, a sense of self-worth based on a stable place in society or on inner values became outmoded, and the traditional faith that hard work led to success was undercut. What was left to replace the earlier sense of self based on one's place in the world was individual gratification and a sense of self based on possessions and personal status. The psychological pattern I am describing is the counterpart in personality of the characteristically individualistic ideology of Third Wave Capitalism. None of the changes in American society required the shift in personality, but by comparison with the America of earlier decades, the characteristic traits of the "me-directed" individual became adaptive. And with them came a new vulnerability to emotional distress.[17]

Social Stress and Unhappiness

So far I have explained the rise in emotional distress in recent decades as the result of personality changes produced directly or indirectly by changes in U.S. society. A much simpler and more direct explanation is that we're more anxious and depressed because we have good reasons to be—because today's America is an ever more insecure and frightening place for all but the super-rich. Old ways of life—manufacturing, farming—have disappeared, and with them the viability of working-class and farming communities, from Appalachia to Detroit. For the poor and for lower-income workers the benefits offered by the social safety net have eroded or been cut back. For the unemployed there is the fear of losing a job in a country in which Congress refuses to extend unemployment benefits. For Blacks and Latinos there is repeated exposure to expressions and consequences of racism, and for young black men there is frequent police harassment and a one in three chance of sooner or later spending time in jail. For undocumented immigrants there is the ever-present threat of deportation, and for many documented immigrants there is the fear of ethnic profiling by police. For students graduation promises only a mountain of debt and no job.

For everyone save those with incomes placing them in the top 10 percent, earnings have stagnated. Only by both husband and wife working and by going more and more into debt (home equity loans, credit cards, car loans, student loans) can many families make ends meet. The price is increased time pressure, marital stress, stress on children, and an ever-present sense of walking on a knife-edge of financial insecurity.

With jobs scarce, especially for those with limited skills, many women in troubled marriages are aware of being "one divorce away from welfare."

For most of the elderly, there is the fear of being one serious illness away from losing their life savings. For many Americans, especially those who are older or less educated, rapid changes in computer and information technology are felt as a threat, menacing their jobs, their sense of competency, and their sense of mastery of the contemporary world.[18]

Even the upper parts of the middle class are not immune. As discussed in chapter 5, public-sector budget cuts, corporate reorganization, and the rise of the Internet undercut the autonomy and job security of teachers, college professors, writers and editors, and social workers. Doctors' independent practices have been absorbed by giant hospitals. Lawyers have found themselves practicing in "mega-firms." Engineers have lost their jobs to outsourcing.

Anxiety has become big business. Doctors urge us to take new medical tests to warn us of the diseases we will develop, even if there is little we can do about it. Schools demand tests, tests, and more tests to ensure the school is effective, driving children to tears and teachers and parents to a permanent state of stress. The 24/7 news media market a tumble of never-ending hysteria. Potential threats from Ebola, ISIS, "illegal immigrants" on the borders, terrorists, genetically modified foods, monster snowstorms, and "polar vortexes" tumble over each other in rapid succession.

At the same time as stresses on middle-class and working-class and poor people were increasing, their sources of social support were decreasing. As the divorce rate and the number of single-parent families rose, families became a less stable source of refuge for both children and their parents. Almost half of all marriages end in divorce, and 28 percent of American children now live with a single parent. (The apparent stabilization of the divorce rate in the last two decades is probably illusory, reflecting the substitution of unmarried couples living together, which can end without a formal divorce, for the more traditional first marriages of the past.)[19]

Nonfamily sources of social support have also faded. White flight, aided and abetted by government and by predatory real estate brokers, emptied white working-class communities. Manufacturing jobs fled the United States, mom-and-pop stores were displaced by big-box stores, and local doctors' practices and community hospitals were absorbed by giant hospital networks. The working-class communities built around these institutions disintegrated. "Relationships" with neighbors in a stable community have been increasingly replaced by more impersonal "transactions," observed

George Soros. Unions declined, as did active involvement in churches. (Evangelistic, fundamentalist churches, especially in the South and Southwest, are the exception.) Robert Putnam has documented the dramatic decline in the involvement of Americans of all social classes in a variety of other face-to-face personal interactions, including direct involvement in political activity, church attendance, membership in community groups, and participation in clubs and athletic leagues. The increasing sense of powerlessness and lack of social engagement made people all the more vulnerable to the highly individualistic, free market oriented ideology promulgated by conservative and centrist media. Americans became more mistrustful of social explanations of individual problems and came to believe that they bore responsibility for their own misery and for doing something about it.[20]

For almost all of us, the sense that we have any control—whether through the political system or thorough unions or other civic organizations—has declined. Government, which once appeared to provide at least some protection against the depredations of corporations, has increasingly seemed more attuned to the needs of Wall Street than of Main Street. The community-based, politically engaged movements of the sixties and early seventies have long faded. The percentage of high school seniors who believe that you can "usually trust people" dropped by half over the latter part of the twentieth century. But isolation breeds loneliness. The number of people reporting that they have "no confidant" in their lives has risen from 10 percent in 1985 to 25 percent in 2004.[21]

The loss of a sense of community and of social connectedness combined with the shift toward "me-centeredness" to create an ever more virulent individualism. Mistrust in collective action and declining community involvement reinforced social isolation and individual anxiety, which in turn begat further loss of faith in community engagement and in the possibility of social solutions to individual problems. Americans' "pursuit of happiness" has hit a roadblock, one that will not be overcome by adding more mental health centers and prescribing more medications.

The Age of Political Rage

Paralleling the rise of individual distress in the United States of recent decades is a rise in political distress—political polarization, anger, and intolerance. Anger at one another is on the rise, often taking the form of action. Americans file some fifteen million lawsuits against one another every year. There is an explosive rise in antigovernment far-right groups. Political partisanship in Congress is at its highest level since the early twentieth century. More than a third of Republicans not merely disagree with Democrats but see the Democratic Party as a threat to the nation's well-being, and more than a quarter of all Democrats express the same hostility toward Republicans. A 2010 poll reported that no less than 24 percent of Republicans believed President Obama "may be the anti-Christ," and 25 percent of all Americans believe he is one of the "domestic enemies" that federal elected officials in their oath of office swear to protect us against.[22]

Why has the country turned so conservative in recent years? Why have the right-wing litanies been so eagerly accepted by millions? Why do so many millions of citizens vote for candidates whose policies appear to contradict their own interests? Why do so many Americans today show what political analyst and journalist Thomas Frank has called a "hair trigger irritability," lashing out at gays, Muslims, immigrants, and—to use Mitt Romney and Paul Ryan's racially coded words—the "47 percent" who are "takers."[23]

I have argued that societal stresses lead to helplessness, passivity, fear, and isolation and that, in turn, these can lead to depression and anxiety. The individual accepts the feelings and lets himself or herself be miserable. But helplessness, passivity, fear, and isolation can also lead to anger and exaggerated egotism. These might be described as "externalized" forms of distress. The individual in these cases acts out his or her distress in the world (perhaps making others miserable).

There is nothing new about extreme conservatism or political expressions of anger in the United States. (Extreme left-wing radicalism, though not unknown, has been far more unusual than right-wing radicalism in recent decades.) From the anti-immigrant, anti-Catholic Know-Nothings of the 1850s and the post–Civil War white supremacist Ku Klux Klan (and its 1920s revival) to the McCarthyite Red Scare of the 1950s and the present-day Tea Party there is a long history of what seems like right-wing wackiness. In 1958 oilman Fred Koch helped found the ultraconservative John Birch Society. Today, Fred's sons, Charles and David Koch, finance the Tea Party and its allies, who say little that was not said by previous generations of conservatives. What is new about the Tea Party and its allies is that they have taken over the entire Republican Party, pulling the party mainstream far to the right and pushing out the few remaining moderate Republicans.

There are many issues on which Americans might in good faith differ. Even though we may disagree passionately about the "right to decide" versus the "right to life," the demand for voter ID requirements versus easier access to voting, or the cost versus the benefits of an increase in the minimum wage, both sides can present reasonably coherent rational or religious arguments. Liberals and conservatives have different beliefs about issues such as the legitimate role of government, the appropriate balance between individual freedom and mutual responsibility, the essential goodness or badness of human nature, and the deference owed tradition. Given these different starting points, it may be hard to reach agreement, but the underlying basis for the disagreement can be perceived, and compromise is not unthinkable.[24]

But other disagreements are much deeper and much harder to comprehend. How are we to understand, for example, the fact that in 2015, 34 percent of Republicans are still "birthers," who insist that President Obama is not a U.S. citizen, that 41 percent of Tea Party adherents believe the earth is not warming, and that 66 percent of self-described "very conservative" Americans believe Muslims are covertly implementing Sharia law in U.S. courts. Viewed from the left, these substantive positions appear to be bizarre distortions of reality.[25]

Freud distinguished between what he called "errors" on the one hand, and "illusions" and "delusions" on the other. Errors, he argued, simply reflect lack of knowledge or poor logic. Aristotle's belief that vermin form out of dung was an error. But illusions and delusions are based on conscious or unconscious wishes, as well. Columbus's belief that he had found a new route to the Indies was based on his wish to have done so. The tenacity of many far-right beliefs, in the face of facts, rational arguments, reason, and common sense, suggests that the beliefs are not merely alternate interpretations of facts but are rooted in unconscious wishes—that is, are rooted in personality.[26]

The left-right differences may extend to differences in belief in empiricism and reason on the one side, faith and trust in revealed truth on the other. Liberals' "rational" arguments to conservatives may fall on deaf ears, not because of the unwillingness of the latter to "face the facts" but because of fundamental differences between them in what constitutes a "fact" and what constitutes evidence. These differences, in turn, are deeply rooted in culture and again, in personality.[27]

The Geography of Belief

A second clue that links the sources of contemporary political anger and exaggerated beliefs to the sources of individual internalized distress lies in geography. The red state–blue state Republican-Democratic divide has become all too familiar. The heartland of the United States—the South, Southwest, Midwest, and Mountain West—has become the homeland of hard-core conservatism, while the Northeast and the Pacific Coast remain bastions of liberalism. The geographical distinction is a vast oversimplification, of course. Rural areas in upstate New York and Pennsylvania are islands of conservatism in larger, safely blue states, and red state cities such as Dallas, Atlanta, and Las Vegas vote Democratic. A demographically based set of distinctions—older, white, less-educated, nonunion, disproportionately male on the one side, and younger, nonwhite, more-educated, unionized, disproportionately female on the other—is equally valid. But "red state–blue state" is a useful shorthand and may help reveal some of the underlying dynamics of the politics that divide us.

The states and regions that are now reliably red historically were predominately agricultural. In the Midwest they also contained great manufacturing cities such as Cleveland and St. Louis. But although U.S. agricultural output has boomed, the number of farms in the United States has dropped almost 70 percent since the 1930s. And manufacturing employment has declined 42 percent from its 1979 peak, 30 percent since 2000 alone, turning the great industrial Midwest into the Rust Belt. The old economies and the old farming and working-class communities built around manufacturing and agriculture are no more. In parts of the South and Southwest, where the economy and population continue to grow, uprootedness is typical and rapid change is king. Elsewhere, out-migration and chronic unemployment loom large. By many measures, these are what *New York Times* writers Annie Lowrey and Alan Flippen in 2014 have called "the hardest places to live," the places with the highest rates of obesity, divorce, teen pregnancy, sexually transmitted diseases, firearm deaths, and alcohol-caused motor vehicle deaths and disability, and the lowest levels of education and income.[28]

Recent years have not been good for many people living in these areas—especially for older white men, the heart of the conservative movement. Even for those who are doing well economically as individuals, their old way of life, their old belief systems, their own expectations of upward mobility for their children, their own sense of themselves as being at the center of the universe in the midst of "the American century" have been torn apart. In a culture that worships individualism, that fervently believes that success comes from character, grit, and hard work, it is hard not to feel a sense of shame, humiliation, and self-loathing, no matter how unjustified in reality.

But shame, humiliation, and self-loathing create intolerable feelings of anxiety and anger, some conscious, some unconscious. The ego must be protected, at all costs. Available cultural values are called on to provide a more acceptable narrative. For some, the feelings are turned inward, in the form of depression and of anxiety. The unhappy feelings may be consciously experienced as due to a specific cause, real or fanciful, or they may take the less specific form of a vague sense of dread or irritability.[29]

But we also want to see the world as making sense, as a fair place where people get their just deserts. We seek a sense that there is order in our lives. So for many, an alternative to internalizing the depression and anxiety is to project the feelings outward. They artificially inflate their own self-esteem with a narcissistic identification with the presumed greatness of the United States: "We're number one!" They scapegoat, letting themselves experience specific groups of others as the source of the problems we experience. They feel anger at the newcomers who did not share in the building of our country, who have not paid their dues, and yet who are offered the rewards. Fear, envy, and shame turn into rage at those who seem to be competing for jobs, such as African Americans, Latinos, and immigrants, documented or undocumented, and at groups who once were vulnerable but now seem empowered, such as women and some Asian immigrant groups.

Anger is also turned against liberal politicians who would reward the very ones responsible for our troubles, and against those who model the very lifestyles that are threatening the traditional ones. Eastern intellectuals with their liberal schemes, Hollywood with its dissolute lifestyles, gays and lesbians with their challenge to traditional sexual mores and family structure, Muslims with their headscarves and other unfamiliar customs, young people celebrating new, openly sexual lifestyles, government bureaucrats fattening themselves off our taxes—all become targets.[30]

The Group Psychology of Red and Blue

Group psychological processes augment the individual processes. We are all motivated to achieve a mutual understanding of reality that will help us regulate interpersonal relationships and permit us to perceive ourselves and our environment as stable and predictable. Identification with a group, whether our family, friends and neighbors, community, or some other group of people perceived to be "like me," helps provide this stability. Maintaining group identity requires a shared sense of reality, however. Evidence that might threaten group identity and cohesion (for example, that evolution or climate change are real or that black people are not enemies but another group of people struggling to get by) is ignored or denied.

Leaders, including individuals who are influential among small groups of people, community leaders such as preachers, business owners, and local politicians, and politicians and media figures with a national reach, contribute to feelings of group identity. They also help provide a language (including both a rhetoric and content) with which to express otherwise inchoate feelings. The language that emerged to express feelings of anger about our society from the early 1970s on was socially, culturally, and politically conservative. It was imbued with support for the "free market" and the view that the individual is superior to the collective, and it often contained deeply encoded racial messages. This conservative ideology didn't just happen to happen. It was developed systematically and self-consciously at the initiative of conservatives in the religious, business, and political communities. It was elaborated by academics, often at think tanks such as the Heritage Foundation, Hoover Institution, and American Enterprise Institute and funded by wealthy individuals, corporations, and foundations. It was assertively promulgated through local and national political campaigns (such as Nixon's 1972 "southern strategy" and

Reagan's 1980 alliance with Jerry Falwell's Moral Majority) and spread by thousands of local and national groups, ranging from the organizations of the religious right such as Pat Robertson's Christian Coalition and James Dobson's Focus on the Family to the local and national Chambers of Commerce, the National Rifle Association, and the Tea Party. Local clergy and televangelists such as Jerry Swaggart and Oral Roberts spread the word further.

The 1987 repeal of the Fairness Doctrine by President Reagan's Federal Communications Commission eliminated the requirement that broadcasters present controversial issues of public importance in a manner that was honest, equitable, and balanced, freeing up local radio and television stations to become right-wing propaganda machines. Right-wing talk radio hosts such as Rush Limbaugh filled the airwaves, and in 1996 Rupert Murdoch and Roger Aile's Fox News debuted, insisting that a lineup made almost entirely of figures such as Bill O'Reilly, Charles Krauthammer, and Sean Hannity provided fair and balanced news.

Those whose traditional identity has been threatened by the changes in the United States of recent decades, regardless of whether they live in red states or blue states, have been especially receptive to conservative ideology and prone to political rage. Such ideology and feelings represented a solution to the need of millions of people to express their frustrations, reduce stress, reduce feelings of humiliation and self-loathing, and make sense of the world.

Several other factors have reinforced the rise of ultraconservatism and rage in the South, Southwest, Midwest, and Mountain West. For one thing, these areas largely coincide with the Bible Belt, the homeland of socially conservative evangelical Protestantism. Protestant theology emphasizes the responsibility of individuals for their own lot in life. Personal success (salvation) or failure (damnation) comes not from social processes but from the individual's personal decision to embrace Jesus as Lord and Savior. In this world, hard work, grit, and sacrifice underlie achievement. Outside groups of people who are seen (realistically or through projection) as sensual and flamboyant, people who do not share an obsession with order and timeliness, people who want the rewards without the pain, are especially alien. Ears are wide open to the messages of fundamentalist preachers, who not only oppose liberal cultural values but urge their followers to use the political system to restore a more just world.

Earlier I suggested that individual personality processes play an important role in how one processes one's experience of the world. Personality studies have shown characteristic differences in the psychology of conservatives and liberals. Those on the right side of the political spectrum (those who tend to support authority and a more-or-less hierarchical social order and who resist shifts toward greater political, economic, and social equality) tend to score higher than those on the left side of the spectrum on measures of adherence to externally imposed conventional norms and to the authorities that impose them. They adhere more strongly to traditional values, and they are more likely to value stability, conformity, and order. They are more accepting of inequality and resist change. They are less tolerant of ambiguity and nuance and less attentive to inner feelings. They are more moralistic and more easily become enraged or vengeful. By contrast, those on the left tend to have greater toleration for novelty, disorder, and change. They show a less strong preference for higher status groups, and they tolerate ambiguity and uncertainty better. They are more able to recognize, apply, and see connections and similarities across divergent perspectives. They are also more impulsive and less "repressed." Not surprisingly, studies of differences in modal personality by region find higher concentrations in the red states of people who are more conventional and more likely to accept authority, precisely the characteristics associated with more conservative political and moral beliefs. Whatever its ultimate source, a larger proportion of people in the red states may be predisposed to accept a conservative worldview.[31]

A third factor intensifying the conservatism of part of the red states and regions is race. Racial beliefs (and by extension, anti-immigrant and anti-minority beliefs, whatever the race of the immigrant or minority group) have a historical persistence. After President Johnson signed the 1964 Civil Rights Act, he reportedly turned to his press secretary and lamented that Democrats "have lost the South for a generation." Though the story may be apocryphal, over the following decades a massive realignment of the parties did take place, and racial issues and attitudes have remained intertwined with U.S. politics in ways subtle and not so subtle. A recent survey of almost forty thousand southern whites found that those who currently live in counties that had a high concentrations of slaves before the Civil War are more conservative on average than those who live in other parts of the South—more likely to vote Republican, more likely to oppose policies favoring greater equality such as affirmative action, and more likely to express racial resentment toward African Americans.[32]

For many, political rage, though irrational in a literal sense (that is, not the result of accurate information and logical analysis), is rational in the sense that it solves a problem. An external enemy—imagined as a malevolent and powerful cause of one's troubles—is created to insulate the self from its shame and inadequacy and to protect against narcissistic injury. Empathy for others, who may objectively share your troubles, goes out the window. The narcissism of recent decades increased vulnerability to narcissistic injury at the same time as threats, real or fantasized, intensified. Faced with these dynamics, politics based solely on economic self-interest and appeals for solidarity across race and ethnic lines carry little weight.

EPILOGUE

And the future? After "the man from Hope" (Bill Clinton) and "the audacity of hope" (Barack Obama's phrase), is there still room for hope? How can we address the issues facing the United States, effectively and sanely? How can we provide economic security for all? How can we create a political system that is transparent, participatory, and responsive to the needs of ordinary people? How can we end the twin atrocities of racism and poverty? How can we re-create a sense of community and collective empowerment? How can we restore the balance between the American traditions of "rugged individualism" and personal freedom and the equally American traditions of providing for the common welfare and ensuring justice for all?

There is no easy, happy ending to the story I have told. If you are looking for an explicit blueprint, a program, a plan of action to spur and hold together a progressive coalition, you will not find it here. In the present political environment, it is hard to imagine *any* progressive changes in American society being feasible, much less sweeping changes to alter the course of recent American history. But before falling into helpless pessimism, it is worth stepping back and exploring, however speculatively, some of the obstacles to change and some potential bases for optimism.

Put pessimism aside for a moment and give yourself permission to imagine the country we could have. Let us not conflate "will" and "way." If we imagine, for a moment, that the will to make changes is there, there are certainly ways. For the most part, there is no great mystery about the reforms that are needed. Everyone has a list. My own list includes progressive tax reform, investment in infrastructure, restoration and expansion of the social safety net and funds for social services, supports for working parents, full enforcement of laws barring discrimination in employment and housing, programs to support affordable housing, regulation of corporate governance, public financing of elections, full restoration of the Voting Rights Act, restoration of rigorous governmental regulation of business, a single-payer health-care system, sentencing and police reform, equitable funding of schools, laws and regulations supportive of union organizing and collective bargaining, and effective action to address climate change. Many other proposals can be offered.

Acknowledging that we do not know how to get to these solutions, that we do not know exactly how our proposals would work out, and that programs to solve existing problems can create new problems does not mean that solutions are impossible. We are not called on here to diagram utopia or to map a detailed route to the end of poverty, inequality, disempowerment, and distress. We *are* called on to demand that "we, the people" make the effort to engage with the problems of society, free of formulas and free of the accepted wisdom as to how things are supposed to be. We *are* called on to reject any contentions that our problems as a nation are unsolvable, that the barriers to action are too great, and that the conservative sway makes even thinking about solutions pointless. To accept these shibboleths as statements of eternal truth is a failure of imagination that disempowers us and accepts the decline of the Republic as inevitable.

Let us start with a cautious faith that change is possible. True, in this age of reduced expectations and political paralysis it seems Pollyannish to propose broad measures to fix the ailments of society. But we are not left with the alternatives of hopelessness and futile grandiosity. Times change. I recall my mother, who had been a radical labor unionist amid the mass political engagement and social upheavals of the 1930s, observing with dismay the cultural conformity and hostility to social change of the late 1950s. "How did the American people change so much?" she would lament. Not five years later, sit-ins spread throughout the South, the Civil Rights Act and Voting Rights Act were before a receptive Congress, the Nuclear Test Ban Treaty had been signed, the War on Poverty was underway, and the turmoil and radical visions of the sixties were beginning to unfold.

If history teaches us anything, it is to expect the unexpected. Outside forces over which we have little control create new, unforeseen challenges or irreversible changes in the context within which we try to meet existing challenges. The likelihood of the rise of political movements, domestic or foreign, of unanticipated foreign policy crises, of threats from non-state actors, of economic crises—all render absurd the fantasy that we can foretell the future, that we can rule out the possibility of more progressive times to come. Many long-term challenges to the conservatism of the moment are already foreseeable, in broad if not specific form. Climate change and globalization in an increasingly interdependent world will set in motion economic instability, intense struggles over resources, political unrest, and massive relocations of people. Policy discussions that may seem impossible now will be unavoidable in the long run. There is no reason to wait to begin the discussion.

Challenging the Liberal Narrative

What are the barriers to change? When those on the left get together to gripe, several themes emerge. First, we recognize that politics is "the art of compromise." However, we complain, Democrats are too ready to compromise, too ready to start negotiations in the middle, while Republicans are far more intransigent. Or we say that politics is about "the art of the deal." As the old adage goes, "Laws are like sausages. It is better not to see them being made." Lyndon Johnson's successes in getting the Civil Rights Act, the Voting Rights Act, and the Economic Opportunity Act through a southern-dominated Congress stand out as masterpieces of successful political dealmaking. Conversely, Barack Obama's failure to achieve more is often laid to his unwillingness to play golf and schmooze with Democratic, much less Republican leaders. Alternately, Obama's failure and

the subsequent Democratic election losses in Congress in 2010 and there-
after are laid to fundamental mistakes in political strategy. Obama, it is
said, should have focused on the economy rather than diverting energy to
health-care reform. He should have taken a more direct lead in the negotiations on the Affordable Care Act, rather than leaving it all to Congress.
He pursued his hope that a more cooperative "new way of doing things,"
less partisan and ideological, was possible for far too long, long after the
Republicans made it clear they were not interested.

Or maybe the problem is that we are just not presenting our ideas
clearly and forcefully enough. The Democratic Party's Victory Task
Force, formed to perform an "autopsy" on why the Democrats lost so badly
in 2014, concluded that the problem is that "there is no single narrative that
unites all of our work and the issues that we care about as a community of
Democrats." The solution, the task force suggested, would be the creation
of "a National Narrative Project to work with party leaders, activists, and
messaging and narrative experts to create a strong values-based national
narrative that will engage, inspire, and motivate voters to identify with
and support Democrats."[1]

Beyond specific political errors, we often believe that the corruption of
our political processes is responsible for the fix the Left is in. The Right
has been triumphant, the story goes, because of big money in politics, gerrymandering by GOP-controlled state legislatures, ceaseless attempts by
Republicans to raise barriers to voting by poor and working people, and
Supreme Court decisions undercutting the Voter Rights Act. At a deeper,
even more intractable level, there are the constitutional provisions over-
weighting the power of small, rural, often southern, and usually conservative states and making the life-termers on the Supreme Court bench
unresponsive to the public will.

All of these explanations of the failures of the Left to stem the conservative tide have validity, and in aggregate they may have contributed to
Democratic defeats and Republican victories. But they are not the basic
causes of the decline of the Left since the 1960s. Somehow, we seem to be
saying, "The Left has good ideas. The reasons the American people haven't
bought them lies not in the ideas but in poor political and electoral tactics
and strategies." Yet somehow the same failings repeat over and over.

So maybe we have to rethink the problem at a more fundamental level.
Why has the Left been so ineffective in winning support for its message?

Perhaps the real problem is that we have never been willing to really take "democracy" seriously. If we did, we would ask ourselves three questions: The first is about the meaning of "self-interest," the second about the political assumptions of the Democratic Party, and third about the barriers to political participation.

The Meaning of "Self-Interest"

The first question is, why do so many Americans appear to vote against their own interests? "What's the matter with Kansas?" Thomas Franks famously asked. How did a state that was once a hotbed of the radical Populist movement become overwhelmingly conservative? "Not long ago, Kansas would have responded to the current situation by making the bastards pay. . . . Not these days." And what's going on in Wisconsin? Why did workers in that historically liberal state, which voted for Obama over McCain in 2008 by 14 percentage points, for Obama over Romney in 2012 by 7 percentage points, vote to reelect Scott Walker despite his antiunion and anti-worker policies? Why did 45 percent of Wisconsin women vote for Walker despite his rollback of reproductive rights programs and repeal of an equal pay for equal work law? Why have Americans gone along with tax cut after tax cut for rich people?[2]

These are not one-time anomalies. They represent a trend in American politics that has now lasted almost fifty years. Abraham Lincoln supposedly quipped, "You can fool all of the people some of the time, and some of the people all of the time, but you can't fool all of the people all of the time." Unless we want to believe that Lincoln was wrong, we have to believe that maybe it is we who are getting fooled all of the time. Maybe one reason is that we are thinking about the idea of "self-interest" in too narrow a way.

Economic well-being does not take in the whole universe of self-interest. Safety, a sense of empowerment, and a belief that government will help take care of you if you need help are also in peoples' self-interest. ("Government Keep Your Hands off My Medicare," read an iconic and unwittingly ironic Tea Party sign.) Despite the ideological glorification of the individual so dear to conservatives, so are feelings of connection to community, pride in tradition and the positive elements of national identity, and faith that one's children face a promising future. And so are the need to ward off feelings of having been had and feelings of envy, shame, and humiliation.

The Left has ceded all of these areas of self-interest to the Right and then acts surprised that people don't act in their own self-interest, defined in purely economic terms.

Unless the Left acknowledges these issues, confronts people's fears openly and directly, and designs programs that address both the underlying social, political, cultural, and economic issues and the fears themselves, it is the Left itself that is failing to address the self-interest of the American people. If we want to expand the realm of possible progressive action, we must acknowledge and address the concrete needs of poorer people, workers, people of color, women, young people, and all others who have been marginalized or stretched to the limits by Third Wave Capitalism. But we must also acknowledge and address the economic insecurity, feelings of psychological and cultural threat and loss, disempowerment, suspicion of government, and regret for lost communities that they share with Middle America.

The Failure of the Democrats

A second question we need to ask is: why do the Democrats consistently fail to enact significant reforms, even when they hold the presidency and both houses of Congress? Under Jimmy Carter, Democratic Party control gave us the Department of Energy and the Department of Education but also gave us airline, railroad, and trucking deregulation. In Bill Clinton's first two years, Democratic control gave us two minor victories, the Motor Voter Registration Act and the Family and Medical Leave Act. Any hope of universal health insurance was defeated, however, and Clinton set up NAFTA and gave us laws to increase the harshness of prison sentences and to begin the current craze for testing schoolchildren in the name of school and teacher "accountability." In the following six years, after the Democrats lost Congress but still had a Democratic president who could wield the veto pen, we got the elimination of welfare, the Defense of Marriage Act, tax breaks for charter schools, and the deregulation of banks and commodity trading. Barack Obama, in his two years of Democratic control of Congress, prevented the financial crisis from turning into all-out Depression and gave us the Affordable Care Act and the Dodd-Frank Act regulating the financial sector. But the economic stimulus was too small to produce a rapid recovery, and the Affordable Care Act barred negotiated drug prices and a government option (and a single-payer system was never seriously considered). And now, although JP Morgan CEO Jamie Dimon may complain that "banks are under assault," Dodd-Frank's protections, compromised to begin with, are being whittled away by Congress and regulators. Somehow, even electing "liberals" doesn't seem to lead to a reversal of the conservative tide.

At the heart of the repeated failure of the Democrats lies their acceptance, whether unknowing or witting, of the transition to Third Wave Capitalism, with its frantic rent-seeking, massive inequality, destruction of countervailing forces, blurring of the lines between business and state, and collapse of faith in our collective power to change our fate.

Compare the assumptions underlying the liberal projects of Roosevelt's New Deal and Johnson's Great Society. Roosevelt, in his 1944 State of the Union address, called for a "second Bill of Rights." "True individual freedom cannot exist without economic security and independence," he insisted. Government must guarantee every American, "regardless of station, race, or creed," the right to a useful and remunerative job, to earn enough to provide adequate food and clothing and recreation, to a decent home, to a good education, to adequate medical care and the opportunity to achieve and enjoy good health, and to adequate protection from the economic travails of old age, sickness, accident, and unemployment. Twenty years later, Lyndon Johnson, in his 1964 State of the Union message, added a few new elements, calling on Congress to provide for civil rights for all, regardless of race, an end to poverty and unemployment, reform of tangled transportation policies, and "more homes, more schools, more libraries, and more hospitals than any single session of Congress in the history of our Republic."[3]

FDR and LBJ, like other past generations of liberals, assumed that the state is not merely the handmaiden of the property-owning classes. Though the state may have disproportionately reflected the needs and interests of the latter, the power of unions, mass protest movements, and elections insured that our government would respond to the needs of "ordinary" people as well. Facilitating these influences on government was part and parcel of what liberals meant by reform. Roosevelt's National Labor Relations Act helped empower working people. Johnson's Economic Opportunity Act sought to empower poor people.

Liberals of earlier generations also took at face value the words of the preamble to the U.S. Constitution, which asserts that our government was established by "*We* the People" in order to "promote the *general* welfare" (my emphases). "Life, liberty, and the pursuit of happiness"—the rights of the individual—were balanced by a collective concern for the common well-being. To be sure, there were those who had been systematically excluded from realizing the American Dream, but these were still part of the dreaming community. One major historical goal of the Left was to include them. Central to the movements of working people in the thirties, of blacks and poor people in the sixties, and of women and gay activists in the seventies and after was the demand that the constituencies of each movement be included in the American Dream and that the words of the Declaration of Independence and the Constitution apply to them.

There is a fundamental difference between these assumptions and the assumptions of Third Wave Capitalism. Poverty provides a case in point. As we saw in chapter 4, the persistence of poverty is not incidental, a mere "failure" of Third Wave Capitalism. It is the direct *result* of Third Wave Capitalism's withdrawal from the very effort to end poverty. Piecemeal, compensatory strategies can, at best, make a dent in the rate of poverty. If we are serious about ending poverty, we must challenge the blurring of the lines between government and private enterprise, the rent-seeking that characterizes the present era, the hegemony of free market and individual-centered ideologies, the structural obstacles to upward mobility, the distribution of wealth, and the destruction of the unions and community movements that were the major forces promoting the various policies associated with lowering poverty rates in the past.

The Disappearing Electorate

The third question we must ask is: why do most Americans not even bother to vote? The great Republican congressional victories of 2014 reflected the active will of exactly 17.6 percent of the eligible voters. Yes, it was more than the Democrats' 15.7 percent, but it was hardly a mandate for the Republican policies much less a vote of confidence in the vitality of our democracy. Back in the late nineteenth century, voter turnout was typically around 80 percent in presidential elections, 65–70 percent in midterm elections. The rates dropped off in the twentieth century, but as recently as the sixties, about 63 percent turned out for presidential contests and 47–48 percent for midterm elections. In the 2014 midterm election, only 34.4 percent of eligible voters voted. Nearly two-thirds of the electorate stayed home.[4]

A good bit of this implicit "none of the above" vote probably reflects a sense that it really doesn't matter which bunch of politicians is in office. A widely publicized 2014 study by political scientists Martin Gilens and Benjamin I. Page studied data from over 1,800 different policy initiatives from 1981 to 2002, looking at cases in which the preferences of economic elites and the stands of organized interest groups differed from those of the average citizen. They concluded, *"The preferences of the average American appear to have only a minuscule, near-zero, statistically non-significant impact upon public policy.* . . . When a majority of citizens disagrees with economic elites or with organized interests, they generally lose. . . . Even when fairly large majorities of Americans favor policy change, they generally do not get it." (Emphasis added.)[5]

In the world of Third Wave Capitalism, which more and more seems to entail "government of the wealthy, by the wealthy, and for the wealthy," it is hardly surprising that a lot of people don't think it is worth their while to vote—even for politicians who profess policies that would benefit them. Many on the left implicitly accept or even cynically promote this position as rational. "Vote 'no' for president," they happily proclaim. But the consequences of elections are serious, for policy, for the makeup of the Supreme Court, and for determining voting districts and election rules at the state and local levels. Electoral politics alone is not enough to produce lasting change, but contempt for or indifference to electoral politics is destructive.

The belief in "government of the people, by the people and for the people" is a core value for most Americans. Our democracy is threatened by big money in politics, gerrymandering, and changes in rules to make voting by poor people and working people more difficult. But no matter how fair the elections, a democracy that systematically ignores the interests of the majority is a democracy in name only. To build a new progressive movement, we must take up the cause of democracy itself.

Challenging the Conservative Narrative

For there to be any possibility of a progressive resurgence, we also have to confront the conservative narrative and address the question of why so many Americans buy in to it. George W. Bush famously told then-Senator Joseph Biden, "I don't do nuance." The right has been very successful at reducing complex issues to simple slogans. The examples are many: the "Contract with America," the "Right to Work," the "Right to Life," "death panels," "If guns are outlawed, only outlaws will have guns," "weapons of mass destruction." Complexity is a confusing issue to the Left. We are caught between wanting to imitate the Right, with its catchy phrases, and a respect for the much more complex truth.

Three sets of simplistic conservative belief stand out, accepted by virtually all Republicans and, unfortunately, by many Democrats. First: "We can't." The most pressing problem in the United States and the key to most of its problems, say conservatives, is our unbalanced budget and the resultant overwhelmingly large national debt. Raising taxes to deal with it is unthinkable. Higher taxes would burden ordinary taxpayers and businesses, the "job creators," and would threaten our international competitiveness. The bottom line is that we simply can't afford to expand government programs (for example, the social safety net).

Second: "The problems are too complex." The belief that complex social problems can be solved through acts of government is widely considered to be foolish. Many years ago, when I was in college, Henry Kissinger, then a professor, would occasionally have lunch with the members of our campus anti–nuclear weapons group. Scoffing at what he saw as the naïveté of our proposals to advance world peace through a nuclear test ban treaty, he would proclaim in his deep German accent, "These things are more complicated than they seem." (We callow youths, out of his presence, would mock him, proclaiming in fake German accents, "These things seem more complicated than they are.")

Third: "We don't want to." To conservatives, freedom is inherently a characteristic of individuals and "big government" is the enemy of freedom and prosperity. Societal constraints on individual freedom put us on the slippery slope to tyranny. It is not government but the "free market" that solves social problems, and the only legitimate goals of public policy are to promote "growth" and serve the needs of businesses (the "job creators," the "drivers of the economic engine").

Let us examine each of these contentions. First, "we can't" and the problem of the debt: Budgetary constraints seem to make it impossible even to consider introducing new and expensive government programs. Many liberal economists have argued that the supposed threat to our economy posed by the national debt has been greatly exaggerated. In any case, the budget surpluses of the later Clinton years were turned into massive deficit neither by something inherent in our system of government nor by the alleged tendency of liberals to throw money at social problems. The causes of the deficit were simple. Government income was deliberately reduced by the Bush-era tax cuts favoring the wealthy and then reduced further, involuntarily, by the recessions of 2001 and 2008. Meanwhile government spending increased, largely due to the soaring costs of the Bush war of aggression in Iraq. Nothing inevitable. All reversible.

There are other, longer-term deficit concerns, to be sure, such as the shortfall anticipated for Social Security. The latter, at least, can be fairly easily fixed by adjusting the payroll tax (most notably by applying it to all earned income, not just income up to $118,500, as it is now).[6] The only relatively intractable part of the deficit is that due to rising costs for Medicare and Medicaid, but, as discussed in chapter 2, what makes health-care costs "intractable" is our unwillingness to confront their real source, the medical-industrial complex.

But leaving the issue of the causes of the deficit aside for a moment, let us embrace complexity. Yes, we do have a moral obligation not to leave our grandchildren with a crippling burden of debt. But that assertion does not end the discussion of what is "moral." We also have a moral obligation not to leave our grandchildren with a decaying infrastructure, not to leave them with the consequences of runaway global warming, not to leave them with the legacy of several generations of bad schooling, not to leave them with an over-expensive and under-effective health-care system, and not to leave them with a society riven by racism and morally tainted by the failure to eliminate poverty.

Then there is the "it's too complex" argument: The irony is great. Americans pride ourselves on our "can-do" attitude, yet right-wing think tanks, media, pundits, politicians, and preachers have drummed into our heads over and over that, while individuals can dream of conquering the world (metaphorically, of course), we must reduce our expectations with respect to public action to meet common needs. The only way to address societal problems is through "free market" solutions, they say.

Things *are* complicated. There are no magical solutions to the world's problems. And no matter how reasonable, clever, or well-crafted proposals for reform are, we can expect fierce opposition, blowback, unanticipated consequences, and unpredicted complications. But things are *also* very simple. It remains possible to imagine a better future for America and to take steps to make this vision real.

Finally: "We don't want to:" The conservative narrative continues with interlinked concerns about the proper roles of government and the proper relationship between government, business, the free market, and the distribution of wealth. Again the ironies are great. Mistrust of our government is perfectly understandable. It has long been bureaucratic, inefficient, wasteful, and opaque. It has long served business interests, although, as we have seen, in recent years it has become increasingly hard to untangle government from business interests. Let us recall the financial crisis of 2008 and the recession that began in late 2007 and, by the economists' definition of recessions, was over by mid-2009. It is hardly a secret that, in reality, by six years later we had still not recovered. Wages remained below their pre-recession levels, unemployment and underemployment remained high, and many of the public services that we had become used to were gone. But it was not the *actions* of government that caused the financial crisis and the recession and the failure to recover rapidly, but the actions of the financial sector and the *inaction* of government at the behest of conservatives and their business allies. It was the failure of government to regulate financial markets that permitted the abuses that led to the crisis, and the failure of government to provide adequate stimulus to the economy, the failure of the government to provide relief for "underwater" homeowners, and the failure of the government to maintain the social safety net that have extended the suffering. Yet somehow the Right has turned that history into blaming the downturn on "big government" itself and into demands to cut government programs even further. In the context of Third Wave Capitalism, in which government and business have become almost indistinguishable, conservatives can get away with blaming government for the sins of the private sector.

It is the same with the vastly increased misdistribution of wealth and income of recent years. It resulted from soaring CEO salaries, monopolistic power over markets, the same predatory lending practices that also brought us the financial crisis and the Great Recession, tax cuts mainly benefiting the rich, government tax subsidies to private corporations, laws passed under corporate influence to weaken unions so that they can't protect the incomes of their members, and so forth. Yet somehow it is okay with the Right for the private sector to engineer a vast redistribution of income but not for the government, acting on all of our behalves, to redistribute it back.

The Problem of Government

Where, exactly, does the problem with our government lie? It is not government per se, but the ability of businesses to use government as a cash cow to generate profits from health care, from military expenditures, from schools. It is not government per se but the fact that, in the absence of countervailing forces such as unions and community protest, government is free to respond to the interests of the wealthy few and not those of the many. And, as for the belief that there is something intrinsic in government (as opposed to private enterprise) that leads to bureaucracy, inefficiency, and lack of transparency, examples of private-sector bureaucracy, inefficiency, and lack of transparency abound. (The cable company and your health insurance company provide easy examples.)

Governments, says the Declaration of Independence, are instituted "to secure" the right to life, liberty, and the pursuit of happiness. The Constitution, the founding document of our government, was established to "establish justice" and "promote the general welfare." How much more explicit can it get? Abraham Lincoln, preemptively rebutting Ronald Reagan's "government as problem" mantra a century before Reagan uttered the words, put it this way: "The legitimate object of government is to do for a community of people whatever they need to have done, but cannot do at all, or cannot so well do for themselves, in their separate and individual capacities."[7]

Take the case of taxes. You alone can't build a road from your house to your workplace. You alone can't underwrite the research to develop a medicine to treat your sick child. You alone can't clean up the toxic waste dump down the street or provide your child's school with audiovisual equipment. And you alone cannot save enough to feel secure if you are laid off from your job and are unemployed for a year. You are actually better off, in any meaningful sense of the words, if your taxes are high enough to pay for all of these things.

Taxes are not intrinsically bad and not intrinsically always too high. The issue is what you get for your taxes. If taxes are raised to let Medicare and Medicaid subsidize the overly high salary of the CEO of a large hospital, or to permit a drug company to make outlandishly large profits, or to let the Defense Department pay for $500 hammers, then yes, taxes are too high. But if taxes are raised to provide you with drinkable water, or to protect you against the insecurity of unemployment, you have experienced a gain, not suffered a loss. Despite the conservatives' refrain about Americans being overtaxed, taxes in the United States are among the lowest in the world. We pay little and we get little. In 2008, U.S. taxes claimed 26 percent of the GDP, compared to an average 35 percent for the thirty-three OECD member countries. The United States ranked thirtieth out of the thirty-three. Only Mexico, Turkey, and Chile had lower tax rates.[8]

What things your taxes will be used for affect your personal calculation of gains and losses, of course. If you are childless, you get no direct gain from school taxes. If you don't own a car, you don't directly benefit from taxes that will be used to maintain roads and bridges. If you have a stable job, you get no immediate benefit from taxes used to pay for unemployment benefits. If you are affluent, you get no personal benefit from Medicaid. But regardless of personal circumstances, you do get indirect benefits from living in a society that has people healthy enough and well-enough educated to perform the jobs that produce the goods and services we all use, from the fact that trucks can deliver your food to the supermarket over bridges that don't collapse, and from living in a world in which unemployed people are not rioting in the streets. As Oliver Wendell Holmes Jr. once said, "Taxes are what we pay for living in civilized society.[9]

E. J. Dionne has argued that throughout our history, at the heart of American politics there have been disagreements about the proper balance between equality and justice, rights and responsibilities, liberty and community, autonomy and interdependence, "private striving and public engagement." But Jefferson and Hamilton, Clay and Jackson, Lincoln and both Roosevelts, Democrats, Whigs, Republicans, Populists, Progressives, and New Dealers all shared the understanding that in a democracy, government is not the realm of "them" but of "us." To all of them, liberty was not just about the freedom of the autonomous individual, oblivious to the needs of others. Liberty was sharing in self-government and deliberating with others about the common good. The unbridled individualism and absolutist rejection of government of the Tea Party and much of the Republican Party today is an historical anachronism, appearing as a dominant ideology only briefly in the Gilded Age of the late nineteenth century and reappearing in the era of Third Wave Capitalism.[10]

The Right has portrayed its glorification of the unfettered individual as the essence of true Americanism. Nothing could be further from the truth. Government and individual liberty are not antithetical. Throughout U.S. history, state action has increased individuals' liberty of action. A person is freer when he or she knows that society will open the doors to opportunity, provide them with an education regardless of their parents' wealth, ensure that jobs are available for all, and pick them up when they fall down.

As for the need for government to look out for business, that's an old shibboleth for conservatives. "The chief business of the American people is business," opined Calvin Coolidge, describing his conception of his role as president and ushering in an earlier era of regulators who did not regulate, of cuts in federal spending, and of ignoring social problems. But it is precisely this blurring of the boundaries between business and government, this subordination of the needs of most people to the needs of business, that has increased qualitatively in Third Wave Capitalism and that has alienated many Americans from their earlier faith in the ability of government to help solve their problems.

Toward a Progressive Resurgence

If there is to be any hope of successfully combating the conservative agenda, both the illusions of the Left and the shibboleths of the Right must be taken on. But the failure of the Left to take democracy seriously and the resistance of the Right to societal efforts to address societal problems are not the only barriers to progressive change. How we confront the issue of race, the alternative narrative we create, and the empowerment of ordinary people all must be addressed.

First, whatever concrete proposals progressives might make, any progressive vision must explicitly address race. Race remains a corrosive factor in American life. For people of color, it is an ongoing barrier to full participation in the American Dream, a source of daily humiliation, and sometimes, a threat to their very lives. For too many white Americans, the fantasy that their own problems are due to preferences given to racial minorities and the belief that programs designed to help poor people are disguised subsidies for people of color at the expense of whites moves American politics further to the right and contributes to a willingness to accept conservative ideologies. For both people of color and whites, race remains a barrier to the political unity that could help both groups meet their economic and cultural needs. Any effort to restore the American Dream must make race part of the national conversation. It must confront the subordination of blacks that has been at the heart of American history since the beginning and the violence that has been used to maintain that subordination, and it must insist that individual racism, structural racism, and systematic racial disparities alike are violations of American ideals.

There are no easy solutions. It is true that many racial barriers have fallen since the early sixties. It is also true that younger people are, on the whole, less tolerant of overt individual racist ideas and behaviors than their elders. But 150 years after the Emancipation Proclamation and fifty years after Martin Luther King's "I Have a Dream" speech, it is no longer enough to hope that time will reduce tensions.

While many white Americans, regardless of age, fail to recognize the degree to which structural racism affects the lives of black Americans, they do support anti-discrimination policies in employment, housing, and other spheres of life.[11] But governmental actions that seem to pit the needs of blacks against those of whites, such as affirmative action for job seekers, forced bussing to integrate schools, or building affordable (read "black") housing in white suburbs, are a harder sell. To be sure, racism plays an important role in triggering this opposition, but so does a sense of fairness. Many whites cannot but be aware of their own unmet needs. Needs, at least when we are talking about the needs of 80 or 90 percent of Americans, are not a zero-sum game in which the benefit of one must be the loss of another. Because one group has serious needs doesn't mean that others' needs just go away. When the government ignores the needs of one group yet seems responsive to the needs of others, or when government calls on one group to make sacrifices (for example, pay higher taxes, miss a chance at a job, or send their children to a distant school) to remediate what seem like sins of the past committed by others, it is not surprising that the former group reacts with anger. Crying "racism" explains little and cuts off discussion.

But policies to redress the consequences of our history of racial oppression also need not be a zero-sum game. Anti-discrimination policies appeal to the sense of fairness of most Americans, and programs that explicitly benefit both black and white can unite rather than divide. Such programs might include efforts to benefit poor and lower-wage workers regardless of race, support families of all sorts, and invest in economically straitened areas, whether Appalachia, the rural South, or inner-city Detroit. "Affirmative action" admissions to college based on income and first-in-family-to-attend-college status can supplement affirmative action addressing race and ethnicity. Programs can be designed to increase the availability of affordable housing (including helping homeowners who are "under water"), improve access to health care, and increase the funding of schools. These are not alternatives to directly addressing discrimination and the enduring consequences of race, but with such programs as context, other policies and programs that disproportionately and explicitly address the burdens people of color bear may become more acceptable.

A less obvious dilemma in addressing race comes from policies that produce a conflict that is nominally between workers and consumers but that also has racial and ethnic implications. If the pay of workers in a fast-food establishment is increased, the price everyone pays for burgers rises, and if bus drivers get a raise, bus fares go up for all. If hospitals lay off staff or reduce their hours, costs to patients may go down, but it is the workers who pay the price. Workers are caught between their need for higher pay and better working conditions and the demands of consumers for lower prices. The conflict is often especially transparent in service industries. Government workers too are caught between their need for stable jobs with decent pay and the demands of taxpayers to cut taxes. In the conflicts, jobs are often at stake. Recall that low-wage jobs and public-sector jobs are disproportionately held by women and by blacks, Latinos, and other people of color.

There is, of course, a third dog in this fight: the owners of the businesses that employ the workers and sell to the customers. Let us return to Walmart, the largest employer in the United States, with 1.4 million workers. Walmart pays low wages, provides meager benefits, and demands of its workers part-time hours and erratic schedules. Consumers get low prices. Consumers win, workers lose . . . and in 2014 Wal-Mart earned $16 billion in profits. Consumers pay indirectly, however, though their payments may seem invisible. Tax-supported programs such as Medicaid, food stamps, and the Earned Income Tax Credit help Walmart workers bridge the gap between their pay and their needs (see chapter 4). On the revenue side, no less than eighteen percent of the entire U.S. food stamp budget is used at Walmart stores, boosting Walmart sales. Walmart also receives $1 billion a year in tax benefits and loopholes. Surely Walmart could raise wages without having to raise prices.[12]

A second issue the Left must address is the need to create an alternative narrative. Those on the left often lament the conservative shift in American politics since the 1970s. It is tempting to reduce our aspirations, to try to make changes at the margins because it seems that that's all that is possible. Part of the apparent shift to the right is a turnout issue, however. The groups most likely to support progressive policies don't turn out to vote at the same rate as those who oppose them, especially in midterm elections. On an issue-by-issue basis, the American population as a whole does not seem as conservative as the electorate. Polls repeatedly show strong support among Americans for governmental policies to address inequality, for maintaining antipoverty spending, for reducing corporate influence, for ensuring that black and white people are treated equally by the courts and by the police, for spending to improve infrastructure and create jobs, for regulating banks, and for giving more resources to schools. On the eve of passage of the Affordable Care Act, 72 percent of the favored a public, single-payer national health insurance plan, and today, despite all of the controversy, over 50 percent still support it.[13]

It's time to develop a comprehensive "Restore the American Dream Program" to compete with the conservative mantras, a coherent body of progressive policy alternatives that directly addresses issues such as inequality, lack of jobs, racial disparities, the persistence of poverty, the power of money in politics, and the threat of climate change, rather than a series of unrelated specific proposals nibbling at the edges of the country's problems.

Beyond their specific content, the purpose of such proposals would be to present an alternative vision of the role of government and an alternative vision of America's future. It would build a counter-narrative to the conservative fairytale that has dominated U.S. politics for well over thirty years. The purpose of these proposals would be to open up a new discussion among the American people, to challenge the Right's domination of center stage, to refuse to let the Right determine the terms of debate, and to rebut the fear that progressive change is unrealistic and that we must settle for being a second-rate society.

Re-empowering Americans

Finally, to expand the realm of the possible, we need to regain our collective faith in the power of the many. Perhaps the central lesson of the history of U.S. social reform is that change doesn't just happen. Throughout our history, progress has come only when ordinary people joined together and poured their hearts and their energy into collective action and broad social movements. In the absence of such movements, the promises of even the most liberal politicians mean little. Earlier, I noted that Jimmy Carter, Bill Clinton, and Barack Obama were unable to produce social reforms of a magnitude rivaling the New Deal or the Great Society. The big difference was not that Carter, Clinton, and Obama were less liberal than FDR and LBJ, or that their political skills were less (though both of these may have been the case). The difference was that FDR and LBJ worked their politics in the context of mass movements demanding change, and Carter, Clinton, and Obama did not. Again and again, when masses of people erupt into protest and action, new institutions and programs, designed at least partly to meet their demands, are created.

Protest and collective action is, in the words of Paul Ylvisaker, one of the architects of the 1960s War on Poverty, "a fourth branch of government." Protest and collective action are not confined to signing petitions and working in electoral campaigns. At times they are unruly. When autoworkers occupied their factories in 1935, when students sat-in in cafeterias in the Jim Crow South in 1960, when students blockaded draft offices in 1967, when black Americans rioted in Watts in 1965 and Detroit and Newark in 1967 and within sight of the U.S. Capitol in 1968, they were not following the rules. Martin Luther King Jr. did not join those who simply deplored the unrest. While worrying that a riot "merely intensifies the fears of the white community while relieving the guilt" and insisting that nonviolence and peaceful protest were the best weapons available in the fight for racial and economic justice, he refused to simply condemn the unrest. "A riot," he said, "is the language of the unheard."[14]

And for better or for worse, that language often is heard. Progressive Era reforms such as the secret ballot, regulation of food and drugs, the progressive income tax, and women's suffrage were a response to growing unrest among poor farmers, workers, immigrants, and women. New Deal reforms such as Social Security, unemployment compensation, the minimum wage, the forty-hour workweek, and the legitimization of labor unions were a response to the massive movements of the unemployed and of workers. The 1964 Civil Rights Act, the War on Poverty, Medicare and Medicaid, the Clean Air Act, Title IX of the Education Act (extending the benefits of federal education spending to women), all would have been unthinkable in the absence of the civil rights movement, the northern urban movements of African Americans and other people of color, the student movements, the feminist protests, and the environmental movement.

In our own time, the post-2012 shift of many Democrats to a more populist rhetoric can be directly traced to the strong, though brief, impact of the Occupy Wall Street movement. The growing acceptance of gay marriage is the result of years of organizing and agitating by gay activists. On the right, the intransigence of Republicans similarly reflects the post-2008 rise of the Tea Party. And as I write, it is not the goodwill of politicians but the strikes and protests of "Fight for $15" that have made raising the minimum wage a national issue. It is the demonstrations of "Black Lives Matter" and the riots in Ferguson (Missouri) and Baltimore that have given urgency to reform of policing. It is the civil disobedience of the "opt out of testing" movement that has thrown a wrench in the plans of corporate school reformers.

The role of social movements is not limited to promoting progressive (or in the case of the Tea Party, reactionary) social policies. To the extent that those movements take on institutional form, they sustain the policies as well. The workers' movements of the thirties became the powerful unions of the postwar era. As the organizational base for the liberal wing of the Democratic Party, they were the major reason that New Deal reforms withstood attack throughout the fifties and they provided major support for Great Society initiatives in the sixties. But the unions have declined and the sixties community movements and issues-based movements did not institutionalize themselves. There was nothing left to protect the gains of the latter decade.

Social movements cannot be planned for, of course. But what happens on the ground is not entirely independent of the way in which leaders lead. FDR's National Industrial Recovery Act legitimized unions (though with no enforcement mechanism), which encouraged United Mine Workers president John L. Lewis to go to the coalfields of West Virginia where—loudly proclaiming, "The President wants you to join the union"—he organized tens of thousands of miners. JFK's "ask not what your country can do for you but what you can do for your country" energized college students to join the Peace Corps, support the civil rights movement, and not long after, oppose the war in Vietnam. Lyndon Johnson's Community Action Program, requiring "maximum feasible participation of the poor" in solving their own problems, bred a generation of community organizers and community-based movements.

If we expect that electing a Hilary Clinton, or even a Bernie Sanders, will solve the serious problems America faces, we will be disappointed. Politicians cannot solve people's problems for them without massive support. Only by engaging people in collective solutions to their own problems is real and lasting change possible.[15]

The Choices We Face

America has changed over the last four decades. Whether these changes represent a net "decline" is arguable. Regardless, there is no going back. But armed with an understanding of the deeper currents of recent history and the great obstacles thrown up to progressive change, the American Dream is still ours to reclaim.

I began this book by reflecting on some apparently contradictory themes in recent U.S. history. There was my childhood memory of glorying in my identity as an American set against my awareness of the many injustices of the America of my childhood. There was the evidence of enormous gains in material well-being, health, education, and human rights over the course of my lifetime set against the "America is in decline" chorus and the reality of a massive shift to the right, a broken political system, a faltering economy, and endless war. And running through it all was the sense that, despite the material gains of the last four decades, something more subtle, more central to what America was or could be, has been lost.

One can't judge history; it simply is. Yet trying to understand what has been lost is an essential part of building a better future.

After finishing a first draft of this epilogue, I gave it to my wife to read, just as she had read drafts of earlier chapters. When I returned some hours later, she greeted me, saying, "You *really* are a patriot, aren't you?" I couldn't decide whether to laugh or to weep. "Yes," I thought, "She really got it."

But then I began to think more soberly. Just what did she and I mean by "patriot"? Certainly not the "the United States is the greatest nation in the history of the world" jingoism of so many American right-wing politicians, or even the "American exceptionalism" professed by President Obama. But equally it did not mean some vague, romanticized vision of democracy or of a fantasized sense of community that existed in earlier days.

I grew up in a left-wing family. My grandfather was active in the radical Jewish labor movement of the early years of the twentieth century. My parents were leaders of the Old Left–led Philadelphia Teachers' Union. Though they were deeply critical of the injustices of capitalism, and though they themselves were the children of immigrants whose personal history lay outside of the U.S., they revered the terribly flawed heroes of American history. There was the slave-owner Tom Jefferson, who penned the immortal words of the Declaration of Independence, words that have inspired people fighting for liberty ever since. There was the Indian-killer Andrew Jackson, demanding that presidents represent the common person, that voting must matter. There was the crazed terrorist John Brown, ready to take the lives of others to end the shame of human slavery. There was sad-eyed Abe Lincoln, ready to deal with the devil if the devil would support the Thirteenth Amendment. There were Frederick Douglass placing the demand for the vote for blacks ahead of the demand for the vote for women, and Susan B. Anthony opposing granting the vote to blacks if it was not also given to women, and later, Carrie Chapman Catt demanding the vote for women while suggesting that uneducated immigrants should be stripped of their right to vote. There was the aristocratic Franklin Roosevelt "saving capitalism in 100 days" but empowering the working class within capitalism. And, in my own memory, there was former segregationist Lyndon Baines Johnson and womanizing Martin Luther King Jr. combining to force the Civil Rights Act and the Voting Rights Act through a reluctant Congress.

As I grew older, I (with or without the flaws) joined in the struggles that made America. At seventeen, I joined in picketing Woolworths in support

of the sit-ins in Greensboro, North Carolina. At twenty-two I helped organize the big New York anti–Vietnam War parades. At twenty-six I joined
a think tank that worked with radical health workers and black and Latino community groups to remake the U.S. health-care system. At thirty,
I went to work at an experimental college that pioneered in opening up
college education to poor people and people of color.

And then the music stopped. The possibilities of change dimmed. De-
voting my life to "the Movement" seemed increasingly quixotic. Even the
later flashes—the brief hopes aroused by the election of Barack Obama
("yes we can"), the incandescent eruption of Occupy Wall Street—proved
ephemeral. What had happened was Third Wave Capitalism.

So what was and what is my patriotism? It is not some belief that the
United States was or is more democratic, free, or prosperous than anywhere else or that America has a mission to correct the wrongs of the
world. It is a vision of America unfolding, striving to be its best self. It is
the memory of pioneers and immigrants leaving home behind, of slave
insurrectionists and abolitionists and suffragists, of Populists and Wob-
blies and militant workers occupying factories, and of students sitting-in
at lunch counters and Freedom Riders riding a bus. It is recalling tens of
millions of people protesting the war in Vietnam in the streets and, for a
moment redeeming America. It is "angry" black militants, "bra-burning"
feminists, and "tree-hugging" environmentalists, and it is gay men and
lesbians working through the legal system to win the right to marry those
they love. It is a vision of people struggling to build an increasingly just
society in which they will have the opportunity to live up to their own
ideals.

When I was a child, we had a scratchy 78 rpm record of Paul Robeson
singing "Ballad for Americans."[16] It proclaimed,

> Our country's strong, our country's young,
> And her greatest songs are still unsung.
> From her plains and mountains we have sprung,
> To keep the faith with those who went before.

In recent years, it has often been hard to "keep the faith with those who
went before." That feeling I started with that something had been lost
was in fact the panic that Third Wave Capitalism had somehow defeated
my America, that land of hope and struggle. The "Ballad for Americans"

spoke to that panic as well: "It will come again. Our marching song will come again," it promised.

Most Americans share common values about what makes a country great. Those values include economic opportunity, the right to live with a sense of personal and economic security, and the right to a quality education, readily available health care, and adequate housing. A great country ensures the right to "equal justice under law," the right to equal treatment regardless of race or ethnicity or gender or sexual orientation, and the right to feel part of a community that looks out for the general welfare. But to turn these shared values into realities will require hard choices.

- We can't be for reducing inequality or ending poverty if we are not willing to restrict the right of a few people to seize a disproportionate part of the wealth we all produce.
- We can't proclaim our "color blindness" if we are not willing to put societal resources into remediating the historical wrongs done to Americans of African descent.
- We can't demand better health and cheaper health care if we are not willing to take on the power of the insurance industry, the drug industry, the processed food industry, the car makers and the cigarette makers, and the polluters and dumpers of toxic wastes.
- We can't insist that our schools must do a better job of educating our children if we are not willing to provide resources for schools and attract good teachers with secure, well-paying jobs, and if we are not able to address the underlying socioeconomic causes of school failure for so many poor children, black children, and Latino children.
- We can't reduce emotional distress if we are not willing to act to reduce economic and social insecurity and organize jobs so that they provide stability as well as a living wage.
- We can't decry the failure of government to respond to popular needs if we are not willing to reform our political system and restrict the influence of money in politics and cut the bonds between business and government.
- We can't demand change if we are not willing to support the messy and unruly movements that bring about change.

We can't bemoan the "decline in America" unless we are willing to ask what is our vision for the United States? What kind of country do we want? What kind of America do we dream of? Will our marching song come again?

NOTES

Introduction

1. David Remnick, "The New Inferiority," *GQ*, May 1988, http://www.gq.com/; Thomas L. Freidman, *That Used to Be Us: How America Fell behind in the World It Invented and How We Can Come Back* (New York: Farrar, Straus, and Giroux, 2011); C. J. Werleman, "Global Rankings Study: America in Warp-Speed Decline," *Salon*, April 19, 2014, http://www.salon.com/; Patrick J. Buchanan, *Suicide of a Superpower: Will America Survive to 2025?* (New York: Thomas Dunne, 2011); Hector Baretto, "Are We the Land of the American Dream, or the American Decline?" *Huffington Post*, November 7, 2013, http://www.huffingtonpost.com/.

2. James Truslow Adams, *The Epic of America* (1931; reprint, Safety Harbor, FL: Simon Publications, 2001).

3. For sources of statistics cited, see chapter 4, notes 14, 34, and 35.

4. For sources of statistics cited, see chapter 1, notes 1,2,3,5, and 6; chapter 3, notes 10, 11, 13, 14; and chapter 4, notes 34 and 35.

1. Third Wave Capitalism

1. Emmanuel Saez and Gabriel Zucman, *Wealth Inequality in the United States Since 1913: Evidence from Capitalized Income Tax Data*, Working Paper 20625 (Washington, DC: National Bureau of Economic Research, 2014), http://www.gabriel-zucman.eu/files/SaezZucman2014.pdf; Emmanuel Saez, "Striking it Richer: The Evolution of Top Incomes in the United States (Updated with 2012 Preliminary Estimates)," 2013, http://eml.berkeley.edu/~saez/

saez-UStopincomes-2012.pdf; Lawrence Mishel, "The Wedges between Productivity and Median Compensation Growth," Issue Brief 330, Economic Policy Institute, 2012, http://www.epi. org/publication/ib330-productivity-vs-compensation; Doug Short, "Five Decades of Middle Class Earnings: June 2015 Update," *Advisor Perspectives*, July 7, 2015; http:// www.advisorperspectives. com/dshort/updates/Employment-Wages-and-Hours-since-1964.php.

2. Elayne J. Heisler, *The U.S. Infant Mortality Rate: International Comparisons, Underlying Factors, and Federal Programs* (Washington, DC: Congressional Research Service, 2012), http://www. fas.org/sgp/crs/misc/R41378.pdf; "NHE Summary including Share of GDP, CY 1960–2013," Centers for Medicare and Medicaid Services, http://www.cms.gov/Research-Statistics-Data-and-Systems/Statistics-Trends-and-Reports/NationalHealthExpendData/NationalHealthAccounts Historical.html; *Health, United States, 2013* (Hyattsville, MD: Centers for Disease Control and Prevention, 2014), Tables 11, 18, 26, and 28, http://www.cdc.gov/nchs/data/hus/hus13.pdf; Sabrina Tavernise, "Life Spans Shrink for Least-Educated Whites in the U.S.," *New York Times*, September 20, 2012.

3. *The Nation's Report Card, Executive Summary* (Washington, DC: National Center for Educational Statistics, 2013), http://nces.ed.gov/nationsreportcard/subject/publications/main2012/pdf/2013456.pdf; *A First Look: 2013 Mathematics and Reading* (Washington, DC: National Center for Educational Statistics, 2013), http://nces.ed.gov/nationsreportcard/subject/publications/main2013/pdf/2014451.pdf; *Digest of Education Statistics* (Washington, DC: National Center for Education Statistics, 2013), Tables 302.60, 104.20, and 302.60, http://nces.ed.gov/programs/digest/2013menu_tables.asp; *The Nation's Report Card, Executive Summary* (Washington, DC: National Center for Educational Statistics, 2013), Figures 7–12 and 23–28.

4. Gary Orfield and Erica Frankenberg, *Brown at 60: Great Progress, a Long Retreat and an Uncertain Future* (Berkeley: Civil Rights Project, 2014), http://civilrightsproject.ucla.edu/research/k-12-education/integration-and-diversity/brown-at-60-great-progress-a-long-retreat-and-an-uncertain-future/Brown-at-60-051814.pdf; Paul Tractenberg, Gary Orfield and Greg Flaxman, "New Jersey's Apartheid and Intensely Segregated Urban Schools" (Newark: Institute on Education Law and Policy, Rutgers University–Newark, 2013), http://ielp.rutgers.edu/docs/IELP%20final%20report%20on%20apartheid%20schools%20101013.pdf; Justin Wolfers, David Leonhardt and Kevin Quealy, "1.5 Million Missing Black Men." *New York Times*, April 20, 2015.

5. *The Poverty and Inequality Report, 2014* (Stanford: Stanford Center on Poverty and Inequality, 2014), http://web.stanford.edu/group/scspi/sotu/SOTU_2014_CPI.pdf.

6. W. M. Compton et al., "Changes in the Prevalence of Major Depression and Comorbid Substance Use Disorders in the United States between 1991–1992 and 2001–2002," *American Journal of Psychiatry* 163, no. 12 (2006): 2141, http://ajp.psychiatryonline.org/doi/abs/10.1176/ajp.2006.163.12.2141; Jean M. Twenge, "The Age of Anxiety? Birth Cohort Change in Anxiety and Neuroticism, 1952–1993," *Journal of Personality and Social Psychology* 79, no. 6 (2000): 1007, http://www.apa.org/pubs/journals/releases/psp7961007.pdf; Miller McPherson, Lynn Smith-Lovin, and Matthew E. Brashears, "Social Isolation in America: Changes in Core Discussion Networks over Two Decades," *American Sociological Review* 71, no. 3 (2006): 353, http://dx.doi.org/10.1177/000312240607100301; Robert B. Putnam, *Bowling Alone* (New York: Simon and Schuster, 2000).

7. On Progressive Era reforms as meeting corporate needs, see James Weinstein, *The Corporate Idea in the Liberal State, 1900–1918* (Boston: Beacon Press, 1968); Gabriel Kolko, *The Triumph of Conservatism* (New York: Free Press, 1977); Martin J. Sklar, *The Corporate Reconstruction of American Capitalism, 1890–1916* (New York: Cambridge University Press, 1988).

8. Tim Worstall, "The Story of Henry Ford's $5 a Day Wages: It's Not What You Think," *Forbes*, March 4, 2012, http://www.forbes.com/sites/timworstall/2012/03/04/the-story-of-henry-fords-5-a-day-wages-its-not-what-you-think.

9. John Kenneth Galbraith, *American Capitalism: The Concept of Countervailing Power* (Boston: Houghton Mifflin, 1952); Gerald Mayer, *Union Membership Trends in the United States* (Washington, DC: Congressional Research Service, 2004), http://digitalcommons.ilr.cornell.edu/cgi/viewcontent.cgi?article=1176&context=key_workplace; Harry Cohani, "Membership of American Trade Unions, 1956," *Monthly Labor Review* 80 no. 10 (1957): 1202, http://www.jstor.org/discover/10.2307/41833628?sid=21105831615533&uid=3739256&uid=2&uid=4.

10. Thomas Piketty and Emmanuel Saez, "Income Inequality in the United States: 1913–1998," *Quarterly Journal of Economics* 118, no. 1 (2003): 1–39, http://eml.berkeley.edu/~saez/pikettyqje.pdf. Claudia Goldin and Robert Margo called this lessening of inequality "the great compression." Claudia Goldin and Robert Margo, "The Great Compression: The United States at Mid-Century," *Quarterly Journal of Economics* 107, no. 1 (1992): 1.

11. The text of the act can be found at 15 U.S.C. § 1021 (1978), Legal Information Institute, Columbia University Law School, http://www.law.cornell.edu/uscode/text/15/1021.

12. See, for example, Robert Gilpin, *The Challenge of Global Capitalism* (Princeton: Princeton University Press, 2000).

13. See, for example, Michael Hudson, *Finance Capitalism and its Discontents* (Dresden: Islet Verlag, 2012).

14. See, for example, Fredric Jameson, *Postmodernism, or the Cultural Logic of Late Capitalism* (Durham: Duke University Press, 1992).

15. See, for example, David M. Kotz, *The Rise and Fall of Neoliberal Capitalism* (Cambridge, MA: Harvard University Press, 2015).

16. Dinah Walker, "Quarterly Update: Foreign Ownership of U.S. Assets," Council on Foreign Relations, January 21, 2015, http://www.cfr.org/united-states/quarterly-update-foreign-ownership-us-assets/p25685; "U.S. Trade in Goods and Services—Balance of Payments (BOP) Basis," U.S. Census Bureau, Economic Indicator Division, 2015, http://www.census.gov/foreign-trade/statistics/historical/gands.pdf; Scott DeCarlo, "The World's Biggest Companies," *Forbes*, April 2, 2008, http://www.forbes.com/.

17. Steven Pearlstein, "When Shareholder Capitalism Came to Town," *American Prospect*, April 19, 2014, http://prospect.org/.

18. Abrams quoted in Robert Reich, "The Rebirth of Stakeholder Capitalism?," *Robertreich.org*, March 12, 2015, http://robertreich.org/post/94260751620; Business Roundtable quoted in Ralph Gomory and Richard Sylla, "The American Corporation," *Daedalus* 142, no. 2 (2013): 102, http://www.amacad.org/pdfs/Sylla_Gomory.pdf.

19. Steven Pearlstein, "When Shareholder Capitalism Came to Town." Also see Steven Pearlstein, "How the Cult of Shareholder Value Wrecked American Business," *Washington Post*, September 9, 2013, http://www.washingtonpost.com/.

20. The "gig" economy has grown rapidly. By 2014, almost 18 percent of all American jobs were performed by part-time freelancers or part-time independent contractors alone, up more than 75% since 2000. Noam Scheiber, "Rising Economic Insecurity Tied to Decades-Long Trend in Employment Practices," *New York Times*, July 12, 2015.

21. The rise of the banks is traced in Jeff Madrick, *Age of Greed: The Triumph of Finance and the Decline of America, 1970 to the Present* (New York: Knopf, 2011). Mark Gongloff, Katy Hall, and Jan Diehm, "5 Years after the Crisis, Big Banks Are Bigger than Ever," *Huffington Post*, September 10, 2013, http://www.huffingtonpost.com/2013/09/10/biggest-banks-even-bigger_n_3900363.html.

22. David C. Hammack, "Introduction: Growth, Transformation, and Quiet Revolution in the Nonprofit Sector over Two Centuries," *Nonprofit and Voluntary Sector Quarterly* 30, no. 2 (2001): 157, http://nvs.sagepub.com/content/30/2/157.full.pdf; Brice S. McKeever and Sarah L. Pettijohn, *The Nonprofit Sector in Brief, 2014* (Washington, DC: Urban Institute, 2014), http://

www.urban.org/UploadedPDF/413277-Nonprofit-Sector-in-Brief-2014.pdf. The difficulty in calculating the contribution of nonprofits to the GDP comes from the fact that the National Income and Product Account surveys of the Department of Commerce confound nonprofits and household activity and treat nonprofit purchases of supplies and services from for-profit businesses as originating in the latter sector. They also exclude volunteer time and effort.

23. "National Football League," *Guidestar*, http://www.guidestar.org/organizations/13-1922622/national-football-league.aspx#financials; "US Chamber of Commerce," *OpenSecrets.org*, http://www.opensecrets.org/lobby/clientsum.php?id=D000019798&year=2014.

24. "The Bayh-Dole Act: It's Working, Association of University Technology Managers, http://www.autm.net/AM/Template.cfm?Section=Bayh_Dole_Act&Template=/CM/ContentDisplay.cfm&ContentID=11603; Ashley J. Stevens et al., "The Role of Public-Sector Research in the Discovery of Drugs and Vaccines," *New England Journal of Medicine* 364 (2011): 535, http://www.nejm.org/doi/full/10.1056/NEJMsa1008268#t=article.

25. Stephanie Strom, "Report Sketches Crime Costing Billions: Theft from Charities," *New York Times*, March 29, 2008; Peter Panepento and Paul Fain, "Insider Deals Are Common among Nonprofit Boards, Study Finds," *Chronicle of Higher Education* 53, no. 44 (2007): A23, http://chronicle.com/article/Insider-Deals-Are-Common-Among/13031.

26. Steven Brill, *America's Bitter Pill* (New York: Random House, 2015), 430.

27. Ira Boudway, "The NFL's Secret Finances: A $10 Billion Mystery," *Bloomberg Business*, September 4, 2014, http://www.bloomberg.com/; Ken Belson, "Goodell's Pay of $44.2 Million in 2012 Puts Him in the Big Leagues," *New York Times*, February 14, 2014; Bob Herman, "CEO Compensation of the 25 Top-Grossing Nonprofit Hospitals," *Becker's Hospital Review*, March 11, 2014, http://www.beckershospitalreview.com/compensation-issues/ceo-compensation-of-the-25-top-grossing-nonprofit-hospitals-2014.html; Tyler Kingkade, "42 Private College Presidents Make More Than $1M, and Harvard's Isn't One of Them, *Huffington Post*, February 11, 2015, http://www.huffingtonpost.com/2013/12/15/private-college-presidents-salary-harvard_n_4433229.html; "Fortune 500 2014," *Fortune*, http://fortune.com/fortune500/wellpoint-inc-38/. Occasionally, profit-making enterprises even turn themselves into non-profits. In 2011, the Keiser family, owners of the for-profit Keiser University (a fifteen-campus school with twenty thousand students), created a nonprofit, Everglades College. Arthur Keiser loaned Everglades $321 million to buy Keiser University, which then operated on a nonprofit basis, while paying Keiser an $856,000 annual salary as president, paying him interest on the loans, and paying him $14.6 million in rent on properties he owns. Patricia Cohen, "Some Owners of Private Colleges Turn a Tidy Profit by Going Nonprofit," *New York Times*, March 2, 2015.

28. To take one somewhat slightly absurd example, Alaskan salmon, caught by U.S. workers in Alaska, is shipped to China, where Chinese workers clean, fillet, and refreeze it, after which it is shipped back to the United States for sale. Paul Greenberg, *American Catch: The Fight for Our Local Seafood* (New York: Penguin, 2014).

29. C. S. Lewis, "The Abolition of Man," in *The Abolition of Man* (New York: Macmillan, 1947), chapter 3, http://72.52.202.216/~fenderse/AbolitionofMan.htm.

30. Jonathan Eig, interview by Terry Gross, "The Great Bluff That Led to a 'Magical' Pill and a Sexual Revolution," National Public Radio, *Fresh Air*, October 7, 2014, http://www.npr.org/.

31. See "Part One: The Media Landscape," in *Information Needs of Communities: The Changing Media Landscape in a Broadband Age* (Federal Communications Commission, 2011), http://transition.fcc.gov/osp/inc-report/INoC-1-Newspapers.pdf; Suzanne M. Kirchoff, *The U.S. Newspaper Industry in Transition*, CRS Report R40700 (Washington, D.C.: Congressional Research Service, 2010), http://www.fas.org/sgp/crs/misc/R40700.pdf; David Carr, "The Fissures are Growing for Papers," *New York Times*, July 8, 2012; Boris Kachka, "The End," *New York Magazine*, September 14, 2008, http://nymag.com/news/media/50279; Williams Cole, "Is Publishing Doomed,"

Brooklyn Rail, November 5, 2010, http://www.brooklynrail.org/2010/11/express/is-publishing-doomed-john-b-thompson-with-williams-cole; Eli Noam, *Media Ownership and Concentration in America* (New York: Oxford University Press, 2009).

32. Bill Moyers, interviewed by Terry Gross, *Fresh Air*, National Public Radio (April 30, 2010); transcript at http://www.wbur.org/npr/126386358.

33. Nixon's "liberalism" reflected the need to respond to ongoing social unrest and the corporate consensus, characteristic of the corporate capitalist era, that regulation and the welfare state were in the long-term interests of business. It was combined, however, with a simultaneous and vicious attack on social movements and with the beginnings of a sharp turn to the right on the part of business.

34. Timothy Noah, "Can Bill Clinton Defend His Record on Inequality?" *MSNBC*, May 2, 2014, http://www.msnbc.com/msnbc/bill-clinton-defends-his-record.

35. This is an oversimplification, of course. For example, using government to weaken labor unions goes back to a Republican Congress's passage of the Taft Hartley Act right after World War II, over President Truman's veto. The Taft Hartley Act made organizing unions more difficult and directly attacked the role of the organized left within unions. The McCarthyite red scare of the late forties and fifties was similarly an attack on militant unions as well as on liberal and Left ideology in general.

36. See Steve Fraser, *The Age of Acquiescence* (New York: Little Brown, 2015), 342–355.

37. "Union Members Summary," U.S. Department of Labor, Bureau of Labor Statistics, 2015, http://www.bls.gov/news.release/union2.nr0.htm. On the destruction of 1960s movements, see David Cunningham, *There's Something Happening Here: The New Left, the Klan, and FBI Counterintelligence* (Berkeley: University of California Press, 2005); Church Committee, *The FBI, Cointelpro, and Martin Luther King, Jr.: Final Report of the Select Committee to Study Governmental Operations with Respect to Intelligence Activities* (1975; repr., St. Petersburg, FL.: Red and Black Publishers, 2015). On attacks on labor, see Gordon Lafer, "The Legislative Attack on American Wages and Labor Standards, 2011–2012," *Economic Policy Institute*, October 31, 2013, http://www.epi.org/publication/attack-on-american-labor-standards; Kate Bronfenbrenner, "No Holds Barred—The Intensification of Employer Opposition to Organizing," *Economic Policy Institute*, May 20, 2001, http://www.epi.org/publication/bp235.

38. On the attacks on Dodd Frank, see, for example, Zach Carter, "Senate Democrats Join GOP Attack on Financial and Environmental Regulation," *Huffington Post*, January 26, 2015, http://www.huffingtonpost.com/2015/01/15/republicans-financial-regulation_n_6549228.html; Dave Clark, Kate Davidson, and Jon Prior, "How Wall St. Got Its Way," *Slate*, December 11, 2014, http://www.politico.com/story/2014/12/wall-street-spending-bill-congress-113525.html.

39. Chris Isidore, "Uncle Sam's Outsourcing Tab: $517 billion," CNN, June 10, 2013, http://money.cnn.com/2013/06/10/news/economy/outsourced-federal-government. Also see, for example, Moshe Schwartz and Jennifer Church, *Department of Defense's Use of Contractors to Support Military Operations: Background, Analysis, and Issues for Congress*, CRS Report R43074 (Washington, DC: Congressional Research Service, 2013), http://www.fas.org/sgp/crs/natsec/R43074.pdf; Dana Priest, *Top Secret America: The Rise of the New American Security State* (New York: Little, Brown, 2011); "About Accenture," Accenture, http://www.accenture.com/us-en/company/Pages/index.aspx; Marsha Gold et al., *Medicare Advantage 2012 Data Spotlight: Enrollment Market Update* (Menlo Park, CA: Kaiser Family Foundation, n.d.), http://kaiserfamilyfoundation.files.word press.com/2013/01/8323.pdf; Jenny Anderson, "Cities Debate Privatizing Public Infrastructure," *New York Times*, August 27, 2008; Phinneas Baxandall, *Road Privatization: Explaining the Trend, Assessing the Facts, and Protecting the Public* (Boston: US PIRG Education Fund, 2007), http://extras.altoonamirror.com/ForTheRecord/Documents/Baxandall.pdf; Geoffrey F. Segal, Adrian

T. Moore, and Samuel McCarthy, *Contracting for Road and Highway Maintenance* (Los Angeles: Reason Public Policy Institute, 2003), http://reason.org/files/344b410e2504a3e41d4f08174311e2b2. pdf. For an international perspective, see Paul A. Grout, *Private Delivery of Public Services* (Bristol, UK: Centre for Market and Public Organisation, 2009), http://www.bristol.ac.uk/cmpo/publications/publicservices/ppfinal.pdf. See also *Government Sector Outsourcing: Transforming Public Service with Outsourced IT Services* (New York: Tholons Advisory Services, 2010), http://www.tholons.com/nl_pdf/Government_Outsourcing.pdf.

40. Paul Chassy and Scott Amey, *Bad Business: Billions of Taxpayer Dollars Wasted on Hiring Contractors* (Washington, DC: Project on Government Oversight, 2011), http://www.pogo.org/our-work/reports/2011/co-gp-20110913.html; Laura Stevens, "For FedEx and UPS, a Cheaper Route: the Post Office," *Wall Street Journal*, August 14, 2014; "Privatization Myths Debunked" (Oakland: In the Public Interest, 2015), http://montrose.co.lwvnet.org/files/itpi_privatization_myths_handout.pdf; Sam Kim, "Research Questions Cost-Efficiency of Privatization," Center for Effective Government, October 10, 2007, http://www.foreffectivegov.org/node/3489; Paul Chassy and Scott Amey, *Bad Business: Billions of Taxpayer Dollars Wasted on Hiring Contractors* (Washington, DC: Project on Government Oversight, 2011), http://www.pogo.org/our-work/reports/2011/co-gp-20110913.html?referrer=http://www.nationofchange.org/2015/03/23/how-privatization-degrades-our-daily-lives.

41. *Federal Individual Income Tax Rates History* (Washington, DC: Tax Foundation, 2013), http://taxfoundation.org/sites/default/files/docs/fed_individual_rate_history_nominal.pdf. Over twelve thousand registered lobbyists spent over $3 billion on lobbying in 2013. The official numbers may underestimate the number of lobbyists and their expenditures by a factor of two, by some estimates. One study found that about half of the lobbyists (registered and unofficial) came out of government service. See Lee Fang, "Where Have All the Lobbyists Gone?" *Nation*, February 19, 2014, http://m.thenation.com/article/shadow-lobbying-complex. The corporate welfare total matches quite closely the combined spending on food stamps, housing vouchers, Supplemental Security Income, Temporary Assistance for Needy Families, the Earned Income Tax Credit, and the Child Tax Credit—i.e., the direct cash transfer programs for poor people. On taxes, see Joseph Stiglitz, "A Tax System Stacked against the 99 Percent," *New York Times*, April 14, 2013; *Who Pays? A Distributional Analysis of the Tax Systems in All 50 States*, 5th ed. (Washington, DC: Institute on Taxation and Economic Policy, 2015), http://www.itep.org/pdf/whopaysreport.pdf.

42. Ken Jacobs, Ian Perry, and Jenifer MacGillvary, "The High Public Cost of Low Wages," UC Berkeley Labor Center, 2015, http://laborcenter.berkeley.edu/the-high-public-cost-of-low-wages/.

43. Joseph Stiglitz and Linda J. Bilmes, "The 1 Percent's Problem," *Vanity Fair*, May 31, 2012, http://www.vanityfair.com/.

44. Ibid.

45. Lawrence Mishel and Alyssa Davis, "CEO Pay Continues to Rise as Typical Workers Are Paid Less," Economic Policy Institute, June 12, 2014, http://www.epi.org/publication/ceo-pay-continues-to-rise.

46. *United States v. Microsoft Corp.*, No. 98-1232 (PTJ), 98-1233 (PTJ) (D.D.C. Nov. 5, 1999). The estimate of the cost per computer user is based on the decision of the Italian courts to require Microsoft to refund consumers the cost of having Windows software bundled into the cost of a new computer. Federico Guerrini, "The Windows Tax Fight Is Finally Over: Buyers Can Get a Refund on Their Microsoft OS in Italy," *ZDNet.com*, October 10, 2014, http://www.zdnet.com/article/the-windows-tax-fight-is-finally-over-buyers-can-get-a-refund-on-their-microsoft-os-in-italy.

47. Ben Stein, "In Class Warfare, Guess Which Class Is Winning," *New York Times*, November 26, 2006.

2. The Health of Nations

1. Jean Dubos and Rene Dubos, *The White Plague: Tuberculosis, Man, and Society* (New York: Little, Brown, 1952).

2. Obama quoted in Jesse Lee, "This is What Change Looks Like," White House Blog, March 22, 2010, http://www.whitehouse.gov/blog/2010/03/22/what-change-looks; Tom Daschle, "The Final Health Care Debate," *New York Times*, January 22, 2011; Sean Sullivan, "Ben Carson: Obamacare Worst Thing 'Since Slavery,'" *Washington Post*, October 11, 2013; Mitch McConnell, interviewed by Chris Wallace, *Fox News Sunday*, July 2, 2012, http://www.foxnews.com/on-air/fox-news-sunday-chris-wallace/2012/07/02/white-house-ready-move-and-implement-health-care-law-mcconnell-we-can-defeat-obamacare-no#p//v/1715106182001.

3. "NHE Fact Sheet," Centers for Medicare and Medicaid Services, December 3, 2014, http://www.cms.gov/Research-Statistics-Data-and-Systems/Statistics-Trends-and-Reports/NationalHealthExpendData/NHE-Fact-Sheet.html; *OECD Health Data 2012: U.S. Health Care from an International Perspective* (Washington, DC: Organization for Economic Co-operation and Development, 2012), http://www.oecd.org/unitedstates/HealthSpendingInUSA_HealthData2012.pdf.

4. National Health Expenditures, Historical (Baltimore: Centers for Medicare and Medicaid Services, 2014), https://www.cms.gov/Research-Statistics-Data-and-Systems/Statistics-Trends-and-Reports/NationalHealthExpendData/NationalHealthAccountsHistorical.html.

5. Robert Pear, "Data on Health Law Shows Largest Drop in Uninsured in 4 Decades, the U.S. Says," *New York Times*, March 17, 2015; "Health Law Sign-Ups Keep Growing; Uninsured Rate Declines," *New York Times*, August 13, 2015.

6. Robin A. Cohen and Michael E. Martinez, *Early Release of Estimates from the National Health Interview Survey, January–March 2015* (Atlanta: Centers for Disease Control and Prevention, National Center for Health Statistics, 2015), http://www.cdc.gov/nchs/data/nhis/earlyrelease/insur201508.pdf.

7. Karen Davis et al., *Mirror, Mirror on The Wall: How the Performance of the U.S. Health Care System Compares Internationally, 2014 Update* (New York: Commonwealth Fund, 2014), http://www.commonwealthfund.org/~/media/files/publications/fund-report/2014/jun/1755_davis_mirror_mirror_2014.pdf.

8. "Life Expectancy at Birth by Race and Sex, 1930–2010," *Infoplease.com*, n.d., http://www.infoplease.com/ipa/A0005148.html; "Infant Mortality Rates, 1950–2010," *Infoplease.com*, 2011, http://www.infoplease.com/ipa/A0779935.html; *75 Years of Mortality in the United States, 1935–2010*, NCHS Data Brief Number 88 (Atlanta: Centers for Disease Control and Prevention, National Center for Health Statistics, 2012), http://www.cdc.gov/nchs/data/databriefs/db88.htm; Rebecca Siegel, Deepa Naishadham, and Ahmedin Jemal, "Cancer Statistics 2013," *CA: A Cancer Journal for Clinicians* 63, no. 1 (2013): 11, http://onlinelibrary.wiley.com/enhanced/doi/10.3322/caac.21166; *Prevalence of Coronary Heart Disease—United States, 2006–2010* (Atlanta.: Centers for Disease Control and Prevention, 2011), http://www.cdc.gov/mmwr/preview/mmwrhtml/mm6040a1.htm.

9. *U.S. Health in International Perspective: Shorter Lives, Poorer Health* (Washington, DC: National Academies Press, 2013).

10. Elayne J. Heisler, *The U.S. Infant Mortality Rate: International Comparisons, Underlying Factors, and Federal Programs* (Washington, DC: Congressional Research Service, 2012), http://www.fas.org/sgp/crs/misc/R41378.pdf.

11. *Health: United States, 2013* (Hyattsville, MD: Centers for Disease Control and Prevention, 2014), Tables 11, 18, 26, and 28, http://www.cdc.gov/nchs/data/hus/hus13.pdf.

12. Sabrina Tavernise, "Life Spans Shrink for Least-Educated Whites in the U.S.," *New York Times*, September 20, 2012; D. A. Kindig and E. R. Cheng, "Even as Mortality Fell in Most US

Counties, Female Mortality Nonetheless Rose in 42.8 Percent of Counties from 1992 to 2006," *Health Affairs* 32, no. 3 (2013): 3451, http://content.healthaffairs.org/content/32/3/451.abstract.

13. Elizabeth Bradley and Lauren Taylor, *The American Health Care Paradox* (New York: Public Affairs, 2013), 2, citing S. H. Woolf and L. Aron, eds. *U.S. Health in International Perspective* (Washington, D.C.: National Academies Press, 2013), and M. Avendano et al., "Health Disadvantage in US Adults Aged 50–70 Years: A Comparison of the Health of Rich and Poor Americans With That of Europeans," *American Journal of Public Health* 99, no. 3 (2009): 540–548, http://www.ncbi.nlm.nih.gov/pmc/articles/PMC2661456.

14. Davis et al., *Mirror, Mirror On The Wall*; "The Long Wait to See a Doctor," New York Times, July 7, 2014.

15. "Improving Health Care Health Care Quality," U.S. Department of Health and Human Services, Agency for Health Care Research and Quality, n.d., http://www.ahrq.gov/research/findings/factsheets/errors-safety/improving-quality/index.html; *Why Not the Best? Results from the National Scorecard on U.S. Health System Performance, 2011*, Commonwealth Fund, 2011, http://www.commonwealthfund.org/Publications/Fund-Reports/2011/Oct/Why-Not-the-Best-2011.aspx?page=all; Katherine Xue, "Superbug: An Epidemic Begins," *Harvard Magazine*, May/June 2014, http://harvardmagazine.com/2014/05/superbug. Hospital errors as third-leading cause of death in the United States: see John T. James, "A New, Evidence-Based Estimate of Patient Harms Associated with Hospital Care," *Journal of Patient Safety* 9, no. 3 (2013): 122, http://www.documentcloud.org/documents/781687-john-james-a-new-evidence-based-estimate-of.html.

16. "World's Best Medical Care?," editorial, *New York Times*, August 12, 2007. Although the comment is now over eight years old, there is little doubt that it still applies.

17. See R. Dubos and J. Dubos, *The White Plague* (Boston: Little, Brown, 1952); Rene Dubos, *Man Adapting* (New Haven: Yale University Press, 1965); Thomas McKeown, *The Role of Medicine: Dream, Mirage, or Nemesis* (London: Nuffield Provincial Hospitals Trust, 1976); Thomas McKeown, *The Origins of Human Disease* (London: Blackwell Publishing, 1988); M. Marmot and R. Wilkinson, eds., *Social Determinants of Health*, 2nd ed. (New York: Oxford University Press, 2005); F. M. Burnet, *Natural History of Infectious Disease*, 3rd ed. (London: Cambridge University Press, 1962); Geof Rayner, *Ecological Public Health: Reshaping the Conditions for Good Health* (London: Routledge, 2012).

18. Denise Riedel Lewis et al., "US Lung Cancer Trends by Histologic Type," *Cancer* 120, no. 18 (2014): 2883, http://onlinelibrary.wiley.com/doi/10.1002/cncr.28749/abstract; *Tobacco Statistics Snapshot* (Bethesda, MD: National Institutes for Mental Health, National Cancer Institute, 2012).

19. Endocrine disruptors are chemicals that may interfere with the body's endocrine system and produce adverse developmental, reproductive, neurological, and immune system effects. See *State of the Science of Endocrine Disrupting Chemicals* (United Nations Environment Programme and World Health Organization, 2013), http://www.who.int/ceh/publications/endocrine/en; "Endocrine Disrupters," National Institute of Environmental Health Sciences, July 18, 2014, http://www.niehs.nih.gov/health/topics/agents/endocrine. On prescription drugs in our water supply, see Melody Petersen, *Our Daily Meds* (New York: Farrar, Straus, and Giroux, 2008).

20. On sources of cancer, see Brett Israel, "How Many Cancers Are Caused by the Environment?," *Scientific American*, May 21, 2010, http://www.scientificamerican.com/; H. Shimizu et al., "Colorectal Cancer Epidemiology: Incidence, Mortality, Survival, and Risk Factors," *Clinics in Colon and Rectal Surgery* 22, no. 4 (2009): 191, http://www.ncbi.nlm.nih.gov/pubmed/21037809; C. Nitsche et al., "Environmental Risk Factors for Chronic Pancreatitis and Pancreatic Cancer," *Digestive Diseases* 29, no. 2 (2011): 235, Ana M. Soto and Carlos Sonnenschein, "Environmental Causes of Cancer: Endocrine Disruptors as Carcinogens," *Nature Reviews Endocrinology* 6 (2010): 363. On other social determinants of health, see D. R. Williams and P. B. Jackson, "Social

Sources of Racial Disparities in Health," *Health Affairs* 24, no. 2 (2005): 325, http://www.ncbi.
nlm.nih.gov/pubmed/15757915; R. F. Schoeni et al., *Making Americans Healthier: Social and Economic Policy as Health Policy* (New York: Russell Sage, 2010); H. Thomson, M. Petticrew, and
D. Morrison, "Health Effects of Housing Improvement" *British Medical Journal* 323 (2001): 187;
C.M. Olson, "Nutrition and Health Outcomes," *Journal of Nutrition* 129, no. 2 (1999): S218, http://
jn.nutrition.org/content/129/2/521S.short; W. T. Gallo et al., "Health Effects of Involuntary Job
Loss among Older Workers: Findings from the Health and Retirement Survey," *Journals of Ger-
ontology Series B: Social Sciences* 55B (2000): 131, http://www.ncbi.nlm.nih.gov/pubmed/11833981;
For the Public's Health: Revitalizing Law and Policy to Meet New Challenges (Washington, DC:
National Academies Press and Institute of Medicine, 2011), http://www.nap.edu/catalog/13093/
for-the-publics-health-revitalizing-law-and-policy-to-meet.

21. Nicholas Freudenberg, *Lethal but Legal* (New York: Oxford University Press, 2014).

22. Susan Boseley, "Sugar Industry Threatens to Scupper WHO," *Guardian*, April 21, 2004;
Evan Halper, "Food Industry Waging a Bitter Battle Over Proposal on Added Sugar Labels," *Los
Angeles Times*, March 17, 2015.

23. Jonathan Shaw, "The Price of Healthy Eating," *Harvard Magazine*, March/April 2014,
http://harvardmagazine.com/2014/03/the-price-of-healthy-eating.

24. Mayuree Rao, Ashkan Afkan, Gitanjali Singh, & Dariush Mozaffarian, "Do Healthy
Foods and Diet Patterns Cost More than Less Healthy Options? A Systematic Review and
Meta Analysis," *British Medical Journal Open* 3, no. 12 (2013): 4277, http://dx.doi.org/10.1136/
bmjopen-2013-004277.

25. Earl S. Ford et al., "Explaining the Decrease in U.S. Deaths from Coronary Disease,
1980–2000," *New England Journal of Medicine* 356, no. 23 (2007): 2388, http://dx.doi.org/10.1056/
NEJMsa053935; Jatoi I. Miller, "Why Is Breast Cancer Mortality Declining?" *Lancet Oncology* 4,
no. 4 (2003): 251, http://www.ncbi.nlm.nih.gov/pubmed/12681269.

26. J.M. McGinnis and W. H. Foege, "Actual Causes of Death in the United States," *Journal of the American Medical Association* 270 no. 18 (1993): 2207–2212, http://www.ncbi.nlm.nih.gov/
pubmed/8411605; Ali H. Mokdad, James S. Marks, Donna F. Stroup, and Julie L. Gerberding,
"Actual Causes of Death in the United States, 2000," *Journal of the American Medical Association* 291
(2004): 1238, http://dx.doi.org/10.1001/jama.291.10.1238; J. P. Bunker, H. S. Frazier, and F. Mo-
steller, "Improving Health: Measuring Effects of Medical Care," *Milbank Quarterly* 72, no. 2 (1994):
225, cited in House et al., "The Health Effects of Social and Economic Policy"; P. Lee and D. Pax-
man, "Reinventing Public Health," *Annual Reviews of Public Health* 18 (1997): 1, cited in Lauren
Taylor, *The American Health Care Paradox* (New York: Public Affairs, 2013), 43–50; M. G. Marmot
and R. G. Wilkinson, *Social Determinants of Health* (New York: Oxford University Press, 2006).

27. "National Health Expenditures by Type of Service and Source of Funds, CY 1960–2013"
(Baltimore, MD: Centers for Medicare and Medicaid Services, 2014), https://www.cms.gov/
Research-Statistics-Data-and-Systems/Statistics-Trends-and-Reports/NationalHealthExpend-
Data/NationalHealthAccountsHistorical.html; total figure for spending excludes investment.
Comparative international figures for spending on the "social determinants of health" can be
found in Elizabeth Bradley and Lauren Taylor, *The American Health Care Paradox* (New York:
Public Affairs, 2013).

28. Oliver Wendell Holmes, *Currents and Counter-Currents in Medical Science, with Other Addresses and Full Essays* (Cambridge: Cambridge University Press, 1860), http://archive.org/stream/
currentscounterc00holm/currentscounterc00holm_djvu.txt. Holmes exempted opium and alcohol for relief of pain and a few traditional medications. Wylie quoted in Paul Starr, *The Social
Transformation of American Medicine* (New York: Basic Books, 1982), 151.

29. Henderson quoted in Peter Conrad, ed., *The Sociology of Health and Mental Illness*, 8th ed.
(New York: Worth, 2009), 191.

30. William G. Rothstein, *American Medical Schools and the Practice of Medicine: A History* (New York: Oxford University Press, 1987), 143; Starr, *The Social Transformation of American Medicine*, 78–144.

31. "What Is the American Medical Association's (AMA) Position on the Affordable Care Act (ACA)?" Medicare News Group, 2014, http://www.medicarenewsgroup.com/; Roger Collier, "American Medical Association Membership Woes Continue," *Canadian Medical Association Journal* 183, no. 11 (2011): E713, http://www.ncbi.nlm.nih.gov/pmc/articles/PMC3153537.

32. My account draws on Barbara Ehrenreich and John Ehrenreich, *The American Health Empire: Power, Profits, and Politics* (New York: Random House, 1970), 3–28; and Ezekiel Emmanuel, *Reinventing American Health Care* (New York: Public Affairs, 2014).

33. Barbara Ehrenreich and John Ehrenreich, *The American Health Empire*, 29–94; Starr, *The Social Transformation of American Medicine*, 430–36.

34. H. Marjorie Valbrun, "Hospital Closings Jeopardize Care in Poor, Urban Communities," *America's Wire*, September 19, 2014, http://americaswire.org/drupal7/?q=content/hospital-closings-jeopardize-care-poor-urban-communities; Alan Sager, "Threats to Urban Public Hospitals and How to Respond to Them," *DC Watch*, March 30, 2001, http://www.dcwatch.com/issues/pbc010330.htm.

35. On the trend to hospital based practices, see the Medical Group Management Association survey, reported in Gregory Mertz, "Hospital Employment vs. Private Practice: Pros and Cons," *Physicians Practice*, June 2, 2013, http://www.physicianspractice.com/blog/hospital-employment-vs-private-practice-pros-and-cons; *Clinical Transformation: New Business Models for a New Era in Healthcare* (n.p.: Accenture, 2012), http://www.accenture.com/SiteCollectionDocuments/PDF/Accenture-Clinical-Transformation-New-Business-Models-for-a-New-Era-in-Healthcare.pdf#zoom=50.

36. For an account of the logic of professionalization, see Barbara and John Ehrenreich, "The Professional-Managerial Class," *Radical America* 11, no. 2 (March/April 1977): 7–31, reprinted in *Between Labor and Capital*, ed. P. Walker (Boston: South End Press, 1979), 5–45. On hospital workers, see Barbara Ehrenreich and John Ehrenreich, "Hospital Workers: Class Conflicts in the Making," *International Journal of Health Services* 5, no. 1 (1975): 43; "May 2013 National Occupational Employment and Wage Estimates United States," U.S. Department of Labor, Bureau of Labor Statistics, http://www.bls.gov/oes/2013/may/oes_nat.htm. On shift of doctors to salaried practice, see John B. McKinlay and Lisa D. Marceau, "The End of the Golden Age of Doctoring," *International Journal of Health Services* 32, no. 2 (2002): 379–416; Gardiner Harris, "More Doctors Taking Salaried Jobs," *New York Times*, March 25, 2010; Robert Kocher and Nikhil R. Sahini, "Hospitals' Race to Employ Physicians—The Logic behind a Money-Losing Proposition," *New England Journal of Medicine* 364, no. 19 (2011): 1790, http://www.nejm.org/doi/full/10.1056/NEJMp1101959.

37. The term "medical-industrial complex" first appeared in print, as far as I know, in articles written by Barbara Ehrenreich and me in the *Bulletin of the Health Policy Center*, November 1969 ("The Medical Industrial Complex" and "The Big Business of Health," available at http://www.healthpacbulletin.org/healthpac-bulletin-november-1969) and in a subsequent article, Barbara Ehrenreich and John Ehrenreich, "The Medical-Industrial Complex" (review of Eli Ginzburg and Miriam Ostow's *Men, Money and Medicine*), *New York Review of Books*, December 17, 1970. The phrase was suggested to us by Dr. Richard Kunnes.

38. Barbara Ehrenreich and John Ehrenreich, "The Big Business of Health"; "National Health Expenditures," Centers for Medicare and Medicaid Services, http://www.cms.gov/Research-Statistics-Data-and-Systems/Statistics-Trends-and-Reports/NationalHealthExpendData/Downloads/tables.pdf; health care employment: "Establishment Data, Table B-1, Employees on Nonfarm Payrolls by Industry Sector and Selected Industry Detail," U.S. Department of Labor, Bureau of Labor Statistics, http://www.bls.gov/news.release/empsit.t17.htm.

39. *NewYork–Presbyterian 2010 Annual Report* (New York: NewYork-Presbyterian Hospital, 2011), http://nyp.org/pdf/annual_report_2010.pdf; Ernst and Young LLP, *Financial Statements: The New York and Presbyterian Hospital, Years Ended December 31, 2013 and 2012* (New York: Ernst and Young, 2014), http://emma.msrb.org/EP810348-EP627652-EP1029431.pdf; Anemena Harticollis, "At NewYork–Presbyterian Hospital, Its Ex-C.E.O. Finds Lucrative Work," *New York Times*, July 15, 2014; Bob Herman, "New York–Presbyterian's Revenue Up 9%," *Becker's Hospital Review*, May 2, 2014, http://www.beckershospitalreview.com/finance/newyork-presbyterian-s-revenue-up-9.html; Bob Herman, "CEO Compensation of the 25 Top-Grossing Non-Profit Hospitals," *Becker's Hospital Review*, September 26, 2012, http://www.beckershospitalreview.com/compensation-issues/ceo-compensation-of-the-25-top-grossing-non-profit-hospitals.html. The high salaries are comparable to those of other top executives in the private sector, of course, and it could be argued that that is what you have to pay to get someone competent to manage such a vast system. But the CEO of New York City's Health and Hospital Corporation, a substantially larger health-care system, with $6.5 billion in annual revenues, was willing to work for only $291,000 a year. Roy M. Poses, "The $9.8 Million Dollar Man," *Health Care Renewal*, December 14, 2009, http://hcrenewal.blogspot.com/2009/12/98-million-dollar-man.html; "Fortune 500 2014," *Fortune*, http://fortune.com/fortune500/ngl-energy-partners-lp-556.

40. On hospital managers' salaries, see Elisabeth Rosenthal, "Medicine's Top Earners Are Not the M.D.s," *New York Times*, May 17, 2014. On hospital real estate holdings and activities, see Michael Stoler, "Hospitals Active in Real Estate," *New York Sun*, January 4, 2007; Janna Herron, "Hospitals Become Real Estate Powerhouses," *The Real Deal*, April 1, 2014, http://therealdeal.com/issues_articles/hospitals-as-real-estate-powerhouse.

41. *Chartbook: Trends Affecting Hospitals and Health System* (Chicago: American Hospital Association, 2015), chapter 4, http://www.aha.org/research/reports/tw/chartbook/ch4.shtml; Bob Herman, "13 Statistics on Hospital Profit and Revenue in 2011," *Becker's Hospital Review*, February 4, 2013, http://www.beckershospitalreview.com/finance/13-statistics-on-hospital-profit-and-revenue-in-2011.html; Brice S. McKeever and Sarah L. Pettijohn, The Non Profit Sector in Brief: Public Charities, Giving and Volunteering, 2014 (Washington, DC: Urban Institute, 2014), http://www.urban.org/publications/413277.html; Helen Gregg, "10 Things to Know about Epic," *Becker's Health Care*, April 17, 2014, http://www.beckershospitalreview.com/lists/10-things-to-know-about-epic.html; "The Healthcare Informatics 100, 2015," Healthcare Infomatics, http://www.healthcare-informatics.com/hci100/healthcare-informatics-100.

42. Elisabeth Rosenthal, "Benefits Questioned in Tax Breaks for Nonprofit Hospitals," *New York Times*, December 16, 2013. The wholly fantastic nature of hospital costs has been well documented. For example, a 2012 New York State Health Department study reported that hospital costs for knee-joint replacement surgery ranged from $1,057 at A. O. Fox Hospital in Oneonta to $33,280 at NYU-Langone Medical Center in New York City, and the cost of routine childbirth and neonatal medical services ranged from $2,603 to $6,692. Nina Bernstein, "New York State Hospital Data Exposes Big Markups, and Odd Bargains," *New York Times*, December 9, 2013. On average, U.S. hospitals charge more than three times their actual cost, and the hundred most expensive U.S. hospitals have a charge-to-cost ratio of 765 percent or more. See "New Data—Some Hospitals Set Charges at 10 Times Their Costs," National Nurses United, press release, January 6, 2014, http://www.nationalnursesunited.org/press/entry/new-data-some-hospitals-set-charges-at-10-times-their-costs.

43. Quoted in Rosenthal, "Benefits Questioned in Tax Breaks for Nonprofit Hospitals."

44. Heather Punke, "Outsourcing Is Exploding in Healthcare—Will the Trend Last?" *Becker's Hospital Review*, October 4, 2013, http://www.beckershospitalreview.com/workforce-labor-management/outsourcing-is-exploding-in-healthcare-will-the-trend-last.html; Martin Stack and Myles Gartland, "Service Industry Evolution: The Offshoring of Radiology," paper presented at the DRUID Summer Conference, Frederiksberg, Denmark, June 18–20, 2006, http://

www2.druid.dk/conferences/viewpaper.php?id=615&cf=8; Nir Kshetri and Nikhilesh Dhola-
kia, "Offshoring of Healthcare Services: The Case of the Indian Medical Transcription Offshoring Industry," *Journal of Health Organization and Management* 25, no. 1 (2011): 94, http://libres.
uncg.edu/ir/uncg/f/N_Kshetri_Offshoring_2011.pdf; Lisa A. Eramo, "Offshore Transcription:
A Seaworthy Choice?" *For The Record* 22, no. 5 (2010): 14, http://www.fortherecordmag.com/
archives/031510p14.shtml.

   45. Heather Punke, "50 Top Grossing For-Profit Hospitals," *Becker's Hospital Review*, June 27,
2014, http://www.beckershospitalreview.com/lists/50-top-grossing-for-profit-hospitals-2014.
html; Bob Herman, "HCA's Profit Up 35% in Q4, Down Slightly in 2013," *Becker's Hospital
Review*, February 4, 2014, http://www.beckershospitalreview.com/finance/hca-s-profit-up-35-
in-q4-down-slightly-in-2013.html; Ezekiel Emmanuel, *Reinventing American Health Care* (New
York: Public Affairs, 2014).

   46. *Health, United States, 2013* (Hyattsville, MD: Centers for Disease Control and Prevention,
2014), Table 114, http://www.cdc.gov/nchs/data/hus/hus13.pdf#114; profits of the big companies
as reported by Thom Hartmann, "11 Major Drug Companies Raked in $85 Billion Last Year, and
Left Many to Die Who Couldn't Buy Their Pricey Drugs," AlterNet.org, April 30, 2013, http://
www.alternet.org/11-major-drug-companies-raked-85-billion-last-year-and-left-many-die-who-
couldnt-buy-their-pricey.

   47. Deana Beasely, "Drug Makers Face More Scrutiny of Discordant U.S. Prices," Reuters, May 10, 2013, http://www.reuters.com/article/2013/05/10/us-usa-health-drugs-analy-
sis-idUSBRE9490MH20130510; Elisabeth Rosenthal, "The Soaring Cost of a Simple Breath,"
New York Times, October 12, 2013.

   48. The $1 billion estimate is based on the work of J. A. DiMasi, Ronald W. Hansen, and
Henry G. Grabowski, "The Price of Innovation: New Estimates of Drug Development Costs,"
Journal of Health Economics 22, no. 2 (2003): 151; Christopher Adams and Van Brantner, "Esti-
mating the Cost of New Drug Development: Is It Really $802 Million?," *Health Affairs* 33, no. 9
(2014): 420, http://content.healthaffairs.org/content/25/2/420.full.html. The $55 million estimate is
from Donald W. Light and Rebecca Warburton, "Demythologizing the High Costs of Pharmaceutical Research," *BioSocieties* 6 (2011): 34; also see Timothy Noah, "The Make Believe Billion,"
Slate, March 3, 2011, http://www.slate.com/articles/business/the_customer/2011/03/the_make-
believe_billion.single.html. The IRS permits drug companies to exclude research and development costs entirely from taxable profits, rather than depreciating them over time like other forms
of investment.

   49. Jeffrey Sachs, "The Pharma Drug that Is Bankrupting America." Alternet, March 17,
2015, http://www.alternet.org/drugs/pharma-drug-bankrupting-america.

   50. Rosanne Spector, "Me-Too Drug: Sometimes They're Just the Same Old Same Old,"
Stanford Medical Magazine, Summer 2005, http://sm.stanford.edu/archive/stanmed/2005summer/
drugs-metoo.html. A more recent study found that drug approvals continue to be "largely driven
by addition-to-class, or 'me too,' drug approvals." Michael Lanthier et al., "An Improved Approach To Measuring Drug Innovation Finds Steady Rates of First-In-Class Pharmaceuticals,
1987–2011," *Health Affairs* 32, no. 8 (2013): 1433.

   51. Eduardo Porter, "A Dearth in Innovation for Key Drugs," *New York Times*, July 22, 2014;
Hester Plumridge, "Drug Makers Tiptoe Back into Antibiotic Research," *Wall Street Journal*,
January 23, 2014.

   52. Melody Petersen, *Our Daily Meds* (New York: Farrar, Straus, and Giroux, 2009), 349; Steven Brill, *America's Bitter Pill* (New York: Random House, 2015), 391.

   53. Among others, Glaxo Smith Kline weathered a criminal conviction and paid a $3 billion
fine for promoting off-label use of its antidepressants (Paxil and Wellbutrin) and for failing to report safety data for its diabetes drug Avandia. Abbott Labs was fined for similar practices with

Depakote, as were Johnson and Johnson for Risperidol and Lilly for Zyprexa. Katie Thomas and Michael Schmidt, "Glaxo Agrees to Pay $3 Billion in Fraud Settlement," *New York Times*, July 2, 2012; Jonathan Stempel, "Pfizer to Pay $325 Million in Neurontin Settlement," Reuters, June 2, 2014, http://www.reuters.com/article/2014/06/02/us-pfizer-neurontin-settlement-idUSKBN0E D1IS20140602; Katie Thomas. "Glaxo Opens Door to Data on Research," *New York Times*, October 11, 2012. Several drug companies have been charged with failing to publish research showing that their drug was no better than placebo or no better than existing drugs. See Petersen, *Our Daily Meds*, 201–205; Brill, *America's Bitter Pill*, 5.

54. Neil Canavan, "Opposition Growing against Azithromycin for Infections," *MedScape Medical News*, February 18, 2014; "Sesame Street-Zithromax Commercial (High Tone)," You-Tube, July 11, 2012, https://www.youtube.com/watch?v=Ftli_ybnEOM. Most other countries do not permit direct to consumer advertising of prescription medications. See C. Lee Ventola, "Direct-to-Consumer Pharmaceutical Advertising: Therapeutic or Toxic," *Pharmacy and Therapeutics* 36, no. 10 (2011), 669–674 and 681–684.

55. In 2015, nearly one-third of all employers will offer only high-deductible plans, up from 10 percent in 2010, and 81 percent will offer such plans as a relatively low-premium choice. Tara Siegel Bernard, "High Health Plan Deductibles Weigh Down More Employees." *New York Times*, September 1, 2014.

56. Charles Ornstein, "How Insurers Are Finding Ways to Shift Costs to the Sick," *New York Times*, September 17, 2004.

57. "National Health Expenditures," Table 3, Centers for Medicare and Medicaid Services, http://www.cms.gov/Research-Statistics-Data-and-Systems/Statistics-Trends-and-Reports/ NationalHealthExpendData/Downloads/tables.pdf.

58. The Food and Drug Administration has been repeatedly criticized for laxness in its regulation of medical devices, conflicts of interest among drug researchers, assessing drug risks, and controlling overuse of antibiotics in animal feeds. See Sabrina Tavernise, "U.S. Aims to Curb Peril of Antibiotic Resistance," *New York Times*, September 18, 2014; Gardiner Harris, "F.D.A. Is Lax on Oversight During Trials, Inquiry Finds," *New York Times*, January 11, 2009; Scott Gottlieb, "FDA Safety Regs Faulted for Lax Oversight," *Forbes*, February 13, 2013, http:// www.forbes.com/sites/scottgottlieb/2013/02/13/fda-safety-regulations-faulted-for-lax-oversight; Rob Stein, "Study of Recalled Medical Devices Faults Lax FDA Testing Methods," *Washington Post*, February 14, 2011.

59. Jim Avila, "USDA to Let Industry Self-Inspect Chicken," *ABC News*, April 18, 2012, http://abcnews.go.com/blogs/headlines/2012/04/usda-to-let-industry-self-inspect-chicken.

60. John Wasik, "Medicare Advantage Isn't Reducing Health Care Costs," *Fiscal Times*, April 16, 2014, http://www.thefiscaltimes.com/Columns/2014/04/16/Medicare-Advantage-Isn-t-Reducing-Health-Care-Costs; Chris Anderson, "GAO Study Finds $5.1 Billion in Medicare Advantage Overpayments," *Healthcare IT News*, March 7, 2013, http://www.healthcareitnews.com/ news/gao-study-finds-51-billion-medicare-advantage-overpayments.

61. Glenn Greenwald, "Obamacare Architect Leaves White House for Pharmaceutical Industry Job." *Guardian*, December 5, 2012.

62. Dante Morra, Sean Nicholson, Wendy Levinson, David N. Gans, Terry Hammons, and Lawrence P. Casalino, "US Physician Practices versus Canadians: Spending Nearly Four Times as Much Money Interacting with Payers," *Health Affairs* 30 (8), 2011, 1443–1450, http://content.healthaffairs.org/content/30/8/1443.full.

63. Pierre L. Yong, Robert S. Saunders, and LeighAnne Olsen, eds., *The Healthcare Imperative: Lowering Costs and Improving Outcomes: Workshop Series Summary* (Washington, DC: National Academies Press, 2010); Christine Stahlecker, "eHealth Spotlight: Understanding Administrative Simplification, Centers for Medicare and Medicaid Services, http://www.cms.gov/

eHealth/ListServ_understandingadminsimplification.html; Bonnie B. Blanchfield et al., "Saving Billions of Dollars—and Physicians' Time—by Streamlining Billing Practices," *Health Affairs* 29, no. 6 (2010): 1248, http://content.healthaffairs.org/content/29/6/1248.full.pdf; Elisabeth Rosenthal, "The Odd Math of Medical Tests: One Scan, Two Prices, Both High," *New York Times*, December 15, 2014.

64. For an account of the impact of the corporatization of hospitals on health workers and, as a result, on patient care, focusing on the effect on "residents"—the doctors in training who provide much of hospital-based medical care—see Lara Goitein, "Training Young Doctors: The Current Crisis," *New York Review of books*, June 4, 2015, pp. 60–62.

65. Crystal L. Hoyt and Jeni L. Burnette, "Should Obesity Be a Disease," *New York Times*, February 21, 2014.

66. On medicine, ideology, and social control, a topic that has been neglected since the late 1970s, see Barbara Ehrenreich and John Ehrenreich, "Medicine and Social Control," in *Welfare in America: Controlling the Dangerous Classes*, ed. Betty Mandel (New York: Prentice Hall, 1975), 138–167; Irving Kenneth Zola, "Medicine as an Institution of Social Control," *Sociological Review* 20, no. 4 (1972): 487, http://dx.doi.org/10.1111/j.1467-954X.1972.tb00220.x; Howard Waitzkin, "A Critical Theory of Medical Discourse: Ideology, Social Control, and the Processing of Social Context in Medical Encounters," *Journal of Health and Social Behavior* 30, no. 2 (1989): 220, http://www.aleciashepherd.com/writings/articles/other/A%20Critical%20Theory%20of%20Medical%20Discourse%20Ideology%20Social.pdf; Peter Conrad, "Types of Medical Social Control," *Sociology of Health and Illness* 1, no. 1 (1979): 1, http://dx.doi.org/10.1111/j.1467-9566.1979.tb00175.x.

3. Getting Schooled

1. "Melinda Gates on the Importance of Evaluations in Shaping Effective Teachers," *PBS News Hour*, June 24, 2012, http://www.pbs.org/newshour/bb/education-jan-june12-m(elindagates_06-04; "Restoring the American Dream: Fixing Education," *Fareed Zakaria GPS*, CNN.com, January 12, 2012, http://transcripts.cnn.com/TRANSCRIPTS/1201/07/fzgps.01.html.

2. "Digest of Education Statistics," National Center for Education Statistics, 2013, Tables 302.60, 104.20, and 302.60, http://nces.ed.gov/programs/digest/2013menu_tables.asp.

3. Bill Gates, "How Teacher Development Could Revolutionize Our Schools," *Washington Post*, February 28, 2011.

4. *Trends in Academic Progress, 2012, The Nation's Report Card* (National Assessment of Educational Progress) (Washington, DC: National Center for Educational Statistics, 2013), http://nces.ed.gov/nationsreportcard/subject/publications/main2012/pdf/2013456.pdf; *A First Look: 2013 Mathematics and Reading*, The Nation's Report Card (National Assessment of Educational Progress) (Washington, DC: National Center for Educational Statistics, 2013), http://nces.ed.gov/nationsreportcard/subject/publications/main2013/pdf/2014451.pdf. In interpreting these tables, note that the format was revised in 2004—it is necessary to compare trends for 1971 to 2004 and 2004 to 2012 separately. Although the overall trend for older (seventeen-year-old) students appears flat, scores for seventeen -year-old white, black, and Latino students taken separately all show significant increases. This apparently paradoxical finding is the result of a larger proportion of the sample in later years being made up of generally lower performing nonwhite students.

5. Lindsay Layton, "U.S. Students Lag around Average on International Science, Math and Reading Test," *Washington Post*, December 13, 2014.

6. *Programme for International Student Assessment (PISA) Results from PISA 2012: United States*, Country Note (Washington, DC: OECD, n.d.), http://www.oecd.org/pisa/keyfindings/PISA-2012-results-US.pdf.

7. Diana Ravitch, *Reign of Error* (New York: Knopf, 2013), 65.

8. "Progress in International Reading Literacy Study (PIRLS): PIRLS 2011 Results," National Center for Educational Statistics, http://nces.ed.gov/surveys/pirls/pirls2011.asp; "Trends in Mathematics and Science Study (TIMSS): Mathematics Achievement of Fourth- and Eighth-Graders in 2011," National Center for Educational Statistics, http://nces.ed.gov/timss/results11_math11.asp; "Trends in Mathematics and Science Study (TIMSS): Science Achievement of Fourth- and Eighth-Graders in 2011," National Center for Educational Statistics, http://nces.ed.gov/timss/results11_science11.asp.

9. For further discussion of the impact the higher proportions of students in the United States from poor families have on the PISA comparisons, see Martin Carnoy and Richard Rothstein, "What Do International Tests Really Show about U.S. Student Performance?," Economic Policy Institute, January 23 2013, http://www.epi.org/publication/us-student-performance-testing; and Ravitch, *Reign of Error*, 75–78, 343–344.

10. Patrick Thibodeau, "Romney Sees Tech Skills Shortage, and H-1B Visa Need," *Computer World*, September 7, 2011, http://www.computerworld.com/article/2510972/it-careers/romney-sees-tech-skills-shortage—and-h-1b-visa-need.html; Barack Obama, "Remarks by the President on Veterans Jobs" (Washington, D.C.: The White House, June 1, 2012), transcript online at https://www.whitehouse.gov/photos-and-video/video/2012/06/01/president-obama-hiring-veterans#transcript. *A National Talent Strategy: Ideas for Securing U.S. Competitiveness and Economic Growth* (Redmond, WA: Microsoft Press, n.d.), http://news.microsoft.com/download/presskits/citizenship/MSNTS.pdf. See also "What We Do: Postsecondary Success Strategy Overview," Bill and Melinda Gates Foundation, 2014, http://www.gatesfoundation.org/What-We-Do/US-Program/Postsecondary-Success. The 80 percent figure comes from a study conducted by the Manufacturing Institute, *2011 Skills Gap Report* (Washington, DC: Manufacturing Institute, 2011), http://www.themanufacturinginstitute.org/Research/Skills-Gap-in-Manufacturing/2011-Skills-Gap-Report/2011-Skills-Gap-Report.aspx. Critical views of the study can be found in "About that Manufacturing Skills Gap: It's Complicated," *Investors' Business Daily*, September 12, 2014, http://www.nasdaq.com/article/about-that-manufacturing-skills-gap-its-complicated-cm390391#ixzz3QbLNataa; Peter Capelli, "What Employers Really Want? Workers They Don't Have to Train," *Washington Post*, September 5, 2014.

11. "In 2005, 36% of US workers were over-qualified for their jobs (against the OECD average of 25%), and 20% were under-qualified (against the OECD average of 22%)." Glenda Quintini, *Right for the Job: Over-Qualified or Under Skilled?*, OECD Social, Employment, & Migration Working Papers 120 (Paris: OECD, 2011), http://www.oecd-ilibrary.org/social-issues-migration-health/right-for-the-job_5kg59fcz3tkd-en.

12. Capelli, "What Employers Really Want? Workers They Don't Have to Train." Occupational areas in which there *is* excess demand, as testified to by rising wages, include certain skilled manual trades, such as boilermakers, welders, and mobile crane operators. Lauren Pinch, "NCCER Survey: Craft Professionals' Wages on the Rise," *Construction Executive*, February 10, 2015, http://enewsletters.constructionexec.com/managingyourbusiness/2015/02/nccer-survey-craft-professionals-wages-on-the-rise.

13. Calculated from figures in "Labor Force Status of 2014 High School Graduates and 2013–14 High School Dropouts 16 to 24 years Old by School Enrollment, Educational Attainment, Sex, Race, and Hispanic or Latino Ethnicity, October 2014," Bureau of Labor Statistics, http://www.bls.gov/news.release/hsgec.t01.htm; *Characteristics of Minimum Wage Workers, 2013*, BLS Report 1048 (Washington, DC: Bureau of Labor Statistics, 2014), Table 6, http://www.bls.gov/cps/minwage2013.pdf.

14. Wesley Robinson, "Most with College STEM Degrees Go to Work in Other Fields, Survey Finds," *Washington Post*, July 10, 2014; Michael Anft, "The STEM Crisis: Reality or Myth?,"

Chronicle of Higher Education, November 11, 2013, http://chronicle.com/article/The-STEM-Crisis-Reality-or/142879; Karen Zeigler and Steven A. Camarota, "Is There a STEM Worker Shortage?," Center for Immigration Studies, May 2014, http://cis.org/no-stem-shortage.

15. Richard Vedder, Christopher Denhart, and Jonathan Robe, *Why Are Recent College Graduates Underemployed? University Enrollments and Labor Market Realities* (Washington, DC: Center for College Affordability and Productivity, 2013) http://centerforcollegeaffordability.org/uploads/Underemployed%20Report%202.pdf; "Occupations with the Most Job Growth," Bureau of Labor Statistics, http://www.bls.gov/emp/ep_table_104.htm; "Where Have All the Raises Gone," New York Times, March 3, 2014.

16. Klaus Schwab, *The Global Competitiveness Report 2014–2015* (Geneva, Switzerland: World Economic Forum, 2014), http://www3.weforum.org/docs/WEF_GlobalCompetitivenessReport_2014-15.pdf; *Creativity and Prosperity: The Global Creativity Index* (Toronto: Martin Prosperity Institute, 2011), http://martinprosperity.org/media/GCI%20Report%20Sep%202011.pdf; *The Global Innovation Index 2014* (Geneva, Switzerland: Global Innovation Index, 2014), http://www.globalinnovationindex.org/content.aspx?page-GII-Home.

17. "Percentage of Persons 25 to 29 years Old with Selected Levels of Educational Attainment, by Race/Ethnicity and Sex: Selected Years, 1920 through 2013, National Center for Education Statistics, http://nces.ed.gov/programs/digest/d13/tables/dt13_104.20.asp.

18. *Trends in Academic Progress, 2012* (Washington, DC: National Center for Educational Statistics, 2013), Figures 7–12, 23–28. The black-white math gap, for instance, narrowed twice as much in the ten years between 1973 and 1982 as in the thirty years that followed.

19. Lyndsey Layton, "How Bill Gates Pulled off the Swift Common Core Revolution," *Washington Post*, June 7, 2014.

20. Sarah Reckhow and Jeffrey W. Snyder, "The Expanding Role of Philanthropy in Education Politics," *Educational Researcher*, May 8, 2014, http://edr.sagepub.com/content/early/2014/05/07/0013189X14536607.full.pdf?ijkey=jxt9LKgVIAKcs&keytype=ref&siteid=spedr; David Sirota, "The Problem with Philanthropy," *In These Times*, June 13, 2014, http://inthesetimes.com/article/16826/the_problem_with_philanthropy; Bill Gates, interview by Arthur C. Brooks, American Enterprise Institute, March 13, 2014, http://www.aei.org/files/2014/03/14/bill-gates-event-transcript_082217994272.pdf.

21. "Facts," American Federation for Children, http://www.federationforchildren.org/ed-choice-101/facts; *The Condition of Education 2014* (Washington, DC: National Center for Education Statistics, 2014), http://www.nces.ed.gov/pubs2014/2014083.pdf; "Digest of Educational Statistics," Table 7, National Center for Education Statistics, 2013; *Parent and Family Involvement in Education, from the National Household Education Surveys Program of 2012* (Washington, DC: National Center for Education Statistics, 2013), http://nces.ed.gov/pubs2013/2013028rev.pdf; Alexandra Usher and Nancy Kober, *Keeping Informed about School Vouchers: A Review of Major Developments and Research* (Washington, DC: Center on Education Policy, 2011), http://www.cep-dc.org/displayDocument.cfm?DocumentID=369; Stan Karp, "Charter Schools and the Future of Public Education," *Common Dreams*, October 13, 2013, http://www.commondreams.org/author/stan-karp; *National Charter School Study: Executive Summary 2013* (Stanford: Center for Research of Educational Outcomes, Stanford University, 2013), https://credo.stanford.edu/documents/NCSS%202013%20Executive%20Summary.pdf; Andrew Maul and Abby McClelland, *Review Of National Charter School Study 2013* (Boulder, CO: National Education Policy Center, 2013), 4, http://nepc.colorado.edu/thinktank/review-credo-2013. See also Bonnie Burn, Jane Asche, and Sue Cain, *For-Profit Virtual Charter Schools: Literature Review and Report* (Las Cruces, NM: League of Women Voters of Greater Las Cruces, 2014), http://www.lwvglc.org/documents/lwvglc_paper_for_profit_virtual_charter_schools.pdf; Elaine Weiss and Don Long, *Market-Oriented Education Reforms' Rhetoric Trumps Reality* (Washington, DC: Broader, Bolder Approach to Education, 2013), http://www.epi.org/files/2013/bba-rhetoric-trumps-reality.pdf.

There is no way to assess the relative values of home schooling and traditional public schooling since the set of children whose parents choose the former is markedly different from the traditional public school population.

More positive readings of the evidence on voucher schools can be found in *Does School Choice Have a Positive Academic Impact on Participating Students* (Indianapolis: Friedman Foundation for Educational Choice, n.d.), http://www.edchoice.org/getattachment/School-Choice/School-Choice-FAQs/How-does-school-choice-affect-public-schools.pdf; Kevin Booker et al., *Charter High Schools Effects on Long Term Attainment and Earnings* (Princeton, NJ: Mathematica Policy Research, 2014), http://www.mathematica-mpr.com/~/media/publications/PDFs/education/charter_long-term_wp.pdf. But see also Valerie Straus, "The Bottom Line on Charter School Studies," *Washington Post*, September 24, 2013; Valerie Strauss, "Major Charter Researcher Causes Stir with Comments about Market-Based School Reform," *Washington Post*, December 12, 2014.

22. Stephen Dyer, *Report: Unfair Funding—How Charter Schools Win and Traditional Schools Lose* (Columbus: Innovation Ohio, 2013), http://innovationohio.org/2013/02/14/report-unfair-funding-how-charter-schools-win-traditional-schools-lose.

23. Sharona Coutts, "Charter Schools Outsource Education to Management Firms, with Mixed Results," ProPublica, April 6, 2011, http://www.propublica.org/article/charter-schools-outsource-education-to-management-firms-with-mixed-results; Marian Wang, "When Charter Schools Are Nonprofit in Name Only," ProPublica, December 9, 2014, http://www.propublica.org/article/when-charter-schools-are-nonprofit-in-name-only?utm_campaign=sprout&utm_medium=social&utm_source=twitter&utm_content=1418148538; Addison Wiggin, "Charter School Gravy Train Runs Express to Fat City," *Forbes*, September 10, 2013, http://www.forbes.com/sites/greatspeculations/2013/09/10/charter-school-gravy-train-runs-express-to-fat-city; Gary Miron and Charisse Gulosino, *Profiles of For-Profit and Nonprofit Education Management Organizations*, 14th ed. (Boulder, CO: National Education Policy Center, 2013), http://nepc.colorado.edu/files/emo-profiles-11-12.pdf.

24. Dyer, *Report: Unfair Funding*; David Arsen and Yongmei Ni, "Is Administration Leaner in Charter Schools? Resource Allocation in Charter and Traditional Public Schools," http://www.ncspe.org/publications_files/OP201.pdf.

25. Helen Zelon, "Why Charter Schools Have High Teacher Turnover," *CityLimits.org*, August 20, 2014, http://www.citylimits.org/news/articles/5156/why-charter-schools-have-high-teacher-turnover/3#.VEAAWildUlZ; *Survey of America's Charter Schools, 2014* (Washington, DC: Center for Education Reform, 2014), http://www.edreform.com/wp-content/uploads/2014/02/2014CharterSchoolSurveyFINAL.pdf.

26. Lyndsey Layton, "In New Orleans, Major School District Closes Traditional Public Schools for Good," *Washington Post*, May 28, 2014; "State Releases Comprehensive Report Cards on Student, School Achievement," Louisiana Department of Education, October 21, 2014, http://www.louisianabelieves.com/newsroom/news-releases/2014/10/21/state-releases-comprehensive-report-cards-on-student-school-achievement (the Orleans and Baton Rouge Recovery and regular school districts are counted as distinct districts); Nick Anderson, "Education Secretary Duncan Calls Hurricane Katrina Good for New Orleans Schools," *Washington Post*, January 30, 2010. Black families in New Orleans, the ones whose children actually attended the post-Katrina schools, disagreed with Duncan's assessment. 62% of African American residents of New Orleans who responded to a poll on the tenth anniversary of the hurricane reported that they thought New Orleans schools were either worse or the same as before the hurricane; only 38% saw an improvement. *Views of Recovery Ten Years After Katrina and Rita* (Baton Rouge, LA: Louisiana State University, August 24, 2015), https://sites01.lsu.edu/wp/pprl/files/2012/07/Views-of-Recovery-August-2015.pdf. Also see Andrea Gabor, "The Myth of the New Orleans School Makeover," *New York Times*, August 22, 2015.

27. Kristin Rawls, "Who Is Profiting from Charters? The Big Bucks behind Charter School Secrecy, Financial Scandal and Corruption," AlterNet, May 8, 2013, http://www.alternet.org/education/who-profiting-charters-big-bucks-behind-charter-school-secrecy-financial-scandal-and?page=0%2C5; Valerie Straus, "The Big Business of Charter Schools," *Washington Post*, August 17, 2012.

28. Rachel Monahan, "Top 16 NYC Charter School Executives Earn More than Chancellor Dennis Walcott.," *New York Daily News*, October 26, 2013; "CMD Exposes America's 'Highest Paid Government Workers,'" *PR Watch* (Center for Media and Democracy), November 19, 2013, http://www.prwatch.org/news/2013/11/12314/cmd-exposes-america%E2%80%99s-%E2%80%9Chighest-paid-government-workers%E2%80%9D; Paul Buchheit, "4 Reasons Why Public Education Is in Desperate Need of Saving (from 'Reformers' Like Michelle Rhee)," *Salon*, April 1, 2014, http://www.salon.com/2014/04/01/4_reasons_why_public_education_is_in_desperate_need_of_saving_and_michelle_rhee_is_wrong_partner/; "K12 Inc., Morningstar, http://insiders.morningstar.com/trading/executive-compensation.action?t=LRN&region=USA&culture=en-US; Allie Gross, "The Charter School Profiteers," *Jacobin*, July 2014, http://www.jacobinmag.com/2014/07/the-charter-school-profiteers/; Addison Wiggin, "Charter School Gravy Train Runs Express to Fat City," *Forbes*, September 10, 2013, http://www.forbes.com/sites/greatspeculations/2013/09/10/charter-school-gravy-train-runs-express-to-fat-city.

29. All of these cities have more than 35 percent of their school-age children enrolled in charter schools. *A Growing Movement: America's Largest Charter School Communities* (Washington, DC: National Alliance for Public Charter Schools, 2013), http://www.publiccharters.org/wp-content/uploads/2014/01/2013-Market-Share-Report-Report_20131210T133315.pdf.

30. Kenneth Lovett, "Cuomo Will Push New Teacher Evaluations, Vows to Bust School 'Monopoly' if Re-elected," *New York Daily News*, October 27, 2014.

31. Valerie Straus, "Texas GOP Rejects 'Critical Thinking' Skills. Really," *Washington Post*, July 9, 2012.

32. Denise Jewell Gee, "Cuomo: State Needs 'Bona Fide' System for Evaluating Teachers," *Buffalo News*, February 3, 2015, http://www.buffalonews.com/city-region/cuomo-state-needs-bona-fide-system-for-evaluating-teachers-20150203. At one level, using reading, writing, and math achievement scores to assess student outcomes is an obvious choice. No one would dispute that teaching reading, writing, and math is one of the major purposes of schooling. But to use reading, writing, and math skills as the sole measure of teacher and school effectiveness depends on several assumptions. First, we must assume that the primary determinants of students' reading, math, and writing skills are the effectiveness of their teachers and the quality of their school. Second, we must assume that we can measure reading, writing, and math achievement in a highly reliable and valid way (i.e., that a score on a single test can unambiguously and reliably reflect all aspects of "reading ability," for example). Third, either the single purpose of schools is to inculcate skills in reading, math, and writing, in which case tests of these skills provide a direct and complete measure of educational "outcomes," or student achievement in reading, writing, and math is so highly correlated with all other school objectives that measuring basic academic skills serves as a useful surrogate for overall learning. If (but only if) all of these assumptions are valid, then we might measure the effectiveness of a particular teacher or of a particular school by determining the gains in their students' scores on standardized tests over the period the students are with that teacher or in that school. In reality, none of them are valid assumptions.

33. Raj Chetty, John N. Friedman, and Jonah E. Rockoff, *The Long-Term Impacts of Teachers: Teacher Value-Added and Student Outcomes in Adulthood*, NBER Working Paper 17699 (Washington, DC: National Bureau of Economic Research, 2011), http://www.nber.org/papers/w17699.pdf. For critiques of the Chetty, Friedman, and Rockoff study, see Moshe Adler, "Review of Measuring the Impacts of Teachers," *Education Policy Analysis Archives* 21, no. 10 (2013): 1, http://epaa.asu.edu/ojs/article/view/1264/1033; Bruce D. Baker, "Fire First, Ask Questions Later?

Comments on Recent Teacher Effectiveness Studies," *School Finance 101*, January 7, 2012, http://
schoolfinance101.wordpress.com/2012/01/07/fire-first-ask-questions-later-comments-on-recent-
teacher-effectiveness-studies; Diane Ravitch, "Columbia Scholar Says Chetty, Friedman, and
Rockoff Are Wrong about VAM," *Diane Ravitch's Blog*, July 28, 2014, http://dianeravitch.
net/2014/07/28/columbia-economist-chetty-et-al-are-wrong-about-vam. See also Raj Chetty, John
Friedman, and Jonah Rockoff, "Response to Adler (2014) Review of 'Measuring the Impacts of
Teachers,'" Harvard University, 2014, http://obs.rc.fas.harvard.edu/chetty/Adler_response.pdf.
The Freidman quote is from Annie Lowrey, "Big Study Links Good Teachers to Lasting Gain,"
New York Times, January 6, 2012.

    34.　Linda Darling-Hammond et al., *Getting Teacher Evaluation Right: A Brief for Policy Mak-
ers* (Washington, DC: American Education Research Association and National Academy of
Education, 2011), http://www.aera.net/Portals/38/docs/News_Media/AERABriefings/Hill%20
Brief%20-%20Teacher%20Eval%202011/GettingTeacherEvaluationRightBackgroundPaper(1).
pdf.

    35.　*Letter Report to the U.S. Department of Education on the Race to the Top Fund Teach-
ers* (Washington, DC: National Academies, 2009), http://www.nap.edu/nap-cgi/skimchap.
cgi?recid=12780&chap=1-14; Henri I. Braun, *Using Student Progress to Evaluate Teachers: A Primer
on Value-Added Models* (Princeton, NJ: Educational Testing Service, 2005), http://www.ets.org/
Media/Research/pdf/PICVAM.pdf. Other critiques of the VAM approach include *The Promise
and Peril of Using Value-Added Modeling to Measure Teacher Effectiveness* (Santa Monica: Rand Corporation, 2004), http://www.rand.org/content/dam/rand/pubs/research_briefs/RB9050/RAND_
RB9050.pdf; Richard Rothstein et al., *Problems with the Use of Student Test Scores to Evaluate
Teachers*, Briefing Paper 278 (Washington, DC: Economic Policy Institute, 2010), http://www.
epi.org/publication/bp278; ASA Statement on Using Value-Added Models for Educational Assessment (Alexandria, VA: American Statistical Association, 2014), http://www.amstat.org/pol-
icy/pdfs/ASA_VAM_Statement.pdf.

    36.　Diane Ravitch, "Breaking News: American Statistical Association Issues Caution on Use
of VAM," *Diane Ravitch's Blog*, April 12, 2014, http://dianeravitch.net/2014/04/12/breaking-news-
american-statistical-association-issues-caution-on-use-of-vam. For an example of uncritical
media acceptance, see Jason Felch, Jason Song, and Doug Smith, "Who's Teaching L.A.'s kids?"
Los Angeles Times, August 14, 2010.

    37.　This is a prime example of what has been called Campbell's Law: "The more any quan-
titative social indicator is used for social decision-making, the more subject it will be to corruption pressures and the more apt it will be to distort and corrupt the social processes it is intended
to measure." Donald T. Campbell, "Assessing the Impact of Planned Social Change," *Evaluation
and Program Planning* 2, no.1 (1976): 67.

    For a critique of the use of student test scores to evaluate teachers, see Ravitch, *Reign of Error*,
107–108. Ravitch, in addition to noting that the average test scores an individual teacher's students
get are unstable from year to year and that teacher ratings based on test scores have huge margins
of error, points out that students are rarely, if ever, tested for their abilities in arts, music, historical
knowledge, and physical education. How, then, are the teachers of these subjects to be assessed?

    38.　"Melinda Gates on the Importance of Evaluations in Shaping Effective Teachers," *PBS
News Hour*, June 24, 2012, http://www.pbs.org/newshour/bb/education-jan-june12-m(elindagates_
06-04/; Eric A. Hanushek, "How Well Do We Understand Achievement Gaps?," *Focus* 27, no. 2
(2010): 5, http://www.irp.wisc.edu/publications/focus/pdfs/foc272c.pdf; Eric A. Hanushek et al.,
The Market for Teacher Quality, Working Paper 11154 (Cambridge, MA: National Bureau of Economic Research, 2005), http://www.nber.org/papers/w11154.pdf.

    39.　On the role of the teacher and the school in determining student achievement, see Bar-
bara Nye, Spyros Konstantopoulos, and Larry V. Hedges, "How Large Are Teacher Effects?,"
Educational Evaluation and Policy Analysis 26, no. 3 (2004): 237, http://dx.doi.org/10.3102/

01623737026003237. See also Meredith Phillips et al., "Family Background, Parenting Practices, and the Black–White Test Score Gap," in *The Black-White Test Score Gap*, ed. Christopher Jencks and Meredith Phillips (Washington, DC: Brookings Institution Press, 1998), 143–145.

40. "Beastly Numbers," *Left Business Observer* 131 (2011), http://www.leftbusinessobserver. com/BeastlyNumbers.html; Max Fisher, "How 35 Countries Compare on Child Poverty (the U.S. Is Ranked 34th)," *Washington Post*, April 15, 2013; *Results from TALIS 2013, United States of America*, Country Note (OECD, 2013), http://www.oecd.org/unitedstates/TALIS-2013-country-note-US.pdf.

41. *Trends in Academic Progress, 2012*; Sean F. Reardon, "The Widening Academic Achievement Gap between the Rich and the Poor: New Evidence and Possible Explanations," in *Whither Opportunity: Rising Inequality, Schools, and Children's Life Chances*, ed. Greg J. Duncan & Richard J. Murnane (New York: Russell Sage Foundation, 2011), 91–116.

42. Kendra Bischoff and Sean F. Reardon, "Residential Segregation by Income, 1970–2009," in *The Lost Decade? Social Change in the U.S. after 2000*, ed. John R. Logan (New York: Russell Sage Foundation, 2013), 208–234; Richard Fry and Paul Taylor, "The Rise of Residential Segregation by Income," Pew Research Center, August 1, 2012, http://www.pewsocialtrends. org/2012/08/01/the-rise-of-residential-segregation-by-income/2012. See also Richard Rothstein, "For Public Schools, Segregation Then, Segregation Now," Economic Policy Institute, August 27, 2013, http://www.epi.org/publication/unfinished-march-public-school-segregation; Richard Rothstein, "Modern Segregation," Economic Policy Institute, March 6, 2014, http://www.epi. org/publication/modern-segregation; Richard Rothstein, "If the Supreme Court Bans the Disparate Impact Standard, It Could Annihilate One of the Few Tools Available to Pursue Housing Integration," Economic Policy Institute, January 9, 2015, http://www.epi.org/publication/ if-the-supreme-court-bans-the-disparate-impact-standard-it-could-annihilate-one-of-the-few-tools-available-to-pursue-housing-integration; Richard Rothstein, "The Making of Ferguson: Public Policies at the Root of Its Troubles," Economic Policy Institute, October 15, 2014, 2014, http://www.epi.org/publication/making-ferguson.

43. Jeff Bryant, "We Must Still Hate Our Kids: Philadelphia and 'Education Reformers' Fight Demented War on Elementary Schools," *Salon*, November 1, 2014, http://www.salon. com/2014/11/01/we_must_still_hate_our_kids_philadelphia_and_education_reformers_fight_ demented_war_on_elementary_schools.

44. Sarah Almy and Christina Theokas, *Not Prepared for Class: High-Poverty Schools Continue to Have Fewer In-Field Teachers* (Washington, DC: Education Trust, 2010), http://eric. ed.gov/?id=ED543217; Kacey Guin, "Chronic Teacher Turnover in Urban Elementary Schools," *Education Policy Analysis Archives* 12, no. 42 (2004): 1, http://files.eric.ed.gov/fulltext/EJ853508.pdf.

45. Michael Leachman and Chris Mai, *Most States Funding Schools Less than before the Recession* (Washington, DC: Center on Budget and Policy Priorities, 2014), http://www.cbpp.org/ cms/?fa=view&id=4011#_ftn1.

46. Bruce D. Baker, David G. Sciarra, and Danielle Farrie, Is School Funding Fair? A National Report Card (Newark, NJ: Education Law Center, Rutgers University, 2014), http://www. schoolfundingfairness.org/National_Report_Card_2014.pdf; Bruce D. Baker, David G. Sciarra, and Danielle Farrie, *Is Funding Fair: A National Report Card* (Newark, NJ: Education Law Center, Rutgers University, 2012), http://www.schoolfundingfairness.org/National_Report_Card_2012. pdf; *Record Setting Inequality: New York's Opportunity Gap Is Wider Than Ever* (Albany, NY: Alliance for Quality Education, 2015), http://www.aqeny.org/wp-content/uploads/2015/01/final-final-record-setting-inequality.pdf; Mitchell Cole and Michael Cassidy, *Unsettling Divide: Education Cuts Hit High-Poverty School Divisions Hardest* (Richmond, VA: Commonwealth Institute for Fiscal Analysis, 2014), http://www.thecommonwealthinstitute.org/2014/12/12/unsettling-divide; Ruth Heuer and Stephanie Stullich, *Comparability of State and Local Expenditures among Schools*

within Districts: A Report from the Study of School-Level Expenditures (Washington, DC: U.S. Department of Education, Office of Planning, Evaluation and Policy Development, Policy and Program Studies Service, 2011), http://www2.ed.gov/rschstat/eval/title-i/school-level-expenditures/school-level-expenditures.pdf.

47. The results of two national surveys of the number of tenured teachers dismissed by public school districts for poor performance, conducted four years apart by the U.S. Department of Education's National Center for Education Statistics, produced estimates of 0.1 percent per year and 1.4 percent per year. *Characteristics of Public School Districts in the United States: Results from the 2011–12 Schools and Staffing Survey*, Table 8 (Washington, DC: National Center for Education Statistics, 2013), http://nces.ed.gov/pubs2013/2013311.pdf; *Characteristics of Public School Districts in the United States: Results from the 2007–2008 Schools and Staffing Survey*, Table 8 (Washington, DC: National Center for Education Statistics, 2009), http://nces.ed.gov/pubs2009/2009320/tables/sass0708_2009320_d1n_08.asp. The explanation for the discrepancy is not clear. Stephen Broughman, the NCES project officer for the school surveys, wrote me that "the total percentage of teachers with tenure is changing over time—this would affect the average number of tenured teachers dismissed over time. Teacher dismissal is a relatively rare event, which means that it is probably unstable over time" (personal communication). Both of these explanations are ridiculous. The total percentage of teachers with tenure was well over 50 percent during both periods and did not change significantly over the four-year gap between the two surveys. And the higher figure, at least, of 1.4 percent, means 45,000 dismissals in a year, which is hardly a "rare" event. My efforts to get further clarification from NCES have gone unanswered. I suspect one or the other figure in the tables is simply an error.

By contrast, nationwide, disciplinary actions against physicians leading to loss or suspension of license totaled 1,905 (about 0.2 percent of physicians) in 2011. See *Summary of 2011 Board Actions* (Euless, TX: Federation of State Medical Boards, 2012), http://library.fsmb.org/pdf/2011-summary-of-board-actions.pdf. Disciplinary actions against lawyers leading to loss or suspension of license totaled 1,248 (about 0.35 percent of attorneys) in 2003. See Patricia Moore and Kevin Simmons, "Are Women More Ethical Lawyers? An Empirical Study," *Florida State University Law Review* 31 (2004): 785, Table 1, http://papers.ssrn.com/sol3/papers.cfm?abstract_id=1285883. On comparison to corporations with more than one thousand employees, the closest counterpart to large public school systems, see Dana Goldstein, *The Teacher Wars: A History of America's Most Embattled Profession* (New York: Doubleday Publishing, 2014).

One former assistant principal at a New York City high school told me, "I could and did get rid of incompetent teachers, including teachers with tenure. You observe them, write them up, work with them, repeat it several times, and if they are incompetent, you can let them go. You just have to be willing to put in the work." Julie Fraad, personal communication.

48. Tenure reform has already happened, for example, in New York City, with the participation of the teachers' union. Susanna Loeb, Luke C. Miller, and James Wyckoff, *Working Paper: Performance Screens for School Improvement: The Case of Teacher Tenure Reform in New York City* (Charlottesville, VA: EdPolicyWorks, 2014), https://cepa.stanford.edu/sites/default/files/31_Teacher_Tenure_Reform_in_NYC.pdf.

49. Summary of Robert M. Carini, "Teacher Unions and Student Achievement," in *School Reform Proposals: The Research Evidence*, ed. Alex Molnar (Charlotte, NC: Information Age Publishing, 2002), 197–213.

50. Bill Gates, "How Teacher Development Could Revolutionize Our Schools," *Washington Post*, February 28, 2011; Duncan quoted in Valerie Straus, "Are American Students Grossly Unprepared for College?," *Washington Post*, March 17, 2014. Remediation figures are from "First-Year Undergraduate Remedial Course Taking: 1999–2000, 2003–04, 2007–08," *Statistics in Brief* (National Center for Education Statistics), January 2013, http://nces.ed.gov/

pubs2013/2013013.pdf; "Digest of Education Statistics," Table 311.40, National Center for Education Statistics, 2013, http://nces.ed.gov/programs/digest/d13/tables/dt13_311.40.asp. CREDO quote in *Charter Schools Make Gains, According to 26-State Study* (Stanford: Center for Research on Education Outcomes, Stanford University, 2013), https://credo.stanford.edu/documents/UNEM BARGOED%20National%20Charter%20Study%20Press%20Release.pdf. CREDO also included a statistically bizarre note equating every 0.1 standard deviation difference to a week of schooling, with no justification provided.

51. Nanci Griffith, *Spin on a Red Brick Floor* (1984), YouTube, https://www.youtube.com/watch?v=2JQxZ4IzaOQ.

52. Haley Sweetland Edwards, "The War on Teacher Tenure," *Time*, November 3, 2014, http://time.com/3533556/the-war-on-teacher-tenure.

53. Anthony York, "List Unmasks Secret Donors to California Initiative Campaigns," *Los Angeles Times*, October 24, 2014; Daniel Denvir, "Secret Corbett Poll Proposing Teachers Union Attack Funded by PennCAN," *Philadelphia CityPaper*, June 19, 2013, http://citypaper.net/Blogs/Secret-Corbett-poll-proposing-teachers-union-attack-funded-by-PennCAN; Susan Jones, "Bill Gates: Raising Minimum Wage 'Does Cause Job Destruction,'" CBS News, January 21, 2014, http://cnsnews.com/news/article/susan-jones/bill-gates-raising-minimum-wage-does-cause-job-destruction; Jeff Reifman, "Where Are Washington's K–12 Dollars? Just Ask Microsoft Shareholders," *Crosscut*, August 22, 2014, http://crosscut.com/2014/08/where-money-k-12-washington-just-ask-microsoft; *Record Setting Inequality: New York State's Opportunity Gap Is Wider Than Ever* (Albany, NY: Alliance for Quality Education, 2015), http://www.aqeny.org/wp-content/uploads/2015/01/final-final-record-setting-inequality.pdf.

54. Gordon Lafer, interview by Jennifer Berkshire, *EduShyster*, November 28, 2014, http://edushyster.com/?tag=gordon-lafer.

55. Lower-income people have fewer resources and opportunities than those of relatively high income. Unsurprisingly, those with more resources tend to believe that external, uncontrollable social forces and others' power have less influence over their lives than do their own personal characteristics. See, for example, Margie E. Lachman and Suzanne L. Weaver, "The Sense of Control as a Moderator of Social Class Differences in Health and Well-Being," *Journal of Personality and Social Psychology* 74, no. 3 (1998): 763, http://dx.doi.org/10.1037/0022-3514.74.3.763.

56. Steven Brill, *Class Warfare: Inside the Fight to Fix America's Schools* (New York: Simon and Schuster, 2011), 303.

57. Jeffrey Aaron Snyder, "Teaching Kids 'Grit' Is All The Rage. Here's What's Wrong with It," *New Republic*, May 6, 2014, http://www.newrepublic.com/article/117615/problem-grit-kipp-and-character-based-education. The "character-based" model of learning of the "no-excuse" model is described in Paul Tough, *How Children Succeed: Grit, Curiosity and the Hidden Power of Character* (New York: Random House, 2012). See also Gary Rubinstein, "The Time KIPP Was Booed Off the Stage," *Gary Rubinstein's Blog*, June 20, 2014, https://garyrubinstein.wordpress.com/2014/06/20/the-time-kipp-was-booed-off-the-stage-at-tfa/; P. L. Thomas, "'No Excuses' and the Culture of Shame: Why Metrics Don't Matter," *Daily Kos*, August 30, 2012, http://www.dailykos.com/story/2012/08/30/1125810/—No-Excuses-and-the-Culture-of-Shame-Why-Metrics-Don-t-Matter#; J. Gonzalez, "Success Academy School Chain Comes under Fire as Parents Fight 'Zero Tolerance' Disciplinary Policy," *New York Daily News*, August 28, 2013; Richard Rothstein, "Grading the Education Reformers," *Slate*, August 29, 2011, http://www.slate.com/articles/arts/books/2011/08/grading_the_education_reformers.html.

58. This is not a matter of deliberate hypocrisy. Those with a direct self-interest in an outcome often vigorously deny that they are biased, and with respect to conscious biases there is no reason to disbelieve them. But decades of research have shown that both financial and psychological preferences for outcome unconsciously affect decision-making and judgment.

59. "Digest of Education Statistics," Table 106.10, National Center of Education Statistics, 2013, https://nces.ed.gov/programs/digest/d13/tables/dt13_106.10.asp?current=yes

60. Stephanie Simon, "Privatizing Public Schools: Big Firms Eyeing Profits From U.S. K–12 Market," *Huffington Post*, October 27, 2014, http://www.huffingtonpost.com/2012/08/02/private-firms-eyeing-prof_n_1732856.html; Alan Singer, "Why Hedge Funds Love Charter Schools," *Huffington Post*, May 20, 2014, http://www.huffingtonpost.com/alan-singer/why-hedge-funds-love-char_b_5357486.html; Kristin Rawls, "Who Is Profiting from Charters? The Big Bucks behind Charter School Secrecy, Financial Scandal and Corruption," AlterNet, May 8, 2013, http://www.alternet.org/education/who-profiting-charters-big-bucks-behind-charter-school-secrecy-financial-scandal-and?page=0%2C5; Duncan Foley, personal communication.

61. Among many other accounts, see Jennifer Job, "The Pearson Monopoly," *newteacher*, April 12, 2013, http://teacherblog.typepad.com/newteacher/2012/11/on-the-rise-of-pearson-oh-and-following-the-money.html; Erik Kain, "The Charter School Movement Quickly Becoming a Backdoor for Corporate Profit," *Forbes*, September 29, 2011, http://www.forbes.com/sites/erikkain/2011/09/29/80-of-michigan-charter-schools-are-for-profits; David Sirota, "The Big Money and Profits behind the Push for Charter Schools," *Pando Daily*, June 19, 2014, http://pando.com/2014/06/19/the-big-money-and-profits-behind-the-push-for-charter-schools; Travis Andrews, "Inside News Corp's $540 Million Bet on American Classrooms," *Mashable*, August 29, 2013, http://mashable.com/2013/08/29/news-corp-education-tablets; Vivek Mural, "A Closer Look at K12 Edtech Venture Funding in 2013," *New Schools Venture Fund*, December 18, 2013, http://www.newschools.org/blog/closer-look-2013; *Opportunities for Innovations that Support our Nation's Education Investment* (Redmond, WA: Microsoft, 2010), http://download.microsoft.com/download/4/1/8/4182DF40-7EA3-4C13-91D0-E3B75D639590/opportunitiesforinnovation_ebook.pdf; "Reimagine Teaching: Technology in the Classroom," Pearson, n.d., http://www.pearsonschool.com/.

62. Layton, "How Bill Gates Pulled off the Swift Common Core Revolution"; Michelle Malkin, "Common Core and the EduTech Abyss," *TownHall.com*, January 8, 2014, http://townhall.com/columnists/michellemalkin/2014/01/08/common-core-and-the-edutech-abyss-n1773298/page/full; David Folkenflik, "News Corp. Education Tablet: For The Love Of Learning?" *NPR*, March 8, 2013, http://www.npr.org/2013/03/08/173766828/news-corp-education-tablet-for-the-love-of-learning; Bill Gates, "Remarks to the National Conference of State Legislatures, Seattle, Wash., July 21, 2009," http://www.gatesfoundation.org/media-center/speeches/2009/07/bill-gates-national-conference-of-state-legislatures-ncsl; Bill Gates, interview by Arthur C. Brooks, American Enterprise Institute, March 13, 2014, http://www.aei.org/files/2014/03/14/-bill-gates-event-transcript_082217994272.pdf; Michael Q. McShane, "Bill Gates at AEI on the Common Core," *AEIdeas* (American Enterprise Institute), March 14, 2014, http://www.aei.org/publication/bill-gates-at-aei-on-the-common-core.

The rise of an education-industrial complex is even more evident at the post-secondary level. Recent decades have seen, for instance, the rapid rise of proprietary (for-profit) post-secondary institutions, guaranteed federal loans to students, government research funds leading to the development of commercially valuable products (such as drugs) on which the university holds the patent, massive involvement in the college sports business, large-scale real estate investment by universities, and massive university endowments.

63. In 2014 a Gallup poll reported that only 26 percent of Americans had "a great deal" or "quite a lot" of confidence in our public schools, down from 37–40 percent between 1991 and 2011, and down from 53–62 percent in the 1970s. "Confidence in Institutions," Gallup Poll, June 5–8, 2014, http://www.gallup.com/poll/1597/confidence-institutions.aspx. At the same time, polls show continued support for more funding for public schools and high ratings by parents of their own children's school and teachers. See, for example, " 'Dems for Public

Ed' Releases Poll Showing Overwhelming Support for Public Schools," Democrats for Public Education, October 2, 2014, http://www.democratsforpubliceducation.com/feature-news/dems-public-ed-releases-poll-showing-overwhelming-support-public-schools.

64. See Rebecca Klein, "GOP Lawmaker: 'Public Education in America Is Socialism,'" *Huffington Post*, October 27, 2014, http://www.huffingtonpost.com/2014/03/14/andrew-brenner-education-socialism_n_4961201.html; Nick Baumann, "Tea Party Frontrunner: Abolish Public Schools," *Mother Jones*, October 13, 2010, http://www.motherjones.com/politics/2010/10/david-harmer-abolish-public-schools.

65. The breach with the labor movement, historically the backbone of more progressive Democratic Party policies, was especially poignant. "Over the years, New Democrats frequently have clashed with organized labor. We've strenuously opposed labor's retrograde agenda for trade protection as well as its attempts to thwart long-overdue reforms in America's underperforming public-sector systems, from welfare to job training to schools. . . . New Democrats also have clashed with labor on the broader question of how Democrats can become America's majority party. . . . Our differences are serious. But we have never believed that conflict between New Democrats and organized labor is immutable or irreconcilable." "Why America Needs a New Labor," *New Democrat*, March 1, 1998, http://www.dlc.org/ndol_ci4e05.html?kaid=107&subid=297&contentid=16030.

66. School doesn't have to be tedious or humiliating. There is a long history of alternative approaches to education, from Jean-Jacques Rousseau to nineteenth-century and early-twentieth-century school reformers such as Johann Pestalozzi, John Dewey, and Maria Montessori to mid-twentieth-century educational radicals such as Paulo Freire, Paul Goodman, and Summerhill's Alexander Neill. These approaches aimed at nurturing children as well as preparing them to meet the demands of adult society and at offering the excitement that a good school can provide to all children regardless of their social origins.

67. For a discussion of the clash of culture between school and children from poor, black communities, see Norman Fruchter, *Urban Schools, Public Will* (New York: Teachers College Press, 2007), 24–45.

68. Jason DeParle, "Harder for Americans to Rise from Lower Rungs," *New York Times*, January 4, 2012.

69. It is true that most people remain more or less in the socioeconomic stratum they were born in. But nothing guarantees that the children of doctors and managers, for instance, will themselves hold professional or managerial positions as adults. The children of the upper middle class are certainly advantaged in their quest to reproduce their parents' class position. Nevertheless, for an individual to remain in the upper middle class, he or she must go to college, get a job, get promotions, etc.

70. Barbara Ehrenreich, *Fear of Falling: The Inner Life of the Middle Class* (New York: Pantheon, 1989).

71. Richard Hofstadter, *Anti-Intellectualism in American Life* (1963; repr., New York: Knopf Doubleday, 2012).

4. Race and Poverty

1. The "poverty threshold" concept was originally devised by Mollie Orshansky, an economist working for the Social Security Administration, in 1963. She started with an estimate of the cost of an "economy food plan" designed by the Department of Agriculture for "emergency use when funds are low." Data from 1955 showed that families of three or more spent one-third of their income on food, so the economy food budget was simply multiplied by three to calculate the poverty line. Since then, the Census Bureau has recalculated the original figures to account for inflation. This approach has been widely criticized for what some see as overestimating and others

see as underestimating "true" rates of poverty. Among other things, since 1955 the proportion of family budgets devoted to food has fallen from one-third to one-fifth. Transfer payments, such as the federal Earned Income Tax Credit and SNAP/food stamps and families' tax liabilities are not taken into account. The poverty thresholds also do not take geographic variations in cost of living into account. They fail to account for the "underground" or informal economy consisting of income, legal or illegal, that falls outside the country's regulations regarding commerce. And the calculations of the number of people below the poverty line excludes people who are in prison, most of whom tended to be poor prior to their incarceration. See Gordon M. Fisher, "The Development and History of the Poverty Thresholds," *Social Security Bulletin* 55, no. 4 (1992): 43, http://www.ssa.gov/history/fisheronpoverty.html; *Measuring Poverty* (New York: National Center for Children and Poverty, 2014), http://www.nccp.org/topics/measuringpoverty.html; *How Is Poverty Measured in the United States?* (Madison, WI: Institute for Research on Poverty, 2014), http://www.irp.wisc.edu/faqs/faq2.htm.

2. Signe-Mary McKernan, Caroline Ratcliffe, and Stephanie R. Cellini, *Transitioning In and Out of Poverty* (Washington, DC: Urban Institute, 2009), http://www.urban.org/uploaded pdf/411956_transitioningpoverty.pdf.

3. Another three million or so immigrants from Europe have entered the United States over the last three decades. While they experience many of the same problems as other immigrants, issues associated with skin color are, for the most part, of lesser concern.

4. See, for example, Matthew Frye Jacobson, *Whiteness of a Different Color* (Cambridge, MA: Harvard University Press, 1999); Karen Brodkin, *How Jews Became White Folks and What That Says about Race in America* (New Brunswick, NJ: Rutgers University Press, 1998).

5. Taken as a whole, the income, rate of poverty, wealth, educational attainment, and rates of incarceration of Latinos, the largest non-black minority group, are between those of whites and blacks but closer to the latter. Latinos' health status, by aggregate measures such as life expectancy, at least, is better than that of non-Latino whites. But all of these figures conflate the experiences of recent immigrants and the U.S.-born descendants of past generations of immigrants, as well as the experiences of Latinos of very different national origins. It is impossible to generalize across varied national origins, class and educational status prior to immigration, immigration histories, legal status as immigrants, English-language facility, and the like. For example, Indian, Chinese, Cambodian, Vietnamese, Korean, and other Asian immigrants have had very different experiences in the United States. Similarly, although two-thirds of the Latino population trace their heritage to Mexico, the experience of recent immigrants, documented or undocumented, differs from that of Mexican Americans who are second or third generation (or more) and from that of Puerto Rican, Dominican, Cuban, Guatemalan, and Colombian immigrants. Even among blacks, there are a variety of differences in self-perception and personal experience between North American–born descendants of slaves and others of African descent whose recent ancestors or own personal history go back to the Caribbean, to Central and South America, or to Africa itself. And while the black middle class that has emerged since the 1960s may have escaped the deficits in education, health, and other social statuses of poorer blacks, it does share in the ongoing experience of discrimination and bigotry and was disproportionately devastated by the 2008 recession and its aftermath.

6. The one group of Americans whose history bears a closer resemblance to that of blacks is American Indians. They too were forcibly uprooted from their homelands, and they too have experienced systematic discrimination and subordination over hundreds of years, and systematic, structural discrimination continues, at least for those living on reservations and trying to maintain their identity and resist assimilation.

7. "People in Poverty by Selected Characteristics: 2012 and 2013," U.S. Census Bureau, http://www.census.gov/hhes/www/poverty/data/incpovhlth/2013/table3.pdf.

8. Lyndon B. Johnson, "To Fulfill These Rights," commencement address at Howard University, June 4, 1965, http://www.lbjlib.utexas.edu/johnson/archives.hom/speeches.hom/650604.asp

9. Martin Luther King, Jr., "I Have a Dream" speech, delivered August 28, 1963, Washington, D.C.

10. Lyndon Baines Johnson, "State of the Union," Washington, D.C., January 8, 1964, http://www.lbjlib.utexas.edu/johnson/archives.hom/speeches.hom/640108.asp; Lyndon Baines Johnson, "Radio and Television Remarks upon Signing the Civil Rights Bill," Washington, DC, July 2, 1964, http://www.lbjlib.utexas.edu/johnson/archives.hom/speeches.hom/640702.asp; Lyndon Baines Johnson, "Speech before Congress on Voting Rights," Washington, DC, March 15, 1965, http://millercenter.org/president/speeches/speech-3386; Economic Opportunity Act of 1964, Public Law 88-452, 78 Stat. 508 (August 20, 1964), Preamble, http://www.gpo.gov/fdsys/pkg/STATUTE-78/pdf/STATUTE-78-Pg508.pdf.

11. See, among others, Alan Aja, Daniel Bustillo, William Darity, and Darrick Hamilton, "From a Tangle of Pathology to a Race-Fair America," *Dissent*, Summer 2014, http://www.dissentmagazine.org/article/from-a-tangle-of-pathology-to-a-race-fair-america; *One Nation, Underemployed: Jobs Rebuild America: 2014 State of Black America* (Washington, DC: National Urban League, 2014), http://iamempowered.com/sites/all/themes/newiae/SOBA/SOBA2014_HTML5/SOBA2014-SinglePgs/index.html; Erik W. Robelen, "Blacks, Latinos See Long Term Progress," *Education Week*, July 10, 2013, http://www.edweek.org/ew/articles/2013/07/10/36naep-2.h32.html; Charles M. Blow, "Inequality in the Air We Breathe?" *New York Times*, January 21, 2015; James Hamblin, "Medicine's Unrelenting Race Gap," *Atlantic*, December 10, 2014, http://www.theatlantic.com/health/archive/2014/12/the-race-problem-in-medicine-race/383613.

12. Polls show, for instance, that there have been rapid declines over the last two decades in the number of whites who think people should be free to refuse to sell their house to blacks or would oppose a family member marrying a black person or believe that whites are more hardworking than blacks. Even blacks are less likely to report that racism is a big problem than was the case in the mid-1990s. *Washington Post–ABC News Poll*, January 13–16, 2009, http://www.washingtonpost.com/wp-srv/politics/documents/postpoll011709.html; Christopher Ingraham, "Chris Rock Is Right: White Americans Are a Lot Less Racist than They Used to Be," *Washington Post*, December 1, 2014.

13. See *Race, Power and Policy: Dismantling Structural Racism* (Grassroots Policy Project, n.d.), http://www.strategicpractice.org/system/files/race_power_policy_workbook.pdf.

14. *Lung Cancer Rates by Race and Ethnicity* (Atlanta: Centers for Disease Control, 2014), http://www.cdc.gov/cancer/lung/statistics/race.htm; *The Racial Wealth Gap* (New York: Institute on Assets and Social Policy and Demos, 2015), http://www.demos.org/sites/default/files/publications/RacialWealthGap_1.pdf; Justin Wolfers, David Leonhardt and Kevin Quealy, "1.5 Million Missing Black Men," *New York Times*, April 20, 2015.

15. Richard Rothstein, "Brown v. Board at 60: Why Have We Been So Disappointed? What Have We Learned?" *Economic Policy Institute*, April 17, 2014, http://www.epi.org/publication/brown-at-60-why-have-we-been-so-disappointed-what-have-we-learned; John R. Logan and Brian J. Stults, "The Persistence of Segregation in the Metropolis: New Findings from the 2010 Census," US 2010 Project, March 24, 2011, http://www.s4.brown.edu/us2010/Data/Report/report2.pdf; Genevieve Siegel-Hawley and Erica Frankenberg, *Southern Slippage: Growing School Segregation in the Most Desegregated Region of the Country* (Los Angeles: Civil Rights Project, 2012), Table 5, http://civilrightsproject.ucla.edu/research/k-12-education/integration-and-diversity/mlk-national/southern-slippage-growing-school-segregation-in-the-most-desegregated-region-of-the-country/hawley-MLK-South-2012.pdf.

16. Richard Rothstein, "The Making of Ferguson: Public Policies at the Root of its Troubles" Economic Policy Institute, October 15, 2014, http://www.epi.org/publication/making-ferguson.

17. Richard Rothstein, "If the Supreme Court Bans the Disparate Impact Standard it Could Annihilate One of the Few Tools Available to Pursue Housing Integration," Economic Policy Institute, January 9, 2015, http://www.epi.org/publication/if-the-supreme-court-bans-the-disparate-impact-standard-it-could-annihilate-one-of-the-few-tools-available-to-pursue-housing-integration; Kendra Bischoff and Sean F. Reardon, "Residential Segregation by Income, 1970–2009," in *The Lost Decade? Social Change in the U.S. after 2000*, ed. John R. Logan (New York: Russell Sage Foundation, 2013); Richard Fry and Paul Taylor, "The Rise of Residential Segregation by Income," Pew Research Center, http://www.pewsocialtrends.org/2012/08/01/the-rise-of-residential-segregation-by-income/2012.

18. Jeff Larson and Nikole Hannah-Jones, "Housing Segregation: The Great Migration and Beyond," *ProPublica*, December 20, 2012, http://www.propublica.org/article/living-apart-how-the-government-betrayed-a-landmark-civil-rights-law. A few months before writing this chapter, my own small Connecticut town voted down a proposal for moderate-income senior housing. Many of the letters to the local newspaper suggested a fear of the "kind of people" who might move in, almost certainly code words for black or poor.

19. Arloc Sherman, *Safety Net Effective at Fighting Poverty but Has Weakened for the Very Poorest* (Washington, DC: Center on Budget and Policy Priorities, 2009), http://www.cbpp.org/files/7-6-09pov.pdf; Colin Gordon, "A Tattered Safety Net: Social Policy and American Inequality," *Dissent*, April 3, 2014, http://www.dissentmagazine.org/online_articles/a-tattered-safety-net-social-policy-and-american-inequality; *Homeless Families with Children*, NCH Fact Sheet 12 (Washington, DC: National Coalition for the Homeless, 2007), http://www.nationalhomeless.org/publications/facts/families.html. The Earned Income Tax Credit was conceived under President Nixon but enacted after his resignation, under President Ford.

20. *The Poverty and Inequality Report, 2014* (Stanford: Stanford Center on Poverty and Inequality, 2014), http://web.stanford.edu/group/scspi/sotu/SOTU_2014_CPI.pdf; Alisha Coleman-Jensen, Christian Gregory, and Anita Singh, "Household Food Security in the United States in 2013," Economic Research Report 173 (Washington, DC: U.S. Department of Agriculture, Economic Research Service, 2014), http://www.ers.usda.gov/media/1565415/err173.pdf; *The State of Homelessness in America, 2014* (Washington, DC: National Alliance to End Homelessness, 2014), http://b.3cdn.net/naeh/d1b106237807ab260f_qam6ydz02.pdf; *Understanding Sub-Standard Housing* (Minneapolis: Thrivent Builds with Habitat for Humanity, 2009), http://www.thriventbuilds.com/homes/issue/simple.html.

21. "Historical Income Tables: Households, Table H-3, Mean Household Income Received by Each Fifth and Top 5 Percent, All Races," U.S. Census Bureau, http://www.census.gov/hhes/www/income/data/historical/household/index.html; *The State of Working America* (Washington, DC: Economic Policy Institute, 2012), http://stateofworkingamerica.org/subjects/overview/?reader.

22. Thomas Piketty and Emmanuel Saez, "Income Inequality in the United States, 1913–1998," *Quarterly Journal of Economics* 128, no. 1 (2003): 1, http://eml.berkeley.edu/~saez/pikettyqje.pdf (tables and figures updated in 2013: http://eml.berkeley.edu/~saez/TabFig2013prel.xls); Josh Bivens, "The U.S. Middle Class Has Faced a Huge 'Inequality Tax' in Recent Decades," Economic Policy Institute, December 11, 2014, http://www.epi.org/publication/the-u-s-middle-class-has-faced-a-huge-inequality-tax-in-recent-decades; Josh Bivens et al., "Raising America's Pay: Why It's Our Central Economic Policy Challenge," Economic Policy Institute, June 4, 2014, http://www.epi.org/publication/raising-americas-pay; Josh Bivens and Elise Gould, "Top 1 Percent Receive Record High Share of Total U.S. Income," Economics Policy Institute, September 12, 2013, http://www.epi.org/blog/top-1-percent-receive-record-high-share-2.

23. *Walmart on Tax Day: How Taxpayers Subsidize America's Biggest Employer and Richest Family* (Washington, DC: Americans for Tax Fairness, 2014), http://www.americansfortaxfairness.org/

files/Walmart-on-Tax-Day-Americans-for-Tax-Fairness-1.pdf; Stephanie Riegg Cellini, Signe-Mary McKernan, and Caroline Ratcliffe, "The Dynamics of Poverty in the United States: A Review of Data, Methods, and Findings," *Journal of Policy Analysis and Management* 27, no. 3 (2008): 557, http://www3.interscience.wiley.com/journal/119817437/issue. The prototypical Walmart worker described would also have gotten another $3,000 from the Earned Income Tax Credit, and Child Tax Credit benefits as well.

24. Economic Opportunity Act, Title II, Pt. A, Sec. 201(a)(2).

25. Sargent Shriver, "Address to the Yale Law School Association," New Haven, Connecticut, April 29, 1966, http://www.sargentshriver.org/speech-article/address-to-the-yale-law-school-association-1966. For a more detailed account, see John Ehrenreich, *The Altruistic Imagination* (Ithaca, NY: Cornell University Press, 1985), 165–185; George Adler, "Community Action and Maximum Feasible Participation: An Opportunity Lost but Not Forgotten for Expanding Democracy at Home," *Notre Dame Journal of Law, Ethics, and Public Policy* 8, no. 2 (1994): 547, http://scholarship.law.nd.edu/ndjlepp/vol8/iss2/6.

26. The OEO itself was abolished in 1974 under President Nixon. Its replacement, the Community Services Administration (CSA), represented a shift in focus from social action to the provision of social services. In 1981, under President Reagan, the CSA was abolished, and the Community Action Agencies were subsequently funded through a grant allocated to each state. Federal funding was no more.

27. David Cooper, "Given the Economy's Growth, the Federal Minimum Wage Could Be Significantly Higher," Economic Policy Institute, April 14, 2015, http://www.epi.org/publication/given-the-economys-growth-the-federal-minimum-wage-could-be-significantly-higher.

28. Arloc Sherman, *Safety Net Effective at Fighting Poverty but Has Weakened for the Very Poorest* (Washington, DC: Center on Budget and Policy Priorities, 2009), http://www.cbpp.org/files/7-6-09pov.pdf; Gordon, "A Tattered Safety Net"; *Homeless Families with Children*; Lauren E. Glaze and Danielle Kaeble, "Correctional Populations in the United States, 2013," NCJ 248479 (Washington, DC: U.S. Department of Justice, Bureau of Justice Statistics, 2014), http://www.bjs.gov/content/pub/pdf/cpus13.pdf.

29. National Research Council, *The Growth of Incarceration in the United States: Exploring Causes and Consequences* (Washington, DC: National Academies Press, 2014), http://www.nap.edu/openbook.php?record_id=18613; *Historical Corrections Statistics in the United States, 1850–1984* (Washington, DC: U.S. Bureau of Justice Statistics, 1986), http://www.bjs.gov/content/pub/pdf/hcsus5084.pdf; *Prisoners in 2010* (Washington, DC: U.S. Bureau of Justice Statistics, 2012), http://www.bjs.gov/content/pub/pdf/p10.pdf; *Jail Inmates at Midyear 2010—Statistical Tables* (Washington, DC: U.S. Bureau of Justice Statistics, 2011), http://www.bjs.gov/index.cfm?ty=pbdetail&iid=2375.

30. A. J. Beck and A. Blumstein, "Trends in Incarceration Rates: 1980–2010," paper prepared for the National Research Council Committee on the Causes and Consequences of High Rates of Incarceration, Washington, DC, cited in National Research Council, *The Growth of Incarceration in the United States: Exploring Causes and Consequences*, 53–55. Also see Marc Mauer, *Comparative International Rates of Incarceration: An Examination of Causes and Trends* (Washington, DC: Sentencing Project, 2003), http://www.sentencingproject.org/doc/publications/inc_comparative_intl.pdf.

31. *The Treatment of Persons with Mental Illness in Prisons and Jails: A State Survey* (Arlington, VA: Treatment Advocacy Center, 2014), http://www.tacreports.org/storage/documents/treatment-behind-bars/treatment-behind-bars-abridged.pdf. In the early 1980s, I served on a committee in western Massachusetts to help decide what should be done with the buildings and grounds of a large state psychiatric hospital that had been closed under the state's deinstitutionalization policy. One witness before the committee, the sheriff of the local county, complained

that the deinstitutionalized patients were living on the streets. Vagrancy and disorderly conduct arrests were way up, and jail space had become overcrowded. Perhaps part of the state hospital buildings, the former residence of many of the new "criminals," could be converted into expanded jail space, he suggested. Today, between 10 and 25 percent of prisoners suffer from severe mental illness. The Los Angeles County Jail is said to be the largest facility for the mentally ill in the United States.

32. Devah Pager, cited in Eduardo Porter, "In the U.S., Punishment Comes before the Crimes," *New York Times*, April 29, 2014; "Crime in the United States, 2009, Table 1," U.S. Department of Justice, September 2010, http://www2.fbi.gov/ucr/cius2009/data/table_01.html; Jennifer Lloyd, *Drug Use Trends* (Washington, DC: White House Office of National Drug Control Policy, 2002), http://www.policyalmanac.org/crime/archive/drug_use_trends.shtml. For a guide to research on whether or not the "broken windows" model of policing actually reduces serious crime, see *Broken Windows Policing* (Fairfax, VA: Center for Evidence-Based Crime Policy, George Mason University, 2013), http://cebcp.org/evidence-based-policing/what-works-in-policing/research-evidence-review/broken-windows-policing.

The use of the police and the criminal justice system to maintain social order is not new, not restricted to black and other minority communities, and not unique to the United States. On the origins of organized police forces, seen as a way of maintaining order in poor communities, see David Whitehouse, "Origins of the Police," *Works in Theory*, December 7, 2014, https://worxintheory.wordpress.com/2014/12/07/origins-of-the-police; Gary Potter, *The History of Policing in the United States* (Richmond, KY: Eastern Kentucky University, 2013), http://plsonline.eku.edu/insidelook/history-policing-united-states-part-1.

33. See, among others, *Banking on Bondage: Private Prisons and Mass Incarceration* (New York: American Civil Liberties Union, 2011), http://www.aclu.org/prisoners-rights/banking-bondage-private-prisons-and-mass-incarceration; Sarah Stillman, "Get Out of Jail, Inc.," *New Yorker*, June 23, 2014, 48, http://www.newyorker.com/magazine/2014/06/23/get-out-of-jail-inc; Rania Khalek, "21st-Century Slaves: How Corporations Exploit Prison Labor," Alternet, July 21, 2011, http://www.alternet.org/story/151732/21st-century_slaves%3A_how_corporations_exploit_prison_labor; Caroline Winter, "What Do Prisoners Make for Victoria's Secret," *Mother Jones*, July/August 2008, http://www.motherjones.com/politics/2008/07/what-do-prisoners-make-victorias-secret; *Justice Expenditure and Employment Extracts, 2012—Preliminary* (NCJ 248628) (Washington, D.C.: Bureau of Justice Statistics, Feb. 26, 2015), http://www.bjs.gov/index.cfm?ty=pbdetail&iid=5239.

34. Oliver Roeder, Lauren-Brooke Eisen, and Julia Bowling, *What Caused the Crime Decline?* (New York: Brennan Center for Justice, 2015), http://www.brennancenter.org/sites/default/files/analysis/Crime_rate_report_web.pdf; Inimai M. Chettiar, "The Many Causes of America's Decline in Crime," *Atlantic*, February 11, 2015, http://www.theatlantic.com/features/archive/2015/02/the-many-causes-of-americas-decline-in-crime/385364; Franklin E. Zimring, "How New York Beat Crime," *OUPBlog*, June 13, 2012, http://blog.oup.com/2012/06/zimring-scientific-american-nyc-beat-crime; Robert H. DeFina and Thomas M. Arvanites, "The Weak Effect of Imprisonment on Crime: 1971–1998," *Social Science Quarterly* 83, no. 3 (2002): 635–653, http://dx.doi.org/10.1111/1540-6237.00106. A few authors argue that imprisonment has contributed significantly to the decrease in crime. See Eric P. Baumer, "An Empirical Assessment of the Contemporary Crime Trends Puzzle: A Modest Step toward a More Comprehensive Research Agenda," in *Understanding Crime Trends*, ed. Arthur Goldberger and Richard Rosenfeld (Washington, DC: National Academies Press, 2008), 127–176; Steven D. Levitt, "Understanding Why Crime Fell in the 1990s: Four Factors that Explain the Decline and Six that Do Not," *Journal of Economic Perspectives* 18, no. 1 (2004): 163, http://pricetheory.uchicago.edu/levitt/Papers/LevittUnderstandingWhyCrime2004.pdf.

35. National Research Council, *The Growth of Incarceration in the United States*, 56–68; Bruce Western, *Punishment and Inequality in America* (New York: Russell Sage Foundation, 2006); Robin J. A. Cox, "Where Do We Go from Here? Mass Incarceration and the Struggle for Civil Rights," Economic Policy Institute, January 16, 2015, http://www.epi.org/publication/where-do-we-go-from-here-mass-incarceration-and-the-struggle-for-civil-rights.

36. Michelle Alexander, *The New Jim Crow* (New York: New Press, 2013); National Research Council, *The Growth of Incarceration in the United States: Exploring Causes and Consequences*, 64–67.

37. National Research Council, *The Growth of Incarceration in the United States*, 202–302; Robert H. DeFina and Lance Hannon, "The Impact of Mass Incarceration on Poverty," *Crime and Delinquency*, 2009, http://dx.doi.org/10.1177/0011128708328864.

38. National Research Council, *The Growth of Incarceration in the United States*, 307. Stephanie Ewert, Bryan Sykes, and Becky Pettit have argued that the government statistics also exaggerate black progress in educational achievement. See Stephanie Ewert, Bryan Sykes, and Becky Pettit, "The Degree of Disadvantage: Incarceration and Racial Inequality in Education," *Annals of the American Academy of Political and Social Science* 651, no. 1 (2014): 24, http://faculty.washington.edu/blsykes/Publications_files/asr_prison_ed_FINAL-1.pdf. See also Derek Neal and Armin Rick, *The Prison Boom and the Lack of Black Progress after Smith and Welch*, Working Paper 20283 (National Bureau of Economic Research, 2014), http://home.uchicago.edu/~/arick/prs_boom_201309.pdf; the conclusion of Ewert et al. has been disputed by Anne McDaniel et al., "The Black Gender Gap in Educational Attainment: Historical Trends and Racial Comparisons," *Demography* 48 no. 3 (2009): 889, http://www.columbia.edu/~tad61/Race%20Paper%2009232009.pdf.

39. *The Morris Justice Report: A Summary of Our Findings* (New York: Morris Justice, 2014), http://morrisjustice.org/report; *City of Milwaukee Police Satisfaction Survey* (Milwaukee: Center for Urban Initiatives and Research, University of Wisconsin–Milwaukee, 2014), http://www.city.milwaukee.gov/ImageLibrary/Groups/cityFPC/agendas4/150122_III_A.pdf. For a nuanced treatment of black community-police relations, see "Cops See It Differently: Part One," *This American Life*, February 6, 2015, http://www.thisamericanlife.org/radio-archives/episode/547/transcript; "Cops See It Differently: Part Two," *This American Life*, February 13, 2015, http://www.thisamericanlife.org/radio-archives/episode/548/transcript; *Race and Punishment: Racial Perceptions of Crime and Support for Punitive Policies* (Washington, D.C.: The Sentencing Project, 2015). http://www.sentencingproject.org/doc/publications/rd_Race_and_Punishment.pdf

40. John Sides, "White People Believe the Justice System Is Color Blind. Black People Really Don't," *Washington Post*, July 22, 2013; Frank Newport, "Fewer Blacks in U.S. See Bias in Jobs, Income, and Housing," Gallup, July 19, 2013, http://www.gallup.com/poll/163580/fewer-blacks-bias-jobs-income-housing.aspx;

41. Black Lives Matter, http://blacklivesmatter.com/about.

42. Matt Bruenig, "How Much Money Would It Take to Eliminate Poverty In America?," *American Prospect*, September 24, 2013, http://prospect.org/article/how-much-money-would-it-take-eliminate-poverty-america; Matt Bruenig and Elizabeth Stoker, "How to Cut the Poverty Rate in Half (It's Easy)," *Atlantic*, October 29, 2013, http://www.theatlantic.com/business/archive/2013/10/how-to-cut-the-poverty-rate-in-half-its-easy/280971. Impact on richest 1 percent calculated from "Current Population Survey, 2013 Household Income, Table HINC-01 Selected Characteristics of Households, by Total Money Income in 2013," U.S. Census Bureau, http://www.census.gov/hhes/www/cpstables/032014/hhinc/hinc01_000.htm; *The Distribution of Household Income and Federal Taxes, 2010* (Washington, DC: Congressional Budget Office, 2013), http://www.cbo.gov/sites/default/files/44604-AverageTaxRates.pdf.

5. The Crisis of the Liberal and Creative Professions

1. Sarah Baxter, "Romney Calls for a Tax Policy That Will Help 'Us' in the Middle Class," *CBS News*, September 21, 2011, http://www.cbsnews.com/8301-503544_162-20109658-503544. html; *Middle Class in America* (U.S. Department of Commerce, Economics and Statistics Administration, 2010), http://www.esa.doc.gov/sites/default/files/middleclassreport.pdf.

2. Conor Friedersdorf, "What Is Rick Santorum's Problem with the Term 'Middle Class'?," *Atlantic*, January 9, 2012, http://www.theatlantic.com/politics/archive/2012/01/what-is-rick-santorums-problem-with-the-term-middle-class/251061.

3. The problem, of course, is that class is not a naturally occurring, objectively existing phenomenon but rather is a category we impose on social realities, social relations, and social processes. People vary in their structural relationship to the polity, economy, and culture, and these variations have major impacts on their lives. The variations, moreover, are not just differences but reflect the fact that some people have power over others in one or another sphere. But class is not a thing. One cannot belong to a class. A class cannot reproduce itself. And classes themselves do not have interests (although the people that make them up may). As a result, depending on the context and our purpose in categorizing people, different approaches to defining "class" may be more or less useful. An index of socioeconomic status is useful in epidemiological studies, giving clues as to the etiology of the disease and providing an essential guide to the allocation of resources. Weberian notions of class, status, and power help understand how and why various more-or-less homogeneous groupings of people appear, with common lifestyles, living conditions, political beliefs, and patterns of education. Marxian ideas about class, based on people's relationship to the means of production, are useful in understanding the nature of grand historical transitions (for example, from feudalism to capitalism) and the sources of political and social conflict in capitalist societies, as well as the dynamics of capitalist development.

4. See John Ehrenreich, *The Altruistic Imagination* (Ithaca, NY: Cornell University Press, 1985), 49–51.

5. Precise figures as to the number of people in professional and managerial roles and accurate comparisons over time are hard to come by. Bureau of Labor Statistics definitions and groupings of occupations and methods of gathering data have changed several times over the years. My data here are from H. D. Anderson and P. E. Davidson, *Occupational Trends in the United States* (Stanford: Stanford University Press, 1940); *Historical Statistics of the United States, Colonial Times to 1957* (U. S. Department of Commerce, Bureau of the Census, 1960); *Statistical Abstract of the United States*, 1973, 1981, 2001, 2008 eds. (U.S. Department of Commerce, Bureau of the Census); Stanley Lebergott, "Labor Force and Employment, 1800–1960," in *Output, Employment, and Productivity in the United States after 1800*, ed. Dorothy S. Brady, Studies in Income and Wealth 30 (New York: National Bureau of Economic Research, 1966), 117, http://www.nber.org/chapters/c1567.pdf.

6. Barbara Ehrenreich and John Ehrenreich, "The Professional-Managerial Class," *Radical America* 11, no. 2 (1977): 7, http://dl.lib.brown.edu/pdfs/1125403552886481.pdf. See also Pat Walker, *Between Labor and Capital* (Boston: South End Press, 1979); Barbara Ehrenreich, *Fear of Falling: The Inner Life of the Middle Class* (New York: Pantheon, 1989). On the relationship between professionals and managers and other classes, see Harry Braverman, *Labor and Monopoly Capital: The Degradation of Work in the Twentieth Century* (New York: Monthly Review Press, 1974); John Ehrenreich, ed., *The Cultural Crisis of Modern Medicine* (New York: Monthly Review Press, 1978); Samuel Bowles and Herbert Gintis, *Schooling in Capitalist America* (New York: Basic Books, 1977); Stewart Ewen, *Captains of Consciousness: Advertising and the Social Roots of the Consumer Culture* (New York: McGraw Hill, 1976).

7. Thorstein Veblen, *The Engineers and the Price System* (New York: Viking Press, 1932); Edward A. Ross, *Sin and Society* (Boston: Houghton Mifflin, 1907), cited in Otis L. Graham, Jr., *The Great Campaigns* (New York: Century, 1922), 171.

8. For further discussion of professionalization as an occupational strategy, see Barbara Ehrenreich and John Ehrenreich, "The Professional-Managerial Class," 26–27; John Ehrenreich, *The Cultural Crisis of Modern Medicine*, 7–8, 28–29; and John Ehrenreich, *The Altruistic Imagination*, 53–57.

9. "Digest of Education Statistics," National Center for Education Statistics, 2013, Tables 103.20, 302.60, 303.10, http://nces.ed.gov/programs/digest/2013menu_tables.asp; Charles T. Clotfelter, Ronald G. Ehrenberg, Malcolm Getz, and John J. Siegfried, *Economic Challenges in Higher Education* (Washington, D.C.: National Bureau of Economic Research, 1991), http://papers.nber.org/books/clot91-1.

10. For a more detailed discussion of the relationship between the professional-managerial class and the movements of the sixties, see Barbara Ehrenreich and John Ehrenreich, "The New Left: A Case Study in Professional—Managerial Class Radicalism," *Radical America* 11, no. 3 (1977): 7, http://library.brown.edu/pdfs/112497719366862.pdf.

11. John Tierney, "The 2004 Campaign: Political Points," *New York Times*, January 11, 2004.

12. Gardiner Harris, "More Doctors Giving up Private Practices," *New York Times*, March 25, 2010; Robert Kocher and Nikhil R. Sahni, "Hospitals' Race to Employ Physicians—The Logic behind a Money-Losing Proposition," *New England Journal of Medicine* 364 (2011): 1790; P. R. Kletke, D. W. Emmons, and K. D. Gillis, "Current Trends in Physicians' Practice Arrangements, from Owners to Employees," *Journal of the American Medical Association* 276 no. 7 (1996): 555, cited in John B. McKinlay and Lisa D. Marceau, "The End of the Golden Age of Doctoring," *International Journal of Health Services* 32, no. 2 (2002): 379.

13. "America's Largest 250 Law Firms," Internet Legal Research Group, http://www.ilrg.com/nlj250/attorneys/desc/1; Marc Galanter, "Old and in the Way: The Coming Demographic Transformation of the Legal Profession and Its Implications for the Provision of Legal Services," *Wisconsin Law Review* 1999, no. 6: 1081–1117, http://www.marcgalanter.net/Documents/oldandintheway.pdf; Abe Krash, "The Changing Legal Profession," *Washington Lawyer*, January 2012, http://www.dcbar.org/for_lawyers/resources/publications/washington_lawyer/january_2008/changes.cfm; *Statistical Abstract of the United States*, 1973, 2001, 2009 eds., U.S. Department of Commerce, Bureau of the Census.

14. "Part One: The Media Landscape," in *The Information Needs of Communities: The Changing Media Landscape in a Broadband Age*, Steve Waldman and the Working Group on Information Needs of Communities (Federal Communications Commission, 2011), http://transition.fcc.gov/osp/inc-report/INoC-1-Newspapers.pdf; *The Decline of Big Media, 1980s–2000s: Key Lessons and Trends* (Cambridge, MA: Shorenstein Center on Media, Politics and Public Policy, Harvard Kennedy School, 2013), http://journalistsresource.org/studies/society/news-media/covering-america-journalism-professor-christopher-daly; Number of U.S. Daily Newspapers, 5-Year Increments (Washington, D.C.: Pew Research Center on Journalism and Media, 2007), http://www.journalism.org/numbers/number-of-u-s-daily-newspapers-5-year-increments/.

15. On the changing media landscape, see ibid.; Suzanne M. Kirchoff, *The U.S. Newspaper Industry in Transition*, CRS Report R40700 (Washington, DC: Congressional Research Service, 2010), http://www.fas.org/sgp/crs/misc/R40700.pdf; David Carr, "The Fissures Are Growing for Papers," *New York Times*, July 8, 2012; Boris Kachka, "The End," *New York Magazine*, September 14, 2008, http://nymag.com/news/media/50279; Williams Cole, "Is Publishing Doomed?," *Brooklyn Rail*, November 2010, http://www.brooklynrail.org/2010/11/express/is-publishing-doomed-john-b-thompson-with-williams-cole; Eli Noam, *Media Ownership and Concentration in America* (New York: Oxford University Press, 2009).

16. On outsourcing, see testimony of Ron Hira, chair, Research and Development Policy Committee, the Institute of Electrical and Electronics Engineers, to the Committee on Small

Business, United States House of Representatives ("Global Outsourcing of Engineering Jobs: Recent Trends and Possible Implications"), June 18, 2003, http://archive.cspo.org/products/lectures/061803.pdf; Linda Levine, *Offshoring (a.k.a. Offshore Outsourcing) and Job Insecurity among U.S.* Workers, CRS Report RL32292 (Washington, DC: Congressional Research Service, 2005), http://fpc.state.gov/documents/organization/46688.pdf; David Wessel, "Big U.S. Firms Shift Hiring Abroad," *Wall Street Journal*, April 19, 2011; Pete Engardio, Aaron Bernstein, and Manjeet Kripalani, "The New Global Job Shift," *Business Week*, February 2 2003, http://www.bloomberg.com/bw/stories/2003-02-02/the-new-global-job-shift; Kletke, P. R., Emmons, D. W., and Gillis, K. D. "Current Trends in Physicians' Practice Arrangements: From Owners to Employees," *Journal of the American Medical Association* 276, no. 7 (1996): 555–560, cited in John B. McKinlay and Lisa D. Marceau, "The End of the Golden Age of Doctoring," *International Journal of Health Services* 32, no. 2 (2002): 550.

17. "Tuition at the University of California (1970)," *Back Bench*, August 16, 2007, http://thebackbench.blogspot.com/2007/08/tuition-at-university-of-california.html; "Cost of Attendance, 2014," University of California Berkeley, Office of Undergraduate Admissions, 2015, http://admissions.berkeley.edu/costofattendance; "Digest of Education Statistics," 2013, Table 330.10, http://nces.ed.gov/programs/digest/d13/tables/dt13_330.10.asp?current–yes; U.S. *CPI Detailed Report: Data for January 2015*, Department of Labor, Bureau of Labor Statistics, Table 24, http://www.bls.gov/cpi/cpid1501.pdf.

18. "Quick Facts about Student Debt," Institute for College Access and Success, March 2014, http://projectonstudentdebt.org/files/pub/Debt_Facts_and_Sources.pdf; *Quarterly Report on Household Debt and Credit*, Federal Reserve Bank of New York, Research and Statistics Group, August 2014, http://www.newyorkfed.org/householdcredit/2014-q2/data/pdf/HHDC_2014Q2.pdf; "Law School Tuition, 1985–2009," American Bar Association, February 7, 2011, http://www.americanbar.org/content/dam/aba/migrated/legaled/statistics/charts/stats_5.authcheckdam.pdf; Dinitra Kessenides, "Jobs Are Still Scarce for New Law School Grads," *Bloomberg Business*, June 20, 2014, http://www.bloomberg.com/bw/articles/2014-06-20/the-employment-rate-falls-again-for-recent-law-school-graduates; Jordan Weissmann, "The Jobs Crisis at Our Best Law Schools Is Much, Much Worse Than You Think," *Atlantic*, April 9, 2013, http://www.theatlantic.com/business/archive/2013/04/the-jobs-crisis-at-our-best-law-schools-is-much-much-worse-than-you-think/274795; Robert Farrington, "Law School and Student Loan Debt: Be Careful," *Forbes*, December 18, 2014, http://www.forbes.com/sites/robertfarrington/2014/12/18/law-school-and-student-loan-debt-be-careful.

6. Anxiety and Rage

1. "NBC News/Wall Street Journal Survey," Study 14039, Hart Research Associates/Public Opinion Strategies, January 2014, http://online.wsj.com/public/resources/documents/wsjnbc newspoll01222014.pdf; "Report: State of the American Workplace," Gallup, September 22, 2014, http://www.gallup.com/services/176708/state-american-workplace.aspx; "Confidence in Institutions," Gallup, June 2014, http://www.gallup.com/poll/1597/confidence-institutions.aspx; David Graham, "What Will America Look Like in 2024?" *Atlantic*, June 1, 2014, http://www.theatlantic.com/politics/archive/2014/07/what-americans-expect-over-the-next-10-years-in-tk-charts/373610.

2. "Understanding the Facts of Anxiety Disorders and Depression Is the First Step," Anxiety and Depression Association of America, 2015, http://www.adaa.org/understanding-anxiety; "Major Depression among Adults," National Institute of Mental Health, http://www.nimh.nih.gov/health/statistics/prevalence/major-depression-among-adults.shtml; Susanna N. Visser et al.,"Trends in the Parent-Report of Health Care Provider-Diagnosed and Medicated Attention-Deficit/Hyperactivity Disorder: United States, 2003–2011," *Journal of the American Academy of Child and Adolescent Psychiatry* 53, no. 1 (2014): 34, http://www.jaacap.com/article/S0890-8567(13)00594-7/fulltext; Ronald C. Kessler et al., "Lifetime Prevalence and Age-of-Onset

Distributions of *DSM-IV* Disorders in the National Comorbidity Survey Replication," *Archives of General Psychiatry* 62 (2005): 593, http://psychology.cos.ucf.edu/childrenslearningclinic/wp-content/uploads/2013/08/Kessler-et-al.-Lifetime-Prevalence-rates-of-disorders.pdf.

3. Marcia Angell, "The Epidemic of Mental Illness: Why?" *New York Review of Books*, June 23, 2011, http://www.nybooks.com/articles/archives/2011/jun/23/epidemic-mental-illness-why; Wilson M. Compton, Kevin P. Conway, Frederick S. Stinson, and Bridget F. Grant, "Changes in the Prevalence of Major Depression and Comorbid Substance Use Disorders in the United States between 1991–1992 and 2001–2002," *American Journal of Psychiatry* 163, no. 12 (2006): 2141, http://ajp.psychiatryonline.org/doi/abs/10.1176/ajp.2006.163.12.2141; Jean M. Twenge, "The Age of Anxiety? Birth Cohort Change in Anxiety and Neuroticism, 1952–1993," *Journal of Personality and Social Psychology* 79, no. 6 (2000): 1007, http://www.apa.org/pubs/journals/releases/psp7961007.pdf; Williams C. Reeves et al., "Mental Illness Surveillance among Adults in the United States," *Morbidity and Mortality Weekly Report Supplements* 60, no. 3 (2011): 1, http://www.cdc.gov/mmwr/preview/mmwrhtml/su6003a1.htm; Amy Novotney, "Students under Pressure," *APA Monitor on Psychology* 45, no. 8 (2014): 36, http://www.apa.org/monitor/2014/09/cover-pressure.aspx; Jonathan Rottenberg, "The Depression Epidemic: Can Mood Science Save Us?," Psychotherapy Networker, November/December 2014, http://www.psychotherapy.org/magazine/currentissue/item/2572-the-depression-epidemic; Robert B. Putnam, *Bowling Alone: The Collapse and Revival of American Community* (New York: Simon and Schuster, 2000), 263.

4. On SSI/SSDI, see E. Fuller Torrey, "How Robert Whitaker Got It Wrong," review of *Anatomy of a Non-Epidemic*, by Robert Whitaker, Treatment Advocacy Center, 2014, http://www.treatmentadvocacycenter.org/component/content/article/2085-anatomy-of-a-non-epidemic-a-review-by-dr-torrey. On ADHD, see Stephen P. Hinshaw and Richard Scheffler, *The ADHD Explosion* (New York: Oxford University Press, 2014). Despite reductions in the stigma assigned to emotional problems, studies of college students have actually shown an increasingly reluctance to seek psychotherapeutic help (as opposed to medication), which may reflect the emphasis on biological causes of mental illness in recent decades. See C. S. MacKenzie, J. Erickson, F. P. Deane, and M. Wright, "Changes in Attitudes toward Seeking Mental Health Services: A 40-Year Cross-Temporal Meta-analysis," *Clinical Psychology Review* 34, no. 2 (2014): 99, http://www.ncbi.nlm.nih.gov/pubmed/24486521. More generally, psychotherapy use in the United States has fallen significantly between 1983 and 2007. M. Olfson and S. C. Marcus, "National Trends in Outpatient Psychotherapy," *American Journal of Psychiatry* 167, no. 12 (2010): 1456–1463, http://dx.doi.org/10.1176/appi.ajp.2010.10040570.

5. Some 214 chemicals are known to be neurotoxic in humans, and some of these have been linked to developmental delays, cognitive deficits, and hyperactivity. Such an explanation may explain some part of the increase in mental and behavioral disorders such as ADHD and schizophrenia, which clearly have a neurodevelopmental course, but do little to explain adult onset depression and anxiety. Philippe Grandjean and Philip J. Landrigan, "Neurobehavioural Effects of Developmental Toxicity," *Lancet*, February 14, 2014, http://dx.doi.org/10.1016/S1474-4422(13)70278-3; Philippe Grandjean and Philip J. Landrigan, "Developmental Toxicity of Industrial Chemicals," *Lancet*, November 8, 2006, http://dx.doi.org/10.1016/S0140-6736(06)69665-7; Rebecca A. Harrington et al., "Prenatal SSRI Use and Offspring with Autism Spectrum Disorder or Developmental Delay," *Pediatrics* 13, no. 5 (2014): 1241, http://dx.doi.org/10.1542/peds.2013-3406. The long-term effect of treatment with psychoactive medications has been proposed by Robert Whitaker, *Anatomy of an Epidemic* (New York: Crown Publishers, 2010). For criticisms and discussion of Whitaker's hypothesis, see Torrey, "How Robert Whitaker Got It Wrong"; John Oldham, Daniel Carlat, Richard Friedman, and Andrew Nierenberg, reply by Marcia Angell, "'The Illusions of Psychiatry': An Exchange," *New York Review of Books*, August 18, 2011, http://www.nybooks.com/articles/archives/2011/aug/18/illusions-psychiatry-exchange.

6. R. Mojtabai, "Americans' Attitudes toward Mental Health Treatment Seeking: 1990–2003," *Psychiatric Services* 58, no. 5 (2007): 642, http://ps.psychiatryonline.org/doi/abs/10.1176/ps.2007.58.5.642; B. A. Pescosolido et al., "A Disease like Any Other? A Decade of Change in Public Reactions to Schizophrenia, Depression, and Alcohol Dependence," *American Journal of Psychiatry* 167, no. 11(2010): 1321, http://ajp.psychiatryonline.org/doi/abs/10.1176/appi.ajp.2010.09121743.

7. Marcia Angell, "The Epidemic of Mental Illness: Why?" *New York Review of Books*, June 23, 2011, http://www.nybooks.com/articles/archives/2011/jun/23/epidemic-mental-illness-why; Gary Greenberg, "The Cult of DSM: Ending Our Allegiance to the Great Gazoo," *Psychotherapy Networker*, March/April 2014, http://www.psychotherapynetworker.org/magazine/currentissue/item/2458-the-cult-of-dsm122.

8. Mary Sykes Wylie, "Falling in Love Again: A Brief History of Our Infatuation with Psychoactive Drugs," *Psychotherapy Networker*, July/August 2014, http://www.psychotherapynetworker.org/magazine/recentissues/2014-julyaug/item/2514-falling-in-love-again; Alan Schwarz, "The Selling of Attention Deficit Disorder," *New York Times*, December 14, 2013; Bruce E. Levine, "How Our Society Breeds Anxiety, Depression, and Dysfunction," Alternet, August 21, 2013, http://www.alternet.org/personal-health/how-our-society-breeds-anxiety-depression-and-dysfunction.

The 1980 third edition of the DSM contained 265 disorders. The 1994 fourth edition contained 365 disorders, a level maintained in the 2013 fifth edition. A recent *New York Times* article describes a campaign undertaken by the drug company Shire to promote awareness of a newly invented "disorder" (what psychiatrists now describe as "binge eating disorder," a diagnosis unknown until the 2014 revision of the DSM) and to instruct patients on how to act to convince a doctor that she or he suffered from it, then to market a drug for it. Katie Thomas, "Shire, Maker of Binge-Eating Drug Vyvanse, First Marketed the Disease," *New York Times*, February 25, 2015.

9. David Riesman, *The Lonely Crowd* (New Haven: Yale University Press, 1950).

10. The theme of increased narcissism is not new, of course. Christopher Lasch, Tom Wolfe, and others described similar patterns in the early 1970s. However, studies comparing scores on various personality measures for adolescents and young adults today and adolescents and young adults in the early 1970s have reported significant increases in narcissism, self-appraisal, focus on immediate gratification and external goals rather than on an internalized goals, materialism, individualism, and unrealistic expectations, as well as the other traits discussed in the text.

Accounts of post-1960s changes in modal personality can be found in Richard Sennett, *The Culture of the New Capitalism* (New Haven: Yale University Press, 2006); Paul Roberts, *The Impulse Society* (New York: Bloomsbury, 2014); Robert Putnam, *Bowling Alone*. Jean Twenge's research provides extensive documentation of a variety of personality shifts over recent years. See Jean M. Twenge, *Generation Me* (New York: Free Press, 2006); Jean M. Twenge and W. Keith Campbell, *The Narcissism Epidemic* (New York: Free Press, 2009); Twenge, "The Age of Anxiety"; Jean M. Twenge et al., "Birth Cohort Increases in Psychopathology among Young Americans, 1938–2007: A Cross-Temporal Meta-Analysis of the MMPI," *Clinical Psychology Review* 30 (2010): 145, http://dx.doi.org/10.1016/j.cpr.2009.10.005; Jean M. Twenge, W. Keith Campbell, and Elise C. Freeman, "Generational Differences in Young Adults' Life Goals, Concern for Others, and Civic Orientation, 1966–2009," *Journal of Personality and Social Psychology* 102, no. 5 (2012): 1045, http://dx.doi.org/10.1037/a0027408. See also Sara H. Konrath, Edward H. O'Brien, and Courtney Hsing, "Changes in Dispositional Empathy in American College Students over Time: A Meta-Analysis," *Personality and Social Psychology Review* 15, no. 2 (2011): 180, http://dx.doi.org/10.1177/1088868310377395. For criticism of Twenge's work, see Jeffrey Jensen Arnett, "The Evidence for Generation We and against Generation Me," *Emerging Adulthood* 1, no. 1 (2013): 5, http://dx.doi.org/10.1177/2167696812466842; Kali H. Trzesniewski and M. Brent Donnellan, "Rethinking 'Generation Me': A Study of Cohort Effects from 1976–2006," *Perspectives on*

Psychological Science 5 no. 1 (2010): 58, http://dx.doi.org/10.1177/1745691609356789; Jean Twenge and W. Keith Campbell, "Birth Cohort Differences in the Monitoring the Future Dataset and Elsewhere: Further Evidence for Generation Me—Commentary on Trzesniewski & Donnellan," *Perspectives on Psychological Science* 5, no. 1 (2010): 81, http://dx.doi.org/10.1177/1745691609357015.

There are differences in patterns between males and females (for example, high-achieving women, at least, are reported to have a lower sense of self-worth than men), but the pattern of *increases* in the traits discussed above over successive birth cohorts crosses gender. See Jean M. Twenge, Sara Konrath, W. Keith Campbell, and Brad J. Bushman, "Egos Inflating over Time: A Cross-Temporal Meta-Analysis of the Narcissistic Personality Inventory," *Journal of Personality* 76, no. 4 (2008): 874, http://dx.doi.org/10.1111/j.1467-6494.2008.00507.x; Jean M. Twenge and Joshua D. Foster, "Birth Cohort Increases in Narcissistic Personality Traits among American College Students, 1982–2009," *Social Psychological and Personality Science* 1, no. 1 (2010): 99, http://dx.doi.org/10.1177/1948550609355719; Jean M. Twenge, "Changes in Women's Assertiveness in Response to Status and Roles: A Cross-Temporal Meta-analysis, 1931–1993," *Journal of Personality and Social Psychology* 81, no. 1 (2001): 133; Jean Twenge and W. Keith Campbell, "Self-Esteem and Socioeconomic Status: A Meta-Analytic Review," *Personality and Social Psychology Review* 6, no. 1 (2002): 59, http://dx.doi.org/10.1207/S15327957PSPR0601_3; Twenge, "The Age of Anxiety?"

There also may be differences in patterns between poorer people and the more affluent. A 2014 study, for example, found that more-affluent people have more of a sense of entitlement and narcissism than those of lower socioeconomic status, are more independent-minded and less emotionally attuned to others, are less concerned with the wishes and expectations of others, and are less concerned with maintaining relationships and fitting in. See Tori DeAngelis, "Class Differences," *American Psychological Association Monitor on Psychology* 46, no. 2 (2015): 62, http://www.apa.org/monitor/2015/02/class-differences.aspx.

11. Twenge, "Generation Me"; Ron Taffel, "The Rise of the Two-Dimensional Parent," *Psychotherapy Networker*, September/October 19, 2014, 19-25, http://www.psychotherapynetworker.org/magazine/recentissues/2014-sepoct/item/2548-the-rise-of-the-two-dimensional-parent. The increasing frequency of single-parent families may also play a role in determining shifts in typical personality. From a psychoanalytic perspective, absence of the father or presence of a stepfather whose authority is weaker than the biological father might be associated with weakness in super-ego development.

12. Patrick O'Connor, "Poll Finds Widespread Economic Anxiety," *Wall Street Journal*, August 5, 2014. Whether social mobility has actually declined is arguable. It is generally agreed that in absolute terms, the United States is a comparatively immobile society, that is, where one starts in the income distribution influences where one ends up to a greater degree than in many other advanced economies. By some estimates, movement between generations from one part of the income distribution to another increased over the 1940–1980 period, but it decreased substantially during the 1980s and is unchanged since 1990 (that is, it stabilized at a lower level than in the decades before 1980). See Linda Levine, *The U.S. Income Distribution and Mobility: Trends and International Comparisons*, R42400 (Washington, DC: Congressional Research Service, 2012), http://fas.org/sgp/crs/misc/R42400.pdf.

13. For discussion of the stakeholder-shareholder distinction and the shift towards the latter in the United States, see Steven Pearlstein, "When Shareholder Capitalism Came to Town," *American Prospect*, April 19, 2014, http://prospect.org/; Robert Reich, "The Rebirth of Stakeholder Capitalism?," *Robertreich.org*, March 12, 2015, http://robertreich.org/post/94260751620.

14. "Number of Jobs Held, Labor Market Activity, and Earnings Growth Among the Youngest Baby Boomers: Results from a Longitudinal Survey," news release, U.S. Department of Labor, Bureau of Labor Statistics, March 31, 2015, http://www.bls.gov/news.release/pdf/nlsoy.pdf.

15. Richard Sennett, *The Culture of the New Capitalism* (New Haven: Yale University Press, 2007).

16. Jean Twenge, "Generation Me"; Paul Roberts, *The Impulse Society*. Adding to the ease of purchasing that credit cards created, Roberts (p. 55) notes that the number of distinct products available in the United States increased manyfold (up to tenfold in a single year) between 1970 and 1996.

17. Psychiatrist R.D. Laing called the loss of security in one's sense of being in the world "ontological insecurity," a concept closely related to Kierkegaard's "dread" and Sartre's anxiety of "nothingness." These writers saw this as a direct source of emotional distress. In the present context, I am only relating it to changes in modal personality patterns, which in turn are related to the rise in emotional distress that has characterized U.S. society in recent decades. See, among others, R.D. Laing, *The Divided Self: An Existential Study in Sanity and Madness* (Oxford: Penguin Books, 1965); Anoop Gupta, *Kierkegaard's Romantic Legacy: Two Theories of the Self* (Ottawa: University of Ottawa Press, 2005).

18. For a review of the impact of socioeconomic status on mental health, see *Report of the APA Task Force on Socioeconomic Status* (Washington, DC: American Psychological Association, 2007), http://www.apa.org/pi/ses/resources/publications/task-force-2006.pdf.

19. Betsey Stevenson and Justin Wolfers, "Trends in Marital Stability," in *Research Handbook on the Economics of Family Law*, eds. Lloyd R. Cohen and Joshua D. Wright (Cheltenham, UK: Edward Elgar Publishing, 2011), http://users.nber.org/~jwolfers/Papers/TrendsinMaritalStabil ity.pdf; Sheela Kennedy and Steven Ruggles, "Breaking Up Is Hard to Count: The Rise of Divorce in the United States, 1980–2010," *Demography* 51, no. 2 (2014): 587, http://link.springer.com/article/10.1007%2Fs13524-013-0270-9; Jonathan Vespa, Jamie M. Lewis, and Rose M. Kreider, *America's Families and Living Arrangements: 2012* (U.S. Census Bureau, 2013), http://www.census.gov/prod/2013pubs/p20-570.pdf.

20. George Soros, *The Crisis of Global Capitalism: Open Society Endangered* (London: Little Brown, 1998); Robert Putnam, *Bowling Alone*. The links between economic and social stress and mental illness are well known. See "Mental Health: Strengthening Our Response," Fact Sheet 220, World Health Organization, August 2014, http://www.who.int/mediacentre/factsheets/fs220/en; M. Harvey Brenner, *Mental Illness and the Economy* (Cambridge, MA: Harvard University Press, 1973); Christopher G. Hudson, "Socioeconomic Status and Mental Illness: Tests of the Social Causation and Selection Hypotheses," *American Journal of Orthopsychiatry* 75, no. 1 (2005): 3; Brian J. Hagan, Bruce D. Forman, and Michael J. Gorodezky, "The Impact of Economic Stress on Community Mental Health Services," *Administration in Mental Health* 10, no. 2 (1982): 104, http://link.springer.com/search?facet-author=%22Brian+J.+Hagan%22.

21. On the decline in trust and the increase in material goals, see Putnam, *Bowling Alone*. On social isolation and lack of confidants, see Paolo Parigi and Warner Henson, "Social Isolation in America," *Annual Reviews of Sociology* 40, no. 1 (2014): 153; Miller McPherson, Lynn Smith-Lovin, and Matthew E. Brashears, "Social Isolation in America: Changes in Core Discussion Networks over Two Decades," *American Sociological Review* 71, no. 3 (2006): 353, http://dx.doi.org/10.1177/000312240607100301. McPherson's conclusions have been disputed by Claude Fischer, "The 2004 GSS Finding of Shrunken Social Networks: An Artifact?," *American Sociological Review* 74, no. 4 (2009): 657. McPherson et al. reply in "Models and Marginals: Using Survey Evidence to Study Social Networks," *American Sociological Review* 74, no. 4 (2009): 670.

22. "Political Polarization in the American Public," Pew Research Center, June 12, 2014, http://www.people-press.org/2014/06/12/political-polarization-in-the-american-public; "New Report: Radical Antigovernment Movement Continues Explosive Growth; SPLC Urges Government to Review Resources Devoted to Domestic Terrorism," Southern Poverty Law Center, March 5, 2013, http://www.splcenter.org/home/splc-report-antigovernment-patriot-movement-continues-explosive-growth-poses-rising-threat-of-v; James Moody and Peter J. Mucha, "Portrait of Political Party Polarization," *Network Science* 1, no. 1 (2013): 119, http://dx.doi.org/10.1017/nws.2012.3; "'Wingnuts' and President Obama," Harris Poll, March 24, 2010, http://www.harrisinteractive.com/

NewsRoom/HarrisPolls/tabid/447/ctl/ReadCustom%20Default/mid/1508/ArticleId/223/Default.
aspx.

23. Thomas Frank, *What's The Matter With Kansas?* (New York: Holt, 2004), 124. Frank notes
that the strongest ultraconservative movement in Kansas was in areas with the lowest incomes
and worst housing.

24. For a discussion of the differing perspectives of liberals and conservatives on the values
ascribed to individuality versus collectivity and their role in political decision-making over the
course of U.S. history, see E. J. Dionne, *Our Divided Political Heart* (New York: Bloomsbury,
2012).

25. "Conspiracy Theories Round Two: Republicans More Likely to Subscribe to Government Conspiracy Theories," *Public Policy Polling*, October 2, 2013, http://www.public
policypolling.com/main/2013/10/conspiracy-theories-round-two-republicans-more-likely-to-
subscribe-to-government-conspiracy-theories.html; "GOP Deeply Divided over Climate Change,"
Pew Research Center, November 1, 2013, http://www.people-press.org/2013/11/01/gop-deeply-
divided-over-climate-change; "Ignorance, Partisanship Drive False Beliefs about Obama, Iraq,"
Fairleigh Dickinson University's Public Minds Poll, January 7, 2015, http://publicmind.fdu.
edu/2015/false. For more general discussions, see Richard Hofstadter, "The Paranoid Style in
American Politics," *Harper's Magazine*, November 1964, http://harpers.org/archive/1964/11/
the-paranoid-style-in-american-politics; Seymour Martin Lipset and Earl Raab, *The Politics of Un-
reason: Right Wing Extremism in America, 1790–1970* (New York: Harper & Row, 1970); Daniel Bell,
ed., *The Radical Right* (Garden City, NY: Doubleday, 1963); Rick Perlstein, "Why Conservatives
Are Still Crazy after All These Years," *Rolling Stone*, March 16, 2012, http://www.rollingstone.com/
politics/news/why-conservatives-are-still-crazy-after-all-these-years-20120316; Mark Lilla, "Republicans for Revolution," *New York Review of Books*, January 12, 2012, http://www.nybooks.com/
articles/archives/2012/jan/12/republicans-revolution/?pagination=false.

26. Sigmund Freud, *The Future of an Illusion* (1927). Freud's distinction between illusions and
delusions was fuzzier, based on the degree of essential conflict with reality. What he called an "illusion" could and sometimes was true, despite its questionable cognitive origin, but a "delusion"
could not be true. Modern day psychologists tend to use the word "illusion" for perceptual mistakes (for example, an "optical illusions"). DSM-5 notes, "The distinction between a delusion and
a strongly held idea is sometimes difficult to make and depends in part on the degree of conviction with which the belief is held, despite clear or reasonable contradictory evidence regarding its
veracity." *Diagnostic and Statistical Manual of Mental Disorders*, 5th ed. (Washington, DC: American Psychological Association, 2013). From this perspective, one is tempted to call climate change
deniers and birthers delusional.

27. The rooting of fact in wish is nowhere so well illustrated as in the contemptuous descrip-
tion by a Bush-era White House aide (commonly believed to be Karl Rove) of "what we call the
'reality-based community.'" "That's not the way the world works anymore," he continued. "We're
an empire now and when we act, we create our own reality." Reported by Ron Suskind, "Faith,
Certainty, and the Presidency of George W. Bush," *New York Times Magazine*, October 17, 2004.

28. "All Employees, Manufacturing," FRED Economic Data, Federal Reserve Bank of
St. Louis, http://research.stlouisfed.org/fred2/series/MANEMP; Annie Lowrey, "What's the Matter with Eastern Kentucky," *New York Times Magazine*, June 26, 2014; Alan Flippen, "Where
Are the Hardest Places to Live in the U.S.?" *New York Times*, June 26, 2014; Robert J. Vanderbei,
"Feeling Blue?," *Topalli.com*, 2010, citing Southern Poverty Law Center, http://www.topalli.com/
blue/intro.html. Ironically, given the red states' opposition to government spending, they tend to
be the states that receive more in federal government benefits than they pay in taxes, unlike most
of the blue states, where the reverse is true.

29. This formulation is much like that of Ernest Becker, *The Denial of Death* (New York:
Simon and Schuster, 1973) and Jeff Greenberg, Sheldon Solomon, and Tom Pyszczynski, "The

Causes and Consequences of a Need for Self-Esteem: A Terror Management Theory," in *Public Self and Private Self*, ed. R. F. Baumeister (New York: Springer-Verlag, 1986), 189, although these authors were trying to explain how humans deal with their realization that death is inevitable.

30. Readers may recognize elements of cognitive dissonance theory, social identity theory, systems justification theory, and the just-world hypothesis in this account. For informal reviews, see "System Justification Theory," *Psychwiki.com*, http://www.psychwiki.com/wiki/System_Jus tification_Theory; "System Justification," *Wikipedia*, http://en.wikipedia.org/wiki/System_justi fication. Compare Theda Skocpol and Vanessa Williamson's account of the factors leading to the rise of the Tea Party, *The Tea Party and the Remaking of Republican Conservatism* (New York: Oxford University Press, 2011).

31. On the personality correlates of conservative ideology, see T. W. Adorno et al., *The Authoritarian Personality* (New York: Norton, 1950); John T. Jost, Brian A. Nosek, and Samuel D. Gosling, "Ideology: Its Resurgence in Social, Personality, and Political Psychology," *Perspectives on Psychological Science* 3, no. 2 (2008): 126; Dana R. Carney et al., "The Secret Lives of Liberals and Conservatives: Personality Profiles, Interaction Styles, and the Things they Leave Behind," *Political Psychology* 29, no. 6 (2008): 807; Peter J. Rentfrow et al., "Divided We Stand: Three Psychological Regions of the United States and Their Political, Economic, Social, and Health Correlates," *Journal of Personality and Social Psychology* 105, no. 6 (2013): 996; Jesse Graham, Ravi Iyer, and Peter Meindl, "The Psychology of Economic Ideology: Emotion, Motivation, and Moral Intuition," *Demos.org*, n.d., http://www.demos.org/sites/default/files/publications/Graham.pdf; Sena Kileva, "Recent Developments in Ideology Research," *Association for Psychological Science Observer* 25, no. 8 (2012), http://www.psychologicalscience.org/index.php/publications/observer/2012/october-12/ideology-research.html.

32. Avidit Acharya, Matthew Blackwell, and Maya Sen, "The Political Legacy of American Slavery," working paper, Harvard University, 2014, http://www.mattblackwell.org/files/papers/slavery.pdf.

Epilogue

1. "Democratic Victory Task Force Preliminary Findings," February 21, 2015, http://www.scribd.com/doc/256467123/Democratic-Victory-Task-Force-Preliminary-Findings.

2. Thomas Frank, *What's the Matter with Kansas?* (New York: Holt Paperbacks, 2004); "Election Results, Wisconsin," *New York Times*, December 9, 2008; "2012 Wisconsin Presidential Results," *Politico*, November 19, 2012, http://www.politico.com/2012-election/results/president/wisconsin; "Decision 2014: Wisconsin, Governor," *NBC News*, 2014, http://www.nbcnews.com/politics/elections/2014/WI/governor/exitpoll.

3. Franklin Delano Roosevelt, "State of the Union Message to Congress," January 11, 1944, text online at http://www.fdrlibrary.marist.edu/archives/images/exerpt_c.jpg; Lyndon Johnson, "Annual Message to Congress on the State of the Union," January 8, 1964, text online at http://www.lbjlib.utexas.edu/johnson/archives.hom/speeches.hom/640108.asp.

4. "National General Election VEP Turnout Rates, 1789–Present," United States Election Project, June 11, 2014, http://www.electproject.org/national-1789-present. The Republicans' 17.6 percent is actually an overestimate, since almost four million people who were in jail or on probation were disenfranchised.

5. Martin Gilens and Benjamin I. Page, "Testing Theories of American Politics: Elites, Interest Groups, and Average Citizens," *Perspectives on Politics* 12 no. 3 (2014): 564, http://dx.doi.org/10.1017/S1537592714001595. Often enough, of course, there is no big difference between what elites and "ordinary" citizens want, so we all get our way and a sense that government is responsive.

6. "The Reformer," Committee for a Responsible Budget, 2012, http://crfb.org/socialsecurity reformer, estimates that subjecting all wages to the payroll tax alone would close 71 percent of the projected gap between Social Security revenues and outlays.

7. Lincoln quoted in E. J. Dionne, *Our Divided Political Heart* (New York: Bloomsbury, 2012): 160.

8. "The Numbers: How Do U.S. Taxes Compare Internationally?," Tax Policy Center, 2011, http://www.taxpolicycenter.org/briefing-book/background/numbers/international.cfm.

9. Holmes, in dissenting opinion in *Compañía General de Tabacos de Filipinas v. Collector of Internal Revenue* (1927), quoted in "Exploring the Origins of Quotations," *Quote Investigator*, April 13, 2012, http://quoteinvestigator.com/2012/04/13/taxes-civilize.

10. Dionne, *Our Divided Political Heart*.

11. For example, 95 percent of whites tell pollsters that the passage of the Civil Rights Act was "very" or "somewhat" important, 69 percent think government should play at least some role in improving the situation of blacks, and more than half disapproved of the Supreme Court's dismantling of the Voting Rights Act. They are less aware of injustices in the criminal justice system, but even there, 42 percent perceive it as functioning inequitably, and by a two-to-one margin whites disapproved of the failure of the Staten Island grand jury to indict the police officer who killed James Garner with a chokehold while arresting him for selling loose cigarettes on the street in 2014. For these results and other polls on race relations, see "Race and Ethnicity," Polling Report.com, http://www.pollingreport.com/race.htm.

12. Walmart officials and the Walton family speak often about the need to improve public education. By one estimate, 105,131 teachers could be hired nationwide with the estimated $7.8 billion in tax breaks and public subsidies going to Walmart and the Walton family each year. "Walmart on Tax Day: How Taxpayers Subsidize America's Biggest Employer and Richest Family," Americans for Tax Fairness, April 2014, http://www.americansfortaxfairness.org/files/Walmart-on-Tax-Day-Americans-for-Tax-Fairness-1.pdf.

13. See Kevin Sack and Marjorie Connelly, "In Poll, Wide Support for Government-Run Health," *New York Times*, June 20, 2009; "Progressive Change Institute Releases Big Ideas Polling Results," Progressive Change Campaign Committee, http://act.boldprogressives.org/survey/pci_bigideas_poll_results.

14. Martin Luther King Jr. Speech at Grosse Pointe (Michigan) High School, March 14, 1968, http://www.gphistorical.org/mlk/mlkspeech.

15. Part of encouraging collective solutions is rebuilding a sense of community. Encouraging collective solutions rather than purely individual solutions (or at least not discouraging collective solutions) should be a consideration in a wide variety of policy decisions. For example, in late 2010 Congress passed President Obama's proposal for a temporary 2 percent cut in the payroll tax. This clearly addressed the material self-interest of American families, each of which was able to go off and spend their tax break as they chose. But suppose that the president had proposed spending the same amount of money on infrastructure projects benefiting communities. That would have been a benefit shared collectively by the community, a very small step toward buttressing battered communities and rebuilding ties among people. Both approaches address self-interest, but the latter conceptualizes in terms of the common welfare rather than of the separate well-being of disconnected individuals.

16. "Ballad for Americans," by John LaTouche and Earl Robinson, © 1939, 1940 (copyright renewed), EMI Robbins Catalog.

INDEX